MUSLIM

A Young Woman's Journey

MUSLIM – A Young Woman's Journey
An Admiral Press book
First edition 2021
© Aisha Wright 2021

This work is based on a true story. The names and descriptions of its characters have been changed.

Cover: Jana Jelovac
Frontispiece calligraphy: © Aisha Wright

This book is typeset in Garamond

Admiral Press
Cape Town, South Africa
admiralpress.books@gmail.com

ISBN: 978-0-620-94986-6

'As for the blessings
of your Lord,
speak out.'

Qur'an

Introduction

This is the story of how I became Muslim.

I come from Norfolk, a largely agricultural county in the east of England. The area is known for its flat landscapes, wide open skies and scenic coastlines. Its ancient history is well documented, as is its flux of peoples – Celts and Romans, Angles, Saxons and Danes. Its historic county town, Norwich, lies about a hundred miles northeast of London, and in the Middle Ages and for some centuries after, it was the largest and most important city in England after the capital.

An immense patchwork of farms blankets the land, and scattered throughout are towns, village greens and ancient woodlands. There are windmills and marshes, footpaths and bridleways, and the Broads, a tranquil network of rivers and lakes.

There's something special about this place. A subtle, age-old richness whispers in the trees and breathes through the wind. Pagan peoples worshipped here. Their standing stones still remain. After them came the Christians, and there are more mediaeval churches here than in the whole of the rest of Britain.

My maternal ancestors have dwelled here for nearly a thousand years. They descend from the Vikings of Scandinavia, then the aristocracy of northern France: my forefather was from Le Quesnay in Normandy, and as a general of William the Conqueror's army he led troops of Normans, Bretons and Flemings onto English soil to defeat King Harold at the Battle of Hastings in 1066 and suppress subsequent revolts in what is now called the Norman Conquest.

My paternal line includes Scottish, Irish and Cornish blood. My grandfather was born in Mysore, India, during the last gasp of the British Raj. I myself was born in Canada and lived there for the first two years of my life.

To the south of Norwich is a village called Cringleford. That is where I was brought up. It is a friendly place, affluent and somewhat picturesque. Its earliest record is Saxon, but its name derives from two ancient Scandinavian words: *kringla*, meaning 'round hill' and likely the rising ground upon which the village church stands, and *ford* referring to the local river Yare, which meanders gently through the lush and fertile landscape.

Not long after finishing school I left this place – and England. I returned some months later, as English as I was before, and perhaps even more so, because I had acquired an insight into the meaning of my life and an understanding of my place in the world. But more than that, I had made sense of the yearning and searching for something that has accompanied me for as long as I can remember.

PART I

April

April in Norfolk. This time of year hums with the exuberance of new life. Fragrant crocus carpets adorn parks and grassy verges. Daffodils sway triumphantly in the breeze. Seasoned acorns announce the secret of the oak, horse chestnut buds unfurl their resinous shoots, and beech, lime and sycamore swell the glorious symphony of England's spring.

I'm parked half up the curb alongside Chapelfield Gardens. It's my hometown's little Central Park, an urban haven bustling with all walks of life at all times of the day. Striding along the pavement, I glance over its hawthorn hedge and through towering trees. I see the Victorian bandstand, its lichened roof crowned by a pretty white dovecote. I see the ugly brick kiosk selling cheap snacks. On the far side, rising on greying neo-Gothic haunches, is the Roman Catholic cathedral, glum cousin to its spired Anglican counterpart down the hill.

The park is busy today. Businesspeople are marching purposefully from one end to the other, their briefcases dangling at their sides. Schoolchildren hang around one of the benches, their laughter bursting over inaudible talk. A homeless man emerges from the shrubbery, his face tanned, his trousers soiled at the knees. I look at him longer than perhaps I should, feeling a pang of concern. Then I see the women from the nearby sweet factory, unmistakable in their pink chequered caps, chatting over cigarettes and watching the comings and goings.

I reach my vehicle, a turquoise camper van. It has no working locks so there's no need for a key. I just haul open the door – it creaks faithfully – and hoist myself into the driver's seat. My feet barely reach the floor so I wear biker boots which give me an extra inch. The ignition is long gone. I reach down for the cables, breathing a faint smell of cinnamon tea and burnt engine oil, and hot-wire it into life. I yank the gearstick into first, check my mirrors and set off.

I drive past the gardens and the ancient city walls, high up enough to look out over the humdrum of local traffic. I can admire the floral gardens hidden from the eyes of cars, and witness, if only fleetingly, the thin branches of trees hanging precariously close to my roof, which dare now and then to give it a tickle or a thwack.

Soon I'm beyond the city's ring road. The engine relaxes into a comfortable hum and the outskirts of suburbia tremor gently in my rear-view mirror. The wind blows through my hair and music blares from the speakers. The speedometer hovers bravely around 55 mph and soon I'm blending and blurring into the quilted fields of an East Anglian countryside.

Beth

I'm headed west. The surrounding land is farming country bordering ancient fen meadows. For miles around, fields of newly cultivated soil are being sown with sugar beet, spring wheat and barley, and the smell of wet earth rests in the air. There are no hills or mountains here, just a pale blue emptiness that extends upwards and outwards as far as my eyes can see.

I'm driving to Beth's house to tell her my decision. It has been on my mind for weeks. Beth is my closest friend. We have never argued, never let each other down, never done awful things to one another. We're like two peas in a pod, but very different-looking ones. Beth is several inches taller than me and voluptuous next to my petite frame. Her chestnut-brown hair contrasts with my blonde, her grown-out fringe – partly dyed red – is drawn up in a beehive, whereas mine is always loose, long and a bit wild. Sun kisses freckle my fair skin while Beth has an olive complexion and a tiny, silver stud in her nose. She's into colourful, baggy clothes with bright green Mary Janes. I'm usually wearing something discovered in a vintage shop: lace-edged blouses with suede hot pants or long swishy skirts.

Beth lives a few miles from a market town amid a warren of far-flung villages. Only recently have I been able to navigate them without having to get out my map: right at the old barn, left at the nameless lane facing a give way sign, second right where for over a mile the road dips into a shallow valley, then right at the fork in the road where an old, red telephone box stands surrounded by tall grass, leaning like the windswept trees behind it.

I turn into Beth's lane. This is deepest Norfolk: wattle and daub, thatch and beams, Peter Rabbit gardens. I pull the steering wheel hard right, navigate a white-painted gateway and stall the van to a stop.

"Hi Ally!" Beth exclaims, running towards me as I jump onto the ground.

Her smile is all kindness and mischief. In hot pursuit is her black Labrador which jumps excitedly about us.

"Hey girl," I croon at the old dog, crouching to stroke her ears.

We walk briskly up the driveway, shingle crunching underfoot. Beth lives with her family in a renovated farmhouse. It looks in one direction over a well-tended hedge, a potholed lane and a row of cottages, and in the other over swathes of farmland. Wisteria clambers about the front of the house. Soon it will be in bloom, and I'll stop and savour the smell of its pendulous violet flowers. At the back door I pull off my boots – the dog sniffs them then curls up in her basket – and we amble through to the kitchen, quarry tiles cold underfoot.

"Something smells good," I remark.

"Bolognese," says Beth. A pot bubbles on the Aga.

She lifts the door latch and we go through to the lounge. Floral curtains hang at lead paned windows, an inglenook fireplace holds wood asking to be lit, and old beams protrude from a low ceiling, their uneven lines like contours on a map. I sink into one of the sofas.

"Here you go," says Beth, prodding me with a bottle of wine.

With schooldays behind us and university still five months ahead, every day is like a weekend. I turn the bottle in my hands, admiring its Gothic label and orange peel surface. Beth gives me a corkscrew and I pop out the cork.

"So you've decided to join me?" Beth enquires, passing me two glasses then making for the record player.

Beth has been talking me into taking a job at the nearby chocolate factory where she has just begun work. She is saving up to travel abroad and has been hoping I'll do the same. I've been ambivalent about it. With the stress of A-levels still working itself out of my system, I've been enjoying the ease of these last months and feeling little compulsion to disrupt it.

"Well," I say, pouring the wine then looking up at her expectant face, pausing a moment for effect: "Yes!" I exclaim with a laugh. "I'm joining you."

Beth whoops and claps her hands together. I'm still surprised at myself too. Something has changed in me recently. I've felt an unseen push, an urge to go.

"I can't believe it!" Beth gasps, eyes lit up and coming to hug me and almost spilling our drinks. "It'll be great to have you at work! It does get a bit dull." Then she catches herself: "Hey, don't let that put you off. When we start travelling it'll all be worth it."

She goes to sift through her dad's LPs. Soon she's holding up an album in either hand. "Neil Young or Santana?"

"Neil, for now," I reply, handing her a glass. We sit facing one another. I feel the chocolate factory and train travel taking shape in my mind.

"What about Chloe?" I say. Chloe's a close school friend. "I'm sure she'd love to come too – what do you think?"

"Yeah, definitely," Beth says. "You want to call her?"

"Sure. I think she'll be back from London at the end of July."

"Just in time for Europe," Beth says, beaming.

"Well," I say, raising my glass, "here's to adventure!"

We clink glasses. Beth goes to place the stylus on the vinyl. A scratchy sound comes out of the speakers, followed by wistful folk-rock. We settle into the mellow ambience, chatting well into the afternoon. Not looking at the clock. Aware of time simply by the sun's movement across the sky.

After some hours, the bottle is almost finished, and the golden light of late afternoon is streaming through the windows. We go to eat some spaghetti then Beth turns on MTV. A bass guitar rumbles like a huge, brooding bumblebee trapped inside the TV set and there is an explosion of frenetic, atonal guitar licks. Beth turns up the volume, and I feel its scrambling pulse electrifying my body.

"Come on!" I shout to my friend, leaping across the room and throwing open the French doors to the garden.

We run into the orchard, and amid apple and pear trees we dance like bacchants. Music like that usually sets me off. It ignites in me an overwhelming urge to be outside under the big open sky and spin round and around, arms outstretched, fingertips skimming the spinning horizon, whirling like a dervish until I'm free of all thoughts and have no sense of body – just an ecstatic, whirring heart.

When it passes we slow down, sinking to the ground in a heap of laughter and disequilibrium. We stay a while, dizzy, giddy, lying on the grass and gazing up at the heavens. Something in me is satiated. But at times like these, something else seems always to linger, wanting. It's as though I'm missing something – something I perhaps once knew, once had, and am longing to get back to. If I'm still enough, I can sense it: a subtle, deep desire, not of my body or of my mind, but dwelling still and silent, waiting, within the very core of my being.

Daylight starts to slip away. The blue colours above are withdrawing, and before long, evening is spreading her cloak. Sober now, I head home while the sky is dimming to mauve, the road hypnotising me with its familiarity and the twilight mingling with my thoughts of travel.

The next day I apply for the job at the factory, and the day after I have packed a bag, left home and moved into Beth's small and cosy spare room.

Eggs

Monday morning. Beth and I head out into crisp, fresh air. Dew covers the fields and glistens in the pale sunlight. In her old red mini, windows open, we twist and turn along country lanes, our cigarette smoke merging with the early morning mists.

The chocolate factory is on the outskirts of town. It's a huge, cement block, similar in size to an aeroplane hangar with skylights in the roof but no windows. Workers trudge towards it in hushed conversation, smokers snatch last-minute drags. We join them. At the entrance, giant jellyfish strips of plastic form a transparent curtain. I push them aside and we walk in.

"Wow, what a smell!" I say, engulfed in a heady air of chocolate.

Beth half smiles, shrugs her shoulders and shows me my punch card. I thrust it into the machine. Clunk. 7.58 a.m. We put on white overalls, gather our hair in blue netted caps and venture out onto the floor. Industrial machinery groans, thuds and booms, echoing off the concrete walls and metal roof. Beth leaves me with a supervisor who takes me to where I'm to start working.

Chocolates of all shapes and sizes are being shunted along a multitude of conveyor belts, and people, motionless from the waist down, stand packaging them. At the end of the floor loom two colossal, metal cylinders.

"Is the chocolate made in those?" I ask the supervisor.

"Nah, that's for recycling," she says. "If ya get any deformed or broken chocolate on the belt, just chuck it in ya bin next to ya, and it'll get taken to them vats." She adds that the molten chocolate inside might be two years old.

The whole factory is producing Easter merchandise. I notice one line producing Easter frogs sporting marzipan crowns and polka-dot bow ties.

I'm shown to my line: miniature cardboard Easter bonnets containing chocolate eggs. A woman wearing a pink hat stands at the head of the line, eyeing me. I diligently begin my task: pick up bonnet, place on lid, turn brim. Pick up bonnet, place on lid, turn brim. I look up at the giant analogue clock on the wall. It's 8.19. Pick up bonnet, place on lid, turn brim.

Gradually I lose track of time. Pick up bonnet, place on lid, turn brim. I try not to look at the clock. When I do it's 8.31.

Ages later, the break-time buzzer barks. We file upstairs to the canteen. Seldom have I looked forward to a mug of tea and sandwich as I do now.

"The first days are the most difficult but you'll get used to it," Beth assures me. "And we'll soon have our travel money."

By the end of the week my feet ache in places I didn't know possible, my fingertips are raw from turning cardboard bonnets and my ears are ringing with dirty-white noise. Sometimes I smell alcohol on the breath of my co-workers. I understand why.

Beth was wrong about getting used to it. The following week I'm having to endure the same pop music played over and over again on the muffled radio – a special form of torture. I try to project my imagination elsewhere, but the music won't let me go. The novelty of working with chocolate has worn right off. I don't even notice its smell.

There's something else too, like a dark cloud creeping up on me. It's not so much a thought as a general sense of foreboding – about Easter and what all this means. I can't help thinking I'm complicit in co-opting the birth of Jesus with chocolate ovoids for the mass market.

It's true I haven't been to church for several years, but I've never lost a reverence for Jesus. Looking across the factory floor and its conveyor belts of endless chocolate riles me. It all seems so ludicrous. Something in my heart recoils. At times I want to laugh out loud to decry it, but that is kept in check by a greater sense of it all being very deeply, very disturbingly wrong.

A couple of weeks have passed. Beth and I have made friends with some of the workers. Julie is the sweetest.

"You goin' ta Naaridge on Sa'urd'y noight?" she'll ask in her strong accent. "Ooh, you're brave, aren'tcha."

Julie likes to share factory rumours. One of the girls, seventeen years old, has just had an abortion. Avoid so-and-so because he sleeps around. But mostly she talks about her little boy whose father left them. Julie dreams of other things, but she's happy to have a job to support her little family. I admire her.

Then there's Mark. "Girls shouldn't wear boots like that," he's said to me four times now. "Just ain't right."

Today I am assigned to the actual egg line. I even get a chair. Ornate boxes pass down our belt and it's my job to place two large egg halves inside them. Sometime around mid-morning I break one up and keep the pieces – partly for comfort, partly because I reckon eating will help pass the time. Soon I feel a bit sick. I swipe the rest of the broken chocolate into the bin beside me and start wondering just how many eggs will be coming down my line today. I try to calculate, using the huge factory clock on the far wall which seems to watch me. Ten every minute, that's about 600 an hour; factoring in our breaks, that's around 4,000 a day. I scan the factory floor and the other conveyor belts and can't quite believe the maths.

Later at Beth's, sitting in bed, I'm poring through one of her brother's books. It's all about paganism, and I come across a section about the celebration of Easter, how it derives from a practice of the Saxons. They worshipped the dawn goddess Eostre – hence the word.

I rest the book in my lap and look over to the window, suddenly drawn to the outside. Curious, I turn off the light and get up, throw open the little curtains and push the window open wide. Cold air rushes in and chills my hands, my face, my chest. I lean over the windowsill, looking out above the fields into the night. The stars are out. Shy and glinting, they appear as pinholes onto some bright wonder.

I recognise Cassiopeia, low in the sky, then Cepheus above it. Ursa Minor. Draco. I think of their stories in Roman mythology, their ancientness rousing my imagination.

Then I think of Jesus. There's no constellation named

after him. I wonder why. But that's fitting, I suppose, since I don't see him as some kind of myth. He was here once, like I am here now. For a moment I try to picture him. I see him walking between rough-hewn houses, bricks the colour of the dusty soil, with companions on his either side swathed in white, and a calm, determined look on his face. Then the image recedes and I see again the night in front of me, and I let my eyes roam its depths, putting legends to more constellations.

Soon I'm shivering. I close the window but leave the curtains open, rub my arms and quickly get back into bed. I feel my blood alive, invigorated. I turn the light back on and continue reading about Eostre and her eggs and rabbits. I was right, I think to myself: eggs have nothing to do with Jesus. Yet he has been reduced to this. I see him again in my mind's eye. He is in the factory, throwing over the conveyor belts like he threw over the moneylenders' tables. I imagine joining in.

Soon I've read enough. I turn off the light and lie looking towards the window, my eyes growing accustomed to the dark. Cassiopeia has fallen a little. I close my eyes and think ahead to tomorrow's work.

On the line the next day, I pick up a chocolate half and rest it in the palm of my hand. With my fingernail I scratch a large cross into the cavity and write: "Did Jesus die for this?" Then I close the egg, set it down in its fancy packaging and watch it glide to the end of the line to join the scores of identical boxes. I feel I'm sending it out to the whole wide world. But I'm not looking for a response – it's more that I want to defend this man of God as well as my own strained sense of integrity.

Jake

Three weeks have passed. The factory bell beeps loudly and another shift is over. I meet Beth at the jellyfish curtains and we march out into the chilly air with a dissipating crowd of workers. I pull my jacket close.

"Do you feel like meeting up with some of my friends?" asks Beth, unlocking the car.

"Who are they?" I ask as we get in.

"Just some folk from around here," she replies. She wiggles the key into the ignition and looks over at me. "Wanna go?"

"Sure," I reply, eager for a change of scene.

Beth reverses in a half loop, then we head into the small local town. In minutes we're circling the square then parking in front of a Georgian town house. We get out and I rap the knocker. A silhouette appears at an upstairs window.

"It's open!" a young woman calls out. "Come on up."

We enter and go up a narrow, unlit staircase to the first floor. A door opens, a friendly girl greets us and we step inside a pale yellow lounge with scant furniture. Two men in their thirties sit in armchairs, one with stubble, the other with scraggly hair, and a couple of girls a few years older than us are chatting on bean bags next to them. A man more our age sits on the floor beside a half-open sash window, strumming a guitar.

"Beth!" he says, eyes lighting up, his right hand slapping his instrument in a gesture of welcome.

"Alright Jake?" Beth grins. "This is my friend Ally."

"Great to see you both," Jake says, nodding his head and looking at me then Beth then at me again. A shard of sunlight nestles beside him.

"Hey, sit down," he says, and we sit next to him and he resumes his playing: folk music, a bit of blues, self-assured. "So what've you guys been up to?"

Beth and I have a moan about the factory.

"Man, I don't know how you do that stuff," he says, dividing his attention between us and his fretboard.

I explain we're saving up to go travelling.

"Cool," he says with a broad smile. "Off to India?"

"Nope, around Europe for a month," says Beth.

Jake stops playing for a moment and looks up at us. "What are you going for?" he asks.

"Why d'you think?" she laughs, and tells him to stop being silly. But I find myself thinking about his question: what *am* I going for?

Jake starts his playing again. I haven't heard a real musical instrument in a while. It's enchanting. Then I hear other sounds. Voices filtering up from the street. Birds. A bus going past. I get up and look out of the window. A war memorial stands in the centre of the square.

I look back at Jake. He has an unusual face, handsome in a way. His dark hair is just past shoulder length, straight like marram grass, flopping down on either side of his face, hiding his temples and reminding me of Iggy Pop. He's wearing a short-sleeved shirt I don't really like, a taupe colour with the two top buttons undone. A colourful eagle tattoo is half apparent on his upper left arm, and a thin, half-smoked roll-up hangs out of one side of his mouth. His eyes appear fixed on a nowhere place while he picks out a melody on his scuffed instrument.

We start talking with the others, all of whom Beth seems to know. It crosses my mind how we haven't hung out with anyone since I started work. Just sitting and chatting like this is a relief from the mind-numbing standing all day, passively listening to the radio.

"Well, it's good to meet you, Ally," Jake says when we get up to leave.

"You too," I say. "And your guitar."

Jake smiles and rests his forearm on the top of his instrument. "So," he says to us both. "You busy this weekend?"

Woods

The end of May heralds the approach of summer. Days and weeks have fallen into a reasonably tolerable rhythm of work, rest and play, and between seeing old school friends, Beth and I meet up with Jake. At last, I finish my time at the factory and have managed to save six hundred pounds for inter-railing. Beth decides to work an extra four weeks and tries to talk me into joining her, but just one more day, one more hour in that place would be impossible.

I decide to move back to my mother's for the while, my childhood home. It's a red-brick house, medium-sized and flanked by pillars and honeysuckle at the porch. Around it is a landscaped garden with such colourful and variegated foliage, it gives the impression of being in bloom even when nothing is. Its approach is bordered by a small field used for grazing highland cattle and small ponies, and populated by rabbits galore. Where the lane bends into a cul-de-sac there is a delightful little wood, worn into pathways by dog-walkers.

I drive up to see Beth at the weekends, and I see Jake too. I see him more than before, in fact. I tag along on visits to his friends but most often we go out for drives in my van. Rumbling along rural lanes beside hedgerows and wild-flower verges, through farms and well-kept villages, we have no particular destination in mind. There's purpose to be found simply in the journeying, and we stop whenever and wherever we feel like it.

We're not 'together'. In fact, the more time we spend together, the more evident is our unspoken, platonic pact. It's uncomplicated and freeing.

Time stretches out with little interruption. Moments like well-placed paintings furnish the backdrop of our drives, disturbed only when we decide to eat or tank up. There's no cause to rush or get anywhere, and when we come to a junction it is the turning that leads deeper into the landscape we choose, sleeping where sunset finds us.

Today I'm fetching Jake from his place on the outskirts of the factory town. He's living there with an older woman, an arrangement he's vague about. He runs upstairs to grab some clothes while I wait in the living room. A framed photograph of him faces me on the windowsill.

"So where are your parents?" I call up, wondering how old the photo is.

"They moved up north," he shouts down. "My dad's in the air force."

"Why didn't you move with them?" I ask, going to look at the figurines on the mantelpiece, observing crocheted doilies on the armchairs.

"Didn't want to," comes the terse reply.

I start wondering if this really is his parents' home.

"So what are you doing in this backwater," I call up from the bottom of the stairs.

"Same as you, man!" he calls back, coming down two at a time.

Jake says 'man' a lot. I imagine it's from some reggae or Rasta influence, or from listening to Woodstock-era artists. Perhaps he picked it up from the American kids he spent time with growing up on airbases. I'm not sure if it annoys me.

We head south-east. The sun is high in the sky. We drive for a while then stop by a field of leafy crops. Beyond is Foxley Wood, a dense swathe of ancient forest. The engine shudders to a halt and we jump to the ground and slam the doors. All is suddenly quiet. A cloud of gnats hovers head-height. Brown skipper butterflies flutter ahead and a silver dew survives the morning's warmth in a strip of shade by the hedgerow. We stroll along the edge of the field, disturbing pheasants. They squawk and spread their wings, airborne for a moment before setting down further off.

I tilt my head back, running my hands through my hair and breathing in the earthy, grassy-smelling air.

"Feels like I've been here before," I sigh.

"We have, haven't we?" says Jake, casually glancing around.

"Pretty sure we haven't," I say.

Jake shoves his hands in his jeans pockets and starts ambling towards the wood.

"Maybe I just feel it in my blood," I call out.

"Farmer's lass are we?" he replies over his shoulder.

I smile at the thought. "My mother was," I say, half to myself.

She's a redhead, my mother. Her skin is even fairer than

mine, rosier too, and her thick, lustrous hair is lightly back-combed into a bob parted on the side. She has always been beautiful. Her large, almond eyes are set wide apart, her generous cheekbones lend her face an open, friendly look, and she's quick to smile. She wears soft jumpers and smart trousers in every hue of cream and beige, and has never pierced her ears. I imagine her as a child, running through fields of ripening wheat under a hot summer sun.

I catch up with Jake and we sit on a grassy bank, the wood beside us.

"Potatoes or sugar beet?" says Jake, nodding towards the leafy crop before us.

"No idea," I say, getting up and crouching at the edge of the field.

I examine a rosette of dark green leaves, attached at the base to some root vegetable. It doesn't look familiar. My mother would know. She's a walking record of a country life now gone. She will tell how the men on their farm would harvest the wheat or barley with a binder then stack the sheaves into shocks, and how her father only let her wear trousers when she was fifteen so she could straddle the Ferguson tractor and drive it across the fields, the men throwing reaped crops onto her trailer.

"I reckon it's sugar beet," I say, rubbing a glossy, sturdy leaf between my fingertips.

"Hmm," says Jake. He puts a stem of grass in his mouth and turns it around with his tongue.

I get to my feet and look up the lines of leaves – green stripes against a dark brown earth, tapering towards the horizon. There is a potency here, and my sense of the seasons and the cycles of sowing and reaping enriches it. Ancestrally, however, I'm a step removed. My grandmother cared for her family and the farmworkers' families, and she managed a huge vegetable garden and produced all manner of pickles and preserves. But she wanted a different life for her daughter, who trained as a secretary, worked twelve years in the city, then broke centuries of family tradition by marrying a businessman, my father. In one generation, the transmission of my grandmother's way of life was broken.

The cry of a far-off bird disturbs my thoughts. I look up. High above the woodland I see a bird of prey, perhaps a buzzard. It cries out again, its sound thin and reed-like, filling the empty sky with high-pitched warning and otherworldly lament. Far from me it appears small, yet its form – like a loaded crossbow – is all predator. Its call echoes. It has an ethereal quality, like whale song on a higher frequency. My mind transfigures the experience so that I'm visualising myself in a line of symmetry between the heavens above and the deep of some undisturbed ocean. I'm mesmerised. Soon there is another buzzard, and together they spiral steadily on the warm air.

"Oh," I say, remembering something in the van. "I want to show you something." I get up and go to fetch it. Walking back, I feel excited.

"Have you read any of these books?" I ask, flashing him the cover of my latest read.

"Shamanism now?" Jake grins.

"So, have you?" I say.

"Everyone's read Castañeda, Ally."

"What? No, they haven't."

"He's a fake, isn't he?" Jake puts another stem of grass in his mouth.

I frown at him, disappointed. But I'm not deterred by his opinions. I sit down cross-legged and open the book. The pages are bright with the sun's reflection. In front of me is an account of a man's spiritual apprenticeship with a Yaqui Indian shaman. It fills me with curiosity and a sense of promise. I like his language of spiritual searching: where God has no name, there's no focus on suffering and redemption and, as I understand it, the attributes of nature – its wildness, spontaneity and innate wisdom – are embodied and used as tools to understand the whole of existence.

Squinting, I read aloud: "*The world of everyday life is not real or out there as we believe it is. Reality, or the world as we all know it, is only a description.*"

"Go on," says Jake, gazing at the horizon.

"Well, he talks about how certain people have unlearnt the world we've been taught to see, and see another they claim to be the real one."

"Our reality isn't really real?" says Jake. "How original."

"I know how that sounds, but..." I put the book down beside me and lean back on my hands. "Come on, you know there's more to the world than what we perceive with our senses."

"How we see this world is part of our being human isn't it?" he says. "Deny that and you deny our humanness."

"But what is our humanness, really?" I ask.

Jake lies down, arms above his head. He's on the verge of saying something, but then he sighs and shakes his head. Then, "I don't know if I can describe it."

"Maybe we've limited what it is to be human," I say, digging my boots into the soil and looking up at the sky. "Why else would we feel there's something more to this world?"

"True," says Jake. "But you won't get answers just reading about it."

"I thought you said you'd read these books?"

"No, man," Jake says, nudging me in the ribs. "I said everyone's read them. You know they're fiction, right?"

"Not necessarily."

Jake smiles. "Go on then. Read us some more."

I pick up the book and continue. *"In the universe there is an immeasurable, indescribable force that sorcerers call the Spirit, the Abstract or Intent, and..."*

"Sorcerers?"

"I know, I know," I say. "But Druids were sorcerers too."

Jake says nothing, slowly nodding his head in thought. I go on regardless.

"Intent is the living connection with everything in the universe."

Then I lie down holding the book as a shield against the sun and reading on aloud about how the busyness of our lives, our relentless interests, our concerns, hopes and fears obscure our link to Intent; how the seeker strives to clarify and revive that link, and that a guide for the path to its knowledge must be taken.

Jake goes quiet. He isn't the kind to look down on spiritual teachings per se. I've seen his book on Buddhism. He flips through it now and then. I appreciate its wisdom. But just as he doesn't really connect to my book, so I have an aversion to his, and because of something quite basic: depictions of divine beings with multiple, bangled arms.

"The thing is," says Jake, "you need a real-life, bona fide teacher for this." He pauses then looks at me. "That's not gonna happen any time soon is it?"

I look at him then look away, saying nothing. He may be right. But I'm not discouraged. I close my eyes and imagine myself with such a teacher: I don't see their face, but I feel their presence – real and somehow majestic. I see myself being somewhere hot. Sure of where I am. And that I'm a student full of yearning for knowledge.

Jake gets up and returns to the van. Soon I hear guitar chords filtering through the air. I stay where I am, reading. The words on the pages transport me to an untranslatable place between worlds. They give me a taste of something I know I want: something beyond myself.

Several chapters on, and the sun's rays have turned golden. The air fills with birdsong. I lay the book at my side and sit up, gazing towards the trees. Beneath them I make out a haze of blue, the last of spring's bluebells.

Leaves

A few days later I'm meeting Beth and Chloe to watch a band at a brick and mirrored-glass venue on the banks of the river in Norwich.

I see Beth in the lobby and we head upstairs to the bar. At the far end is a huge wall of glass offering an unnerving view to the river below. In the middle, sitting at one of the black designer tables, is our friend and fellow traveller-to-be Chloe, back in town for the weekend.

I'm happy to see her. "Hope you haven't been waiting long?" I say.

"Just got here," she replies with her big, enigmatic smile, taking off a plum jacket.

Chloe is half a foot taller than me. She's wearing quirky velvet culottes, long satin gloves and multiple silver rings. She has mousey hair which falls in thick cascades around her pale, heart-shaped face, and when she makes up her cat-like eyes with black liner they appear impossibly huge. She pronounces her S's crisply, reminding me of her Swedish mother, and part of her is given over to an indefatigable love of Prince and all things purple. She's quiet, but I wouldn't say she's shy or insecure. It's rather that she'd sooner listen than talk.

"So, you've got our journey mapped out already?" she asks, taking a menthol cigarette from a mother-of-pearl case.

"No way," replies Beth. "We've got as far as Amsterdam and roughly how to get to France and Spain. Maybe Italy too."

"Sounds great," says Chloe, puffing a stream of smoke upwards out of the right corner of her mouth. "I can't wait."

There's always been a good energy between Beth, Chloe and me. I'm closer to each of them than they are to one another but it's to no one's detriment. I visualise our route, wondering what experiences will come our way.

"Can you come to Beth's next week?" I ask Chloe. "We'll be looking at the map and you need to give us your input."

"Oh, I forgot to say," Beth interjects. "I've got a friend with a place outside Valencia. She's there with her boyfriend at the end of July and we're welcome to kip with them if we like."

"Are you arranging that before we leave?" asks Chloe.

"Don't think so," says Beth. "Let's just see how our route pans out."

"We haven't actually arranged anything," I say, rolling a cigarette.

"You don't think we should?" says Chloe.

"We'll have a travel guidebook," I say. "We can decide as we go along."

"Hey!" exclaims Beth, standing up and waving.

A friendly-looking young man on the far side of the

room waves back and makes his way through the jostling crowd. He's wearing a pale orange T-shirt, brown collarless leather jacket and blue 501s. "Matt," says Beth, "you know Ally and Chloe?"

"More or less," he grins, acknowledging us and taking a chair from the adjacent table. "How're you all doing?"

Matt is on the shorter side of medium height, a few inches taller than me. He has short brown hair and small, dark brown eyes that move quickly, darting if he's not sure of something, exuding warmth and kindness when he's relaxed. He's the kind of bloke everybody seems to know and like.

We chat for a bit. He talks in succinct, well-pronounced bursts, most often ending his sentences with a touch of humour and smiling so that small dimples appear in his cheeks. Soon he excuses himself, returning with light beers for the four of us. Leaning in, forearms on table, he listens attentively as we chat about our imminent travels.

Beth checks the time to see when the band are starting up. "Shall we drop them now?" she says.

"Sure," I say, getting out a tiny plastic bag and passing it around. We each take out a tiny square of cartridge paper stamped with a strawberry and put them under our tongues.

We tell Matt our travel plans.

"Well, if you're leaving in a few weeks I'll be beating you to it," he smiles. "I'll be in Spain this weekend."

"Spain?" I say. "Which part?"

"Somewhere in the south."

Beth checks the time again. "Hey, we've got five minutes," she says excitedly.

Downstairs there's a bustling atmosphere of fans and groupies. The band are fiddling with last minute tuning, the drummer taps out rhythms. Soon the stage blasts into sound, people are jumping all around and the whole place has gone wild.

Twenty minutes in, everything becomes rather strange. The music starts dissolving into jumbles of sounds. The lights are blurring into streaks of bright colour.

I feel Chloe tugging at my arm. "Ally, I'm really starting to trip, aren't you?" and before I can reply she's yelling in my ear, "We need to get out of here!" We find Beth and Matt who are feeling the same and we all agree to leave straight away.

Matt lives on the other side of town on the third floor of a Victorian terraced house. We tumble into his high-ceilinged room, disoriented and half-laughing. The pale blue walls are rippling slowly from corner to corner and the ceiling seems to be breathing.

"Nice room," I say, still capable of pleasantries.

"Thanks," says Matt, going to draw the curtains closed. The pupils of his eyes are so dilated that his irises are no longer visible. In their blackness are red whirling spirals.

"My mouth tastes metallic," I say, smoothing my tongue over my palette. "Does yours?"

"Yep," he says. "Here." He passes me a bottle of mineral water and it leaves a glimmering trail as it glides to my outstretched hand. Swallowing feels odd.

We sit down and get comfortable, remarking on the band we're missing and how our teeth feel brittle. I look at the posters on the wall. One of them is a large print of Jimi Hendrix playing Monterey. No sooner has my glance lingered than the legend himself is hurdling slow-motion out of the wall towards me. "Look! It's..." but then I think better of it.

"This is really strong stuff," says Chloe.

None of us says much after that. It's not so much that we feel comfortable enough with one another not to talk, but we've slipped away into our separate worlds. Thoughts cascade into themselves with helical precision and I watch them happen. It feels like I'm watching 'me' happen.

Soon, the whole room and everything in it is alive and moving. Whatever I look at starts dripping onto the floor or changes appearance completely. I can barely tell what is real. But this sense of separation from content and form is liberating, thrilling in fact.

"Let's go outside!" I say to the others, scrabbling to my feet. "Let's go and explore."

No one answers. Chloe is transfixed with her lavish doodling, Matt is staring at the cupboard and Beth has spent ages under a huge, red blanket. I poke it and she punches out a limb.

"Well I'm going out there," I say.

Matt offers me his Walkman and I gratefully accept it. Gripping the thing tightly I leave the room and make my way downstairs. I feel I'm leaving the world behind.

Outside is dark and misty. A warm glow throbs from the streetlamps. I start walking. During the day this area bustles with life. Now it's eerily silent. I come to a junction and am about to cross it when I sense something fall to the ground – a battery from the Walkman. I go to pick it up but my hand passes through the tarmac, the white paint of the crossing rippling around it. I jerk my hand back, watching open-mouthed as the liquid road stills. Then I reach down again, the white paint and black tarmac swirling around my forearms like marbling oils on water. My heart beats faster. I locate the battery by touch and quickly step back onto the pavement. I shouldn't be alone, I think to myself.

Back inside, upstairs, Matt agrees to join me. We head out. The night is still and yielding. Overhead, a starry blackness seems to protect us. We walk and walk. My whole being is full of joy and wonder, like a child at a fairground. I can't stop effusing about all the weird and wonderful things I'm seeing. Matt politely endures my commentaries. His vision is unaffected, but says his thoughts most definitely aren't.

Striding down a gravelly lane, we pass affluent properties and gardens spilling with shrubs and tall-stemmed flowers. My hallucinations are preposterous now. Tall fox-gloves morph into welcoming alligators standing on their tails. But more than all this, it's my sense of self that is now in change. It's become tenuous, and to keep some semblance of hold on it I keep telling myself my name, my age, my address. My body feels like it's merely a glove. A visible husk. And I sense similar superficiality in all of the external world, intuiting greater reality in its underlying, intrinsic presence. I sense something truly unfamiliar: objects offering up the very essence of themselves, their *is*-ness.

We come to a long, lamplit avenue, the end of which I can scarcely make out. On either side are mature lime trees, their lowest branches hanging just out of reach. I admire the majesty of their trunks, their boughs, the miniature canyons etched in their bark. I'm drawn closer to one of them and go to stand at its broad, sturdy girth looking upwards, marvelling at its round, glimmering leaves.

Something captivates me: I observe with awe how every single leaf is animated while remaining most definitely a leaf. I perceive some kind of emission coming from them. There are no words but I understand it to be a kind of language – a secret, perpetual outpouring as though I've tuned into a frequency, a radio channel I've never noticed.

Everything – the avenue, the street lamps, Matt, the trees – all of it fades into the background except this all-pervading perception. It is – in contrast to the events leading up to it – lucid, immediate. Distilled. Then something of this experience intensifies such that I can scarcely register what is happening. I feel I'm being drawn through a black hole, my consciousness both compressed and expanding. In the next moment I feel I've come out the other side. All is absolutely still, as though suspended.

Time seems no longer to pass. It exists in a state of constant present. All is quivering and pulsing with serene emanation, fundamental to all and everything. I feel I'm standing in what is unseen, observing some otherwise hidden phenomenon which is always all around me, and which always, simply, is. I'm not merely witness to it, I am intimately connected to the whole of it. For a timeless moment, my whole being is bathed in it. Saturated.

I thought the approach of day would break the spell. But as the first light of dawn gives way to a powder blue sky, primrose sunshine and the banter of people meeting for Sunday coffee and croissants, I'm still marvelling at my shape-shifting surroundings.

Matt and I return to his pad where Beth and Chloe are asleep. Inside, I feel claustrophobic and smaller – I can't bear it. I look around, and part of me suddenly fears that if I stay here a moment longer I'll lose the meaning of my inner experience.

"I think I'm going to head home, Matt. Thanks so much for having us over... and for walking with me."

"You don't want some tea before you go?" he says, putting the kettle on.

"No, I'm fine thanks. I need to leave." I glance again at Beth and Chloe. "Say goodbye to them for me. And hey, have a great time in Spain."

Back home, I withdraw to my bedroom with my watercolours, the chemicals withdrawing from my system. I paint a watery abstract of pink, mauve and violet trees, their branches hanging like willows over a lake of limpid blues. In my mind, I keep coming back to that lime tree. Those leaves. That language. I recall the sense of having been let in on a secret and can still inhabit its meaning – like I've been gifted an insight into the very nature of existence, how everything is constantly voicing something and that I, as a part of the natural world, am no exception.

Then I wonder if this is really the case. The doubt bothers me and prompts mixed feelings. I start picking apart the night: pinpointing moments of insight, then recalling my hallucinations – mostly nonsensical – and trying to ascertain whether the insight was merely a part of that.

But intuition says it wasn't. I did witness something. And dwelling on it again, a wash of longing for its essence seeps through me, colouring me like my paintbrush water.

I think about revisiting the experience, but something in me rejects the idea. Then I start wondering: surely there are ways of more deeply perceiving that don't involve chemicals? The question lingers while I flood the page with colour.

Intent

Chloe is back down in London and Jake and I are now spending most of our time together. The warmth of July invites us ever more outside and accompanies us for walks on beaches and strolls through woods. We come upon a village fair and a festival, dance at a country reggae gig and in the still moments we share reflections on life. We have little food but lots of time to tiptoe and trample around the meadows of our minds, groping at mysteries and wonders, me seeking something I'm unable to name.

Recently I bought a two-inch-wide leather wristband. With the blunt side of my pocketknife I inscribed along its top side the word INTENT. Something is calling me, and though I don't know what I'm being called to, I don't want to be distracted from it.

I glance at the wristband as I grip the steering wheel. I'm driving south with Jake towards Suffolk. The road we're on is straight, Roman, and on the horizon is a broad silhouette of pine trees, dense like tightly packed spears. Above it, a shield of cloud covers the sun. But not entirely. Sunlight escapes around its edges, bright and blazing like molten magnesium, paling to bronze as it spills towards us, bathing the fields in a rich amber glow.

I open my window and breathe in the dry, dusty smell of barley. Its mature, whiskered ears are hanging down, bowing to the coming harvest. An energy of potential is in the air.

"I feel good about this direction." I say. "You want to keep going?"

"Sure," Jake replies. "Maybe we can park in those woods ahead."

Soon we're on the cusp of the forest, the road in front cutting through as if parting an ocean.

Tall pine trees tower on either side and cast a deep shade on the undergrowth. I take a right turn, setting off a cawing clamour of rooks, then turn off-road, wheels juddering as we lurch into an area of deciduous trees, their leaves translucent with sparkling sunlight.

"How about over there?" Jake says, tapping his window.

The perfect clearing. I cut the engine and park. We step down onto the fertile mulch of the woodland floor. Sounds of the forest emerge and greet us. Jake wanders off to explore. With book in hand, I walk over to a fallen tree and clamber onto its trunk, its roots unearthed and exposed like an Arthur Rackham painting. Soft and sprawling plants grow round and about. Shafts of sunlight here and there illuminate floating pollen and dust. Birds are singing and squirrels romp along branches high above. Were we to stay long enough I'm sure every living inhabitant of the forest would show itself.

A twig snaps a little way off. Jake. I open my book.

"Are you there?" I shout out.

"Yep, over here," comes Jake's voice from behind a huge oak.

"*A warrior needs focus*," I call half joking into the undergrowth. "*Heightened awareness is like a springboard.*"

"A springboard to what?" Jake calls back, rustling towards me through the bracken.

I don't answer him.

Jake comes to sit with me, his hair loose around his face. He looks thoughtful and stares ahead as though looking at something he can't get into focus.

"I think I understand what he means," I say.

"Me too," says Jake, "but only in my head."

He pauses.

"What do you think it is that'd take us from a mental understanding to real experience?"

I try to respond but can't. I realise I'm using the same faculty in my mind to ask and to answer the question – like a dog chasing its tail.

"I just..." I exhale, puffing out my cheeks. "All I know is that I want to know."

"Sure," says Jake, his tone kind. "But man, maybe you should try reading something else."

"Maybe it's the translation?" I suggest limply. I lift up my book again and read: "*People have no idea of the strange power they carry within. At this moment, for instance, you have the means to reach Infinity.*" I clasp the book to my chest. "I'm not sure if we can reach the petrol station tomorrow morning." Silence. We burst out laughing. "I'm serious!" I continue, "I should have filled up this morning."

"Guess we'll find out tomorrow," Jake says, yawning.

Evening is drawing in. Trees transform into silhouettes against an orange sky and owls twit-twit-awhoo a duet. A cold breeze blows through my clothes and gives me goose-bumps. I go back to the van, grab a blanket and climb up onto the roof. Following close behind, Jake reaches through the window, pulls out his guitar and clambers up beside me. I feel that mellow, alive feeling from being outside all day. Together we watch an amber sun descend behind the green-wood. Streaks of pink blaze across a purple skyscape. Jake strums a few chords, then he sets on a tune that seeps into the twilight; soulful cadences merging with the fading of the day.

"I'm going inside," Jake says eventually, putting his guitar across his lap. "You coming?"

"In a bit," I say, looking beyond our clearing to darkening trees.

Jake clambers down, his guitar twanging, and gets inside the van, rocking me on top. I hear him put on his jacket. I pull my blanket tighter around me. There's still some light left and I stay to witness it and the forest life withdrawing, the birds fluttering their wings as they settle to roost.

I used to come here with my family and our caravan. I remember being five and allowed to cycle off into the forest by myself for the very first time. The sense of independence was exhilarating. Thrilling. I have a photo of me then, on my bike next to the Swingball. Hair in bunches. Paused deep in thought.

Inside the van, a candle burns atop the cooker and Jake is asleep. I climb in and see my dim reflection in the back window. I blow out the candle and pinch the wick in my fingers. It sizzles for a split second. Jake moves a little. I look over to him and in the darkness I make out his pouch of rune stones lying next to him. I wonder about the long-ago people who might have used them: Vikings, Saxons. I think of the Celtic Iceni tribe who governed this whole area and trod this very soil. Their queen, Boudicca, a flame-haired warrior, led her people in revolt against the incursive Romans. One of my cousins now farms what was once her land, her fort, her marketplace.

I lie down and look out of the window into the blackness. Moonlight glimmers through a weave of treetops.

"Hey," says Jake.

I don't answer.

He turns towards me and clears his throat. "You okay?" he says sleepily.

"I'm fine," I whisper, turning to look at his face, its contours barely recognisable in the darkness. For a moment, I'm acutely aware of our proximity, our physicality. But something stops me from moving into that world – something tentative – and the words come out of my mouth: "Go back to sleep."

Jake turns to face the other way and soon the sound of his breathing becomes heavy again.

I love this time, the depths of night. These are the hours when reflections come thick and fast, when darkness sheds light on thoughts daytime obscures. My mind wanders. It settles again on the ancients. I see them as signposts, showing me the way to some age-old, natural law. My thoughts bear no nostalgia. Rather, they give form to a deep-down longing, a yearning *to know* that radiates out from my solar plexus, causing my heart to beat a little stronger and making me all the more aware of my own breath.

My book comes to mind. I see Native Americans, arid plains and strange rock formations. I see shamans shape-shifting into the spirit world. And I incline to those images: their vast open space and sun-like warmth, but I concede that for me, now, they are a fantasy.

I think of Jesus again. What of him? And what of Buddha? What of all the prophets?

I reach for the book and read: '*When a warrior learns to stop the internal dialogue, everything becomes possible.*'

Suddenly I feel out of place. I sit bolt upright, disturbed. What the hell am I doing here? The thought is energised by a tightness in my chest, then it shoots again and again at some inner point-blank range. I catch myself not breathing. My lungs feel tight. *Please God, stop these thoughts*, I think to myself. Then a voice from a deeper place says: *Let me find it.* What that means I cannot say. With answers to nothing, I eventually fall asleep.

"Wake up."
I open my eyes.
I'm suspended in pure light.
"Wake up."
There is an absence of everything except this light.
Where am I?
Nothing seems to exist but this.
I hear the voice again: "Wake up."
And I realise the voice is my own.

I wake with a gasp, into darkness. My body is uncovered, cold. I prop myself up and peer through the windows. It's still dark. Trees and bracken stand in still silhouette. I watch the motionless scene, expecting something to happen. I feel alarmed, but more than that, relieved. In my mind's eye I see that light, more a vision than a dream. I keep peering through the window. Silence. Yet in this silence those words still resonate – wake up – and they linger on, reflecting in the pool of my mind, demanding something of me. But what? Where do I go from here? I try to reinhabit the experience. I can't. Only a subtle tension remains, a luminous residue.

I look over at Jake and admire for a while his sleeping, boyish face. I reach out to touch him but then think better of it, preferring to stay within the confines of my own self, cautious lest the power of that advice, that command, be lost.

Slowly and carefully, not wanting to disturb him, I pull a blanket over my body, lie down again and try to get back to sleep. It must be around four, nearly dawn. Warmer now, my muscles relax. For a while I gaze at the treetops and the limpid black sky between. I imagine myself journeying up and out into the empty-full, dark beyond, rolling like a wave, on and on into unseeable expanse, restless to arrive at some distant, starlit shore. And yet, the warmth of my blanket pulls me back, returns me to my body and its limitations. I close my eyes and imagine the whole universe inside me.

Then I recall that vision of pure light.

I think of God.

God can't 'look like' anything, I think to myself. *Can't 'be like' anything*. I wonder how to think about God, my thoughts lapping at some inner ocean.

I pick up the book and feel on it the dampness of the night. I fumble for my lighter and rub its flint, its flame burning steadily with a hiss. I read: *'A man of knowledge lives by acting, not by thinking about acting.'* I look away from the page. I realise how tired I am of thinking. I'm so tired of trying to work it all out. I close the book and muse its cover, a scorched Dali-esque desertscape. A giant cactus in the foreground forms the shape of a closed hand and its index finger points upwards to the sky where white clouds form a mouth.

I let the flame die and toss the lighter to the side.

Inspiration seizes me. With book in hand, I carefully creak open the back door of the van just enough to let myself out. In the darkness, I tread barefoot towards the trees, feet wet with dew, face moist with mist. As my eyes grow accustomed to the night and the black of its shapes and forms, paler objects begin to emerge as though lit from within: the trunk of a silver birch, grey flints and nubs of chalk on the ground, and the brass Celtic bangle which hugs my upper right arm and seems almost to glow. I spot a hole in an oak tree and carefully make my way over. Standing on tiptoes and leaning against the damp, humus-smelling bark, I reach up and place the book into the recess. I confer a blessing on it and on the next person who may find it. Then I step back, satisfaction coursing through my veins.

I turn around and face towards the clearing. I'm about to make my way back to the van when something stops me. I decide to stay a while at the foot of the oak, wanting to mark this special letting go. I stand up straight and close my eyes.

I breathe in the forest; its mulchy, woody, earthy, sweet-smelling, cool and sensual air. I breathe out. Moments pass. I feel night relinquishing its hold. I open my eyes and look up, resting my eyes on the leaf-laden, moon-a-glow boughs and branches that stretch out over me. Then, through the trees, I see the first glimmer of dawn.

I hear creatures rousing and rustling in the undergrowth. Birds; first one, then two, three and more begin to sing. Still and alert, I watch the darkness recede and listen with delight to the sounds of the forest growing louder and louder, proclaiming with abandon the break of day.

Maps

It's the weekend and we're making plans at Beth's house. The afternoon is overcast and chilly, and a map of Europe lies unfurled across the table. Jake hovers beside me.

"Okay!" says Beth, pushing her fringe from her face and tracing her finger over the train routes. "Train to Harwich, ferry to the Hook of Holland..."

"I can't believe you're really going," Jake interjects.

"You'd better believe it!" I reply. "Train through Belgium to France," I continue. "Shall we stop in Paris?"

Jake plonks himself in a chair at the far end of the table and rolls a cigarette.

"I think we should get the night train through," says Beth. "Down to Bordeaux maybe..."

"Then on to Spain and Italy," I suggest.

"Italy's a push," says Beth. "But we could manage it."

Jake drops some irreverent comments about sleeping rough, spending all our money and ending up broke.

"We'll see, won't we," I say, smiling at him and shrugging my shoulders.

He blows a perfect smoke ring in my direction. I open my travel guide to compare maps.

"Where's Chloe got to?" says Beth.

"She'll be here soon I reckon," I say. "Meanwhile folks, I'm going to make some tea. Who wants some?"

I go to the kitchen and put the kettle on. In the orchard the trees are swaying. Beyond them is a view of the fields stretching to the horizon. A wind buffets the wheat this way and that and the sky is darkening. Lightning flashes in the near distance.

"Did you see that?" I gasp.

The others hurry to the window. There's a rolling boom of thunder, then cracking sounds as though the far off sky is being split apart. We stare outside and wait. But nothing more comes. Beth and Jake wander back to the table. I remain at the window, watching, hoping for the storm to break and rains to come, but the sky grows quiet. In the distance, however, storm clouds are still gathering, latent with energy. Expectant. The light in the sky slips further. Then headlights appear in the driveway.

"Chloe's here!" I call out.

Beth goes out to greet her. I take another mug from the cupboard, set about making tea for four and hunting for some biscuits.

Lank

It's a couple of weeks later. Nearly August. I'm in a smelly, red telephone box calling my mother. The van has broken down and is parked up at a mechanic's in a rundown part of the city. I've been high for four days and haven't slept.

No answer.

I hang up and push open the door. A feverish tingle rushes up through my blood and my face suddenly feels numb and puffy.

"Do I look odd to you," I say to Jake, letting the door shut and smoothing my hands over my temples and staring at the cold moisture on my palms.

Jake frowns a little. "Maybe we should eat something." He jogs to a convenience store over the road and returns with some bananas.

"When was the last time we ate?" I say, peeling one.

"It's been a while," says Jake, chomping and studying my face. He half-smiles, concern in his eyes.

I feel slightly panicked. I start imagining I'm about to overdose and wonder whether I should be calling my mother and brother to tell them I love them. Something in me overrides it.

"Feeling any better?" Jake asks.

The banana feels sludgy and alien in my mouth.

"Hmm?" says Jake.

I glance up at his eyes, looking to see if he's still worried. Then I feel my body responding to nutrients, absorbing them, assimilating them.

Jake grins. "Man, I reckon you're okay," he says, bending his knees so that his eyes are level with mine. "Hey?"

"Hope so," I say, meeting his gaze and eating some more.

Two bananas and half a bottle of flat Coke later, we're walking into the city. I have to get passport photos for my interrail ticket. We stand outside a booth on the second floor of a department store, waiting for my photos to appear in the shoot. I catch myself in the mirror: my eyes are sunken and my hair hangs lank and lifeless over my shoulders. I'm horrified. Hopefully it won't show in the photos. An electric rolling sound diverts my attention and the booth spits out a set of four pictures. I grab them impatiently, the colours developing in my hand.

"Where's that sweet girl gone?" Jake says smiling but clenching his jaw. He takes the glossy strip out of my hands and looks repeatedly between it and me.

"I'm still here," I say, annoyed at him, but mostly with myself.

I whisk the photos out of his hand, barely looking at

them, and stuff them into my bag. Suddenly, I don't want to be seen like this.

"I think I'm going to go home," I say quickly.

"Yeah?" says Jake tentatively, looking straight into my eyes, making me feel exposed. "You mean, right *now*?"

"I need to get it together before going away, okay? Take a bath... see my mother."

"Well, I guess that's probably a good idea." He smiles, but I feel his disappointment. "What about the van though?"

"It can stay where it is for now. Hopefully I'll get it sorted before I leave."

"I'll come and see you before you get on that train, okay?" His posture and smile are awkward all of a sudden, as though he's feeling rejected.

"Sure," I say brightly, not wanting to hurt his feelings.

He hesitates a moment. "You sure you're okay?" His eyes are full of concern.

"I think I will be."

We part with friendly words. I stay put, watching as he turns and walks towards the lift. For a moment I wonder where he will go and what he will do. He's just moved into Norwich but he's not familiar with the city. I notice his shirt untucked and his jeans baggy around his thighs. He's got thinner lately. I see him pressing the button for the lift, sinking his hands into his pockets, turning to smile at an old man hobbled beside him and tilting up his head to watch the lift numbers change. It feels odd looking at him from afar. I'm usually right next to him. I wonder what I'd think of him if I were seeing him now for the first time. Something about him feels like a stranger. I think back to meeting him in that flat, me striking up conversation, him strumming his guitar. Just reminiscing about it makes me feel like something has come to an end.

The blue light says '2', our floor, and I quickly turn and walk away. I hear the lift open with a 'ching' then close. He's gone. I walk towards the stairs, retrieving the photo strip from my bag and hoping I don't look so bad after all. I scrutinise the wan image. I look awful. How hadn't I noticed? My heart sinks again. I thrust it back in my bag, the images still gnawing at me, and head down the stairs.

Leaving the entrance lobby, I push open one of the glass doors and inhale the fresh air on my face. Then something makes me look back. Behind me, an elderly lady dressed in a tweed jacket and skirt with a small silk scarf around her neck is approaching the door. I wait a moment, holding it open.

As she walks through, she looks straight at me, longer than a glance, and says quite clearly and deliberately: "You will have your reward in heaven." Before I can think of how to reply, she's making her way out onto the street, the lane curving to the left and taking her out of sight.

I walk out into the street, full of the image of the lady's face and her words. I walk past the foot of the Guildhall then alongside the open-air market and its multicoloured striped roofs, all the time with the warm feeling of a stranger's kindness.

You'll have your reward in heaven, I think to myself. Straight out of the blue.

The bus station is a few minutes away. I decide to take the route that goes past where my father used to work. Soon I'm approaching the building: majestic, Palladian – I can't take my eyes off it. I admire its limestone pagoda and columns, its ornamental urns atop pillars. As I get closer I see gold, bare-bosomed dragons, their outstretched wings guarding the ground floor windows.

It's strange to think that many years ago my father used to come here every day. I feel a pang of sadness. I don't remember much about him. I do remember feeling safe when he was around. He taught me basic woodwork and we assembled model aircraft kits together. He encouraged me to run – "*faster, faster!*" – and how to ride a bike. He wore yellow flip-flops around the house, perhaps a leftover from working in India. He exercised every morning before going to work and in the afternoons I'd watch at the window for him to come home. At night he read me bedtime stories.

I stop in front of the building, my eyes roaming its grand details. Back then, before my father died, I felt God to be good and kind. All things were bright and beautiful. But when he passed away, I came to understand God in another, deeper way: not just as something I'd heard people talking about, but as All-Encompassing.

Inescapable.

A young man in a smart grey suit with a black briefcase pushes out of the front doors. He jogs down the steps, smoothing down his tie, and hurries purposely onto the street. I imagine my father doing the same – coming out of those same doors and hastening down those same steps.

For years after he died, there was a painful, grief-carved chasm. It had neither form nor limit, yet some invisible, unconscious barrier which prevented me from expressing it to anyone. Those who tried talking to me about it felt like intruders. Thieves after treasure. Part of me grew to be alone, separate and private.

Daytime was full of school and lots of friends, sports, music lessons and children's TV, and I was seemingly a happy, fun-loving child. I let myself cry only after swimming lessons, reckoning that whoever saw my blotchy, tear-stained face would think it was the chlorine.

Night however, was another land. My heart ached and caved so much that at times it felt as though my lungs were punctured. But in all that there was something else.

A secret.

Sometimes at night, lying in bed, the pain would give way, and for a timeless moment I would be floating, suspended, in the vastness of the universe. I remember seeing stars – lights – all around me. My whole being would become flooded with peace. I knew God then. And my heart would be mended and I would fall straight to sleep.

I turn back to the pavement. Nearly opposite the building is the entrance to the bus station. I walk through it to the top end and sit down on a metal bench next to a woman with a pram. I've got a ten-minute wait before my bus comes. The air is cooling and I don't have a warm coat. I cross my arms and hug my body, looking up and down the road and its slow-moving traffic. I miss my van.

Jake's probably home now, I think to myself. I recall our conversations in the van about life, death and the afterlife. I used to talk to my father about those things. He was good at listening, and what I loved was that his answers always left me wanting more. When I could no longer ask him, I tried imagining what his answers might be so that I might walk in the footprints of his thoughts. In time though, I found the sand was too close to the sea.

At home I call Beth. We talk about leaving at the end of the week. After calling Chloe to check with her, we have our departure date. I tell my mother our plan and her mood brightens; I can tell she's been worried about my van life. She puts the kettle on and over a quick cup of tea I tell her our interrail ideas. It all seems quite abstract.

Later, I go upstairs and run a bath. I stand naked in front of the wide bathroom mirror. I lean in and examine my sunken eyes. My irises are pale grey-blue with a pronounced navy ring encircling them. Beneath them, the whites are looking somewhat yellowed.

"You will get your reward in heaven," I hear the old lady say.

Looking now at my worn-out reflection, I feel I've let myself down. I've strayed from the person I feel myself to be. I'm out of sync.

I brush my teeth for longer than usual. My eyes rest on the African violets standing in a pot next to the sink. Evening sunlight catches their mist-like surface. I lean down and scoop handfuls of cold water into my mouth, surprised at how refreshing it is. I straighten up and stare again at the mirror, at the person who for all these years has stood faithfully looking back.

Bench

A few days later I'm making a trip into the city for last minute bits and pieces. Besides the interrail ticket and traveller's cheques, I have mosquito repellent, plasters and a compass on my list. It's morning and the air is crisp. I'm wearing my grey cowboy hat and blue-lensed sunglasses and I feel bright and energised by the sunshine on my face and smiles from passers-by. It takes me only half an hour to get what I need. I decide to take the scenic route back to the car park.

The stroll takes me though one of the city's oldest parts. The ground here is cobbled, the houses timber-framed and askew. The last vehicles that drove down these quaint, narrow lanes were horse-drawn. It's a pedestrian area now.

On my left I pass a church that overlooks a small green. Its walls are clad with flint from the north Norfolk coast and above its arched doorway is a square blue sundial with gold hands and numerals shining in the sunlight. It's larger than my village church at Cringleford, where my mother would take my brother and me every Sunday when we were small. Dressed in our best clothes – I remember a grey woollen coat with velvet collar and cuffs – we would sit in pews close to the front. I loved the history of the place: generations of villagers coming together Sunday after Sunday until death obliged them, like my father, to rest in the graveyard outside.

The church I'm passing is now an antiques and collectibles shop. I see a couple coming out and sitting on a bench in front, going over their purchases.

At a widening of the footway is a cluster of clothing boutiques, a bookstore, a health-food shop and a couple of New Age places – one called *Head in the Clouds*, a survivor from the 70s. Above are upper stories whose Tudor beams jut precariously over the street.

I pass an old tavern, and further along is another church, this one guarded by black railings and a row of chained-up bikes. I glance up at its arched windows, their latticed panes in need of a clean, its tall tower adorned with a crenelated parapet full of cooing pigeons.

Cringleford church is much older than these ones. I haven't been in a while, but I remember the sense of it. If I arrived early for Friday evening choir practice, I'd stand at the back in the musty silence, alone, and for as long as I could bear the spookiness I would let my eyes roam the stained-glass windows of haloed saints, the dark grey ledger stones on the floor in the aisle, and a faded Saxon mural on one of the walls. If I was sure no one was watching, I'd trace my fingertips around the 500-year-old font. There was a presence there then, more immediate than when the rest of the choir came in and the practice began.

Back in the present, a couple brush past me, laughing, nudging my hat askew. I take it off, shake out my hair and put it back on. Then I start wondering how many people have passed this church here: all the life it has seen. The most curious feature in Cringleford church was a hole chiselled in an oblique direction through its thick, outside wall to the altar. It's called a leper's squint, and it let the diseased and other undesirables witness the service from the outside without disturbing the rest of the congregation. Many a time I peered through that two-metre-long scope, imagining the plight of people forced to weather the elements and worship as outcasts. I imagined how *they* might have felt the presence of God. It gave me goosebumps.

I pass the black-railed church and its boarded-up door. Nobody prays there anymore. I don't think it's used for anything.

I'm nearly on the street that will take me up to the gardens and back to where the van is parked. A little way ahead and to the right I notice a man sitting squarely on a bench. He has tanned skin, thick, dark blonde hair and strong features. He's leaning forward a little, resting his forearms on his thighs, hands lightly clasped and looking directly at me with steady blue eyes. His gaze unsettles me and I'm struck by a strange thought:

He's a man of God.

Something inside me comes to a halt.

A man of God? The thought comes as a surprise. But more surprising is how it doesn't seem silly or odd. It feels significant. I become acutely aware of my breathing, how my heart is beating faster. The recognition shoots down my veins and stirs up a well of feeling. For as long as I remember, I've been wanting to know someone who truly knows God.

I remember when I was eleven, I watched a TV series about the life of Jesus. It was a cinematic blend of the four New Testament accounts. For the six weeks before Easter, our family sat glued to the television set watching Jesus's life and the events leading up to his death play out before us. I was gripped from start to finish, often concealing my tears.

Come to think of it, since an early age I was always curious about Jesus. In fact, I longed to meet him; to be like Mary of Bethany and pour perfumed oil on his feet and wipe them with my hair; to be one of his disciples; to spend just one moment in his presence. I asked God that I might come to know him, to see him even. I told myself it wasn't possible. But I would still ask.

Years later, I read an interview with the series' lead actor. He said that filming had been boring. When he was on the cross between shots, he'd be in his dressing gown and slippers and his wife would hand him cigarettes; brandy when it got cold. The Hollywood bubble burst. But the hidden longing remained.

And now this man in front of me. I feel self-conscious and force myself to look away, part of me thinking how ridiculous I'm being. But my intuition is so strong I cannot help but look back, and when he glances at me again I feel the same powerful jolt at my core. Then I notice the footsteps of passers-by, a cosmetic smell wafting out of a hair salon, bright sunlight. A voice inside me says: *Go up to him!*

The next thing I know, I've walked right past him and I'm at the junction of another lane. I stop abruptly and feel the yearning of my younger years. Spinning around, I hasten back to the bench where I saw him. But he has gone. I look up and down the length of the street – he's not there – then, breaking into a run, I start looking up all the nearby lanes and alleyways.

He's nowhere to be seen. My heart is pounding and I'm out of breath. The part of me that scoffed at my gut feeling now scoffs again at my searching. But I ignore it. In the middle of the street amid the people to-ing and fro-ing, I tilt my head to the sky. "Please, give me another chance," I find myself whispering. "I won't miss it again. I *promise.*"

Tarot

We have one day left in beautiful, summery England. One more day of nettles and daisies, swallows and skylarks, of stout corn bales adorning the fields. I spend it with Beth and Jake at my mother's house; drinking tea, washing clothes, but mostly flicking through my travel guide with Beth, reading up on European history, culture and sights. Jake doesn't say much.

In the late afternoon, my mother returns from playing bridge with friends. Beth chats with her in the kitchen, their upbeat voices filtering through to the games room where I play a few rounds of pool with Jake. When we tire of it we join them for tea and toast.

"Alison, I was just telling Beth I'd really appreciate you keeping in touch," my mother says, going to put her cup and saucer by the sink. "You think I'm silly, but I do worry." She glances at Beth apologetically.

"Mum, we're going away for a month, not a year."

"My dear, when you're a mother you'll know what it's like. Mark my words."

She often says this. I'm not a mother, so I can't disagree with her. But her worrying irritates me. I try not to react, but I let out a big sigh. She comes to sit down. Her face is lined but her warmth of spirit gives it a youthful quality. "Just please be careful and…"

"Mum, I *know*!" I look to Beth and roll my eyes. She's smiling at the familiar exchange.

"Beth's mother is concerned too, you know."

My mother looks at me, waiting for something. I don't want to distress her, so with a conceding tone I say, "I know, Mum," then I get up and try to reassure her with a hug. "Sorry," I say, squeezing her tight.

Upstairs in the bathroom, I brush my teeth, splash my face with water and peer at myself in the mirror. In my bedroom I slide open the cupboard. On the left hang my clothes and on the right are shelves of books. I consider what to take. Imagining long train journeys, I decide on a tatty biography of Jimi Hendrix and his band. I decide to take my Tarot cards too, and reach up to where I keep them on the long shelf atop the wardrobe, a place to which I'd often climb in hide-and-seek games with my brother.

The cards aren't where I remember leaving them. I step up onto the bottom shelf of the cupboard, straining to feel them. I come across my collection of family Bibles. I take one of them down. The book in my hand is large and heavy and has a rich brown, tooled-leather cover. I carefully lift its brass clasp and open it to the inside page. I notice its date: 1868. Elegantly handwritten words are dedicated to my great, great grandmother: "With earnest wishes and prayers for her spiritual and temporal welfare."

I put my nose gently to the page and breathe in. I love that musty, old-paper smell. I reread the words and feel them warm me. They seem bound to another time, when belief was a given and words such as these were commonplace. I imagine how special it must have felt to receive such a magnificent book, and how special it must have felt to give it. I wipe off the dust and place it back where I found it. Then I stand on my tiptoes and spot the Tarot deck at the back.

"Hey," says Beth, poking her head around the door. "Chloe called. We're meeting at half six, yeah?"

"Bright and early, yep."

"How's the packing going?" she asks, going to sit on my rocking chair.

I step down onto the carpet. "Haven't started, to be honest."

I hold out the Tarot cards, an Arthurian set in pre-Raphaelite style.

"Fancy a quick reading?"

"It's getting late, Ally. We should..." Beth's voice trails off as I sit down, shuffle the cards and lay them out.

"Oh, alright."

I turn my cards over one by one. Beth moves to the edge of the chair.

"Hey, I didn't want to mention it in front of your mum," she says, her voice lowered, "but have you heard about Matt? Word is he's been brainwashed by some people he hooked up with abroad."

"What?" I make a face. "Who?"

"Dunno. Something to do with an old school friend."

"That's odd," I remark, thinking back to the last time I saw him. "Doesn't sound like him."

"I know," says Beth, frowning.

Our attention returns to the cards.

"You see those ones?" I say, pointing to three of the seven cards. "They're turning up all the time. Chloe got them the other day too."

"I'm looking up what they mean," Beth says, taking the Tarot book.

Jake knocks gently on the bedroom door and comes in. "You okay?" he says, sitting down next to me. I point to my card reading.

"Again?" he says, staring at it. "What d'you make of it?"

I shrug my shoulders. "It feels significant but I can't imagine what it could mean."

Then Beth gasps, her eyes on a page in the book. "Shit, Ally! The Apple Woman is actually the Death card. What the hell?"

"Don't freak out," I say, amused. "After death comes life. New beginnings. It's a positive card."

I return the cards to the deck, hoping I'm right. The readings I've been getting lately indicate change, the giving up of things, transition. The prospect is exciting. At the same time, I don't put much stock by it all. Tarot is just a bit of fun, a novelty really.

"Do Beth's," says Jake.

"Yeah, let's!" says Beth, putting down the book.

I hand her the cards. She shuffles vigorously then lays them out. The same three cards appear in the same positions.

"Weird," she says, shaking her head.

I leave Beth and Jake reading the book's definitions while I turn to packing. With warmer weather in mind, I get out my black gym shoes from the cupboard and throw some light tops, shorts and a silk minidress into my rucksack along with my passport – a last-minute temporary one but it'll do – then my traveller's cheques and train ticket.

It's nearing ten o'clock when night descends. I offer to drive Jake home.

"Come on, merry prankster," I joke as he shuts the front door behind us and I run ahead to my mended van.

"You're the prankster Ally," he calls out, catching me up and trying to pinch my cheek.

It's chilly out. Rain clouds are gathered overhead. We climb into the van and I wire it into life. Soon we're on the main road heading into town. We don't talk much. I want to say something but I can't – our parting has crept up on me and got me feeling self-conscious. I pull up outside his house and leave the engine running.

"Thanks for the ride, Ally," says Jake. "So, have a really great time." He looks at me awaiting some acknowledgment.

"Sure," I manage.

This is more than a goodbye. It's a letting go. But I don't want to let go. I turn off the engine and a roar of quiet engulfs us.

"You're not going to kiss me goodbye?" I venture, summoning the courage and struggling for the first time in his presence to get words out of my mouth.

Jake smiles and we lean towards each other over the warm hood of the engine between our seats, and like a scene from a black and white movie we politely kiss goodbye. He pulls away, the leather of his seat squeaking loudly in the darkness. But I don't pull away – I'm stuck on freeze-frame, pinned in place by a resistance to separate.

I imagine him inclining towards me, kissing me again and me kissing him back; him pushing my hair off my cheek and resting the palm of his hand on the side of my face, his guitar-calloused fingers pressing lightly into my skin. Siren thoughts whisper: *this is no ending, don't get on that train* – and I imagine reaching out in the darkness and putting my hand around his neck and drawing him closer so that I'm breathing his scent of musk and tobacco and sawdust, breathing in our woods and forests and skyscapes, breathing in...

Jake leans towards me ready to kiss me. This time I know it's how I want him to. I close my eyes.

Something stops me. With a gasp I pull back. This isn't what's meant for me. I know it. I look into Jake's enquiring face; his kind, handsome-in-a-way face cast half into shadow by the lamplight, and all I want to do is keep on looking. Still, I turn away. I feel his eyes on me, and everything in me wants to turn back to him. But I fix my gaze through the windscreen in front of me. It's starting to drizzle.

"Bye Ally," Jake says softly. He clears his throat. "Call me when you get back."

And with that he opens his door and jumps down onto the street. I feel him walk around the back of the van, my skin prickling at the sound of his footsteps. He raps one of the back doors twice by way of a second goodbye then I hear the lock turn in his front door. I will myself not to look. Before the door closes I'm starting up the engine and pulling away.

Driving home, I'm shocked by what just happened. I stick a cassette of harp music into the tape deck, but within seconds its delicateness irritates me and I swap it for some hardcore Nirvana. That's better.

I drive off the ring road then the heavens open. Squalls of rainwater pound the roof and lash at the windscreen, the sound duelling with lurching guitar cadences and raspy vocals. I drive faster and turn on my wipers. Rhythmic thudding comes at me while I struggle to see through a windscreen clear for only brief moments. Water sprays up from the tyres with a crescendoing hiss and the sounds from the speakers pale to noise. Too much noise. I feel for the eject button and toss the tape onto the empty passenger seat.

Now the confines of my van are an echo chamber of rainfall, amplifying my conflicted feelings: curious longing for Jake's touch, excitement at the thought of it and annoyance at wanting it too late. Then there's the self-reproach: did I just betray our friendship? Our platonic, spiritual-questing, music-loving, nature-soaked companionship? Street lights cast jagged reflections in puddles. I swish through them all.

But I'm still caught. I keep replaying what just happened, spellbound by fantasies of where it could have gone. Imagined sequences play out, and I let them. I enjoy them. Then ahead, a traffic light turns red and I reach out my foot to brake. Paused, waiting at the junction, I look up at the light and stare directly into its red, fiery glare, defiant in the downpour, its brightness hurting my retinas and daring me to look away. Is that actually what our time was about? Was I that oblivious to my desires?

The traffic light turns amber and I redirect my gaze to the road in front. Was I in denial, fooling myself all along? Green. I drive away into rain so heavy, it's like bullets on a steel drum. Then a thought comes to me, more striking than the others: I didn't *want* to get together with him in that way. I was wanting something else – something of another nature. The whole boyfriend-girlfriend thing would have short-circuited a journey, a quest; an advancement towards something I know deep down.

The road is straight now. For a moment I rest my forearms on the large, thin steering wheel. An image comes to mind: Jake and I standing side by side looking out to the horizon. I see how he was a companion with whom I searched for something. I just didn't find what I was looking for.

The rain is letting up. I pass Cringleford church then make a right onto the road towards my mother's house. Soon I'm turning off downhill, my wipers starting to squeak against a rainless windscreen. I switch them off. Now there is just the familiar hum of the engine, the rumble of the wheels and the warm air blowing from the vents. I think of my book hidden in the oak. I think of the ancients. The shamans. The prophets. I'm still searching.

I turn into the drive along the field. Behind the hedgerow I see dark outlines of grazing ponies, and beyond them the black mass of woodland. Then I'm home. I ease the van up the driveway and park alongside the conifers. I get out and tread lightly towards the porch. Honeysuckle scents the air. The security lights come on and I pause a moment. In the floodlit garden I see the leaves of the maple and the walnut, fully grown now, and the grass cut long for summer. The evening's rain has settled on the lawn and assumed the appearance of dew.

I stretch out my arms and reach up into the night. The clouds are dispersing and directly above is a swathe of clear sky. The lights click off and my eyes grow accustomed to the dark. Constellations emerge – patterns as familiar as the freckles on my face. How reassuring they are: in perpetual movement yet eternally constant. I wonder if I'll see them in French and Spanish skies. Then I wonder where I might be when I do see them, and whether I'll be happy to have left all this behind.

Depart

There's something about trains. Sitting on board the service to Harwich looking out of the window across the platforms, I feel it. I visualise myself from the outside of the carriage looking in and imagine how others might see me.

Beth and Chloe sit opposite. We're listening for the stationmaster's whistle, because in two minutes it will turn seven o'clock and our journey will begin. The carriage is warm and full. I look around, wondering where our fellow passengers are headed. Doors at either end open and close for last minute passengers, and with them a stale odour of bleach and cigarette butts wafts down the aisle.

Then the whistle echoes loudly in the station rafters. There's a lurch, the screech of metal on metal, and we're slowly pulling out of Norwich station. My palms are sweating. I press them into the seat and feel the synthetic roughness of public-transport fabric. A man's voice announces the itinerary over the tannoy. Beth and Chloe chat excitedly. I try to join in but my mind is elsewhere: Where am I going? *Why am I going?*

I feel the rattling acceleration of the train, the jolt and sway of our carriage. Faster and faster, warehouses, power cables and misshapen shrubs pass by our window. What am I going *for?* I recall idle days spent out in the van; reading into the early hours, transported to far off places, and I want to be there again, not here. My stomach churns. I feel sick from lack of sleep. I wonder if I should tell my friends how I feel, whether I should apologise and get off at the next stop. But I can't think how to broach it and nothing comes out of my mouth. I feel wrenched from my beautiful familiar; outside are colourless skies, pylons and ugly buildings.

We ride further and further from the city. What *can* I say to Beth and Chloe? That I'd prefer to hang out with some guy I met just a few months ago?

Then I think back to those long weeks of factory work and recall the intention behind taking the job. I remember how that urge to leave England had gripped me; that gut feeling to just go. I look down at my wristband and study its carved word: INTENT. I mull over what it means to me now. Outside the window, the countryside comes and goes. My eyes flick from one scene to the next. Marshlands and meadows. Geese on a river. A man walking his dog.

A decision surfaces: I'm setting out on this journey. I *intend* it. I refocus and see my reflection in the window. My eyes are still sunken. *I intend this,* I say to myself, and somehow I know it's the right thing to be on this train.

I lean back in my seat and smile at Beth and Chloe. *Plus, it's only for a month,* I tell myself. And I do love travelling. I breathe out slowly, willing myself to submit to the journey. I'll feel better soon. I rest my hand on my stomach. Just four weeks.

The outskirts of the city pale and shrink into the distance. I see violet hues in the clouds. I watch fields, grazing animals and spinneys whizz past. Chloe gets out her travel book and pores over possibilities. I see the occasional windmill, and sometimes the train slows so that I can see clearly the hedgerows which hug the train tracks just metres away: hawthorns tangled with flowering dog rose and threaded with thorny brambles hanging heavy with blackberries – thousands of them – some red and ripening, some deep purple and bulbous. The clickety-clack of our carriage lulls me into daydreams, punctuated now and then by brief hollow roars as we pass beneath bridges.

Later we arrive at Harwich. From there we take the ferry to the Hook of Holland. I'm seasick all the way. On the train to Utrecht, we're holed up in the bicycle carriage. Sitting on the floor amid a trove of wheels, frames and handlebars, we share our plans with a cheery group of Dutch backpackers whose friendliness is the best welcome to their country we could have wished for.

We disembark at Utrecht. I try to get interested in the history of the place, reading in my guidebook how it has been the religious centre of the Netherlands since the eighth century and that its history dates back to the year 47, when Emperor Claudius ordered his general to build defences along the Rhine, which bordered his Empire. But I don't really care.

We spend the day strolling aimlessly through the city centre. It begins to bucket down with rain and we take shelter under trees in a park. We get thoroughly soaked. I'd happily spend more time with the likes of those Dutch travellers, but here in this grey, wet place there are none to be seen.

The next hours are a sodden limbo-land. We try to laugh it off – there are moments when it does feel fun – but I can't help wondering what on earth I'm doing here. The thought weighs on my heart and seems to prick my conscience.

In the early afternoon we're getting on our next train. As it pulls away from the station, I look down at my wristband, rotating it this way and that, reading and rereading its letters.

PART II

Amsterdam

"This is it," exclaims Beth as our train hisses to a halt. "Amsterdam."

We hoist on our rucksacks and I start feeling excited as we step down onto a busy subterranean platform, joining a stream of fellow passengers and a babble of foreign languages. We jostle our way upstairs along vinyl floors, plastic banisters and inaudible announcements then surface into a large sunlit atrium.

"Hello Amsterdam!" I say, putting my arms around the shoulders of my friends and pulling them close as we walk towards the bright entrance.

"He-hey!" chimes Beth. Chloe's mouth is agape.

Arm in arm, we walk out and find ourselves at the edge of an enormous square. In front of us the sky is blue with a few wisps of cloud, and the late afternoon sun is shining on a hoard of folk to-ing and fro-ing in front of us. Groups of people our age are all over the square, huddled around rucksacks and chatting; some of them watching street performers or listening to buskers. The sight of them makes me happy. A strong optimism comes over me for the first time since leaving home, to do with who we might meet along the way, what we'll see, what we'll experience.

I stretch my arms wide and slowly turn round and around, delighting in our surroundings and this newfound ambience of freedom and possibility. Beth and Chloe grin at my antics and we mosey into the square, weaving our way among fellow travellers.

"The *size* of this place," says Beth, looking around with her hands on her hips.

"The smell of it!" I grin. Marijuana wafts through the air. There is also the smell of sausages frying at a nearby stand and the subtler scents of hops and seawater.

We sit down on warm cobbles.

"And you see that," says Chloe, looking up from the travel guide and pointing to the red and white station behind us. "It's neo-Renaissance, apparently."

It reminds me of the Jacobean stately homes to which my mother would take me in north Norfolk. Thinking of England, I realise the unease about leaving has completely left me.

Chloe continues, reading: "Amsterdam rests on three man-made islands, themselves resting on thousands of wooden piles driven deep into muddy soil." She pauses and looks up at us.

"Uh-huh," says Beth, and we burst into laughter.

"Shall we get something to eat?" I suggest eventually.

Restaurants and cafés line the square. We choose a simple

one at the far end and eat sandwiches. Looking out, the area is quiet for its size, then I notice the lack of vehicles. Instead there is a constant swish and rattle of bicycles. The place is teeming with them.

Afterwards we stroll past a war memorial surrounded by tourists taking photos, a palatial building with a green copper dome and scores of elegant windows, and a large Gothic-looking church. It feels good to stretch our legs. My senses are heightened, hooked by hearing passers-by chatting in Dutch, the sight of unfamiliar number plates, and my first time seeing a tram. There is also the freedom of being a complete stranger: nobody knows us and we know no one. Everything is whittled down to the immediacy of the present moment.

Evening sets in and our thoughts turn to where we can spend the night. It's not as easy as we'd assumed: the backpacker lodges are full and the bed and breakfasts and guesthouses are booked up too. We ask at a hotel but it's far too expensive. At another, the rates are even higher.

"Shall we try over there?" Beth says, pointing towards an area away from the square.

"Looks a bit dodgy don't you think?" I reply.

"Let's go and see," says Beth, and we head for an area of dirty-cream housing blocks. Soon we're wandering through cramped, concrete streets. Twilight is yielding to darkness.

"I hope somewhere has room," I mutter, noticing figures emerging from the shadows.

"Shit, Ally," Beth exclaims. "Let's have another look at the book."

"Maybe we should go back and look on the other side of the square?" says Chloe.

We come to a halt and I let down my rucksack. I'm opening the top zip to retrieve the travel guide when a group of men appear in front of us.

"Hello girls!" one of them ventures with some kind of accent, not Dutch. "Are you lost?"

"Er, no. Just looking for something, thanks," I say hurriedly, keeping my eyes down. The men approach and my heart starts pounding. They're just metres from us now. I pretend to keep searching for 'something' although the book is just under my hand. I glance up at them for a split second. I sense Beth and Chloe tensing up and wonder if instead of concealing our panic we should be running as fast as we can.

"You're lost!" another of them says. "No problem. You need a place to stay?"

"No thanks." "Yes." "NO!" We look at each other.

"Let's go," Beth whispers, inching backwards.

"Don't worry. Bismillah." the man says. "We take you where you can stay. Good place, clean. Not too expensive. Come! We are your hosts."

Beth looks at me and I look at Chloe who's looking at Beth. Something tells me the men genuinely want to help. Then one of them looks like he's going to walk away. I hoist my rucksack onto my back.

"Okay!" I call out, walking towards them.

The men break into smiles. Beth hisses my name under her breath.

"Come on," I say to her over my shoulder, and she and Chloe hoist up their packs and follow.

"You just arrived, yes?" one of the young men continues. "Welcome!" he says enthusiastically.

"And where are you from – not here?" I continue, judging by their darkish skin, hair and eyes.

"From Morocco. But now we live here. Helping travellers like you!" he laughs.

In a couple of minutes, we arrive at an inconspicuous hostel set back from the street. A matronly lady in a grey pinafore appears and greets us, and after formalities that include holding our passports until morning, our attention returns to the three men. We thank them and they smile and wish us well. I wonder if we should give them some money, but they say goodbye, turn their backs and disappear into the night.

It's dark. A dim amber light glows at a wide, horizontal window high up in the wall. My bed is fresh and warm and there's a smell of mildew and soap. I roll onto my back and my eyes roam the ceiling, the other beds – some with outlines of breathing bodies – and the window, open just a little. I'm tired, but traces of adrenalin tremor in my veins. Beth and Chloe are close but I don't speak to them. It might wake someone up. I think of woods and forests and how moonlight is colder than the light here, but better at telling stories.

Someone opposite me coughs. Another sighs loudly. Then all is quiet except for a humming sound – air conditioning perhaps, or a fridge.

Canal

I wake up in a small white dorm with metal bunk beds and over a dozen females in various states of sleep, dress and departure. The novelty jolts me. Too self-conscious to sleep more, I get up. Beth and Chloe are still asleep. I head for the showers. The hot water is luxurious, and for the first time in twenty-four hours I feel clean.

I find Beth and Chloe in the cafeteria, queuing for muesli and orange juice. Beth has ditched her baggy trousers for shorts and is in a turquoise top with a neckline she cut wider herself. Chloe is in shorts too, her velvets swapped for pretty cottons.

A huge cross hangs on the wall behind the main buffet area, and a group of fully garbed nuns sit at a nearby table engrossed in grapefruit, surrounded by a mixed crew of backpackers and possibly homeless people.

We reclaim our passports then wander back to the square, which is still full of the same kind of people as yesterday. But it's drizzling now. We check the map then head south from the station, cross a bridge over a tree-lined canal and reach the oldest part of the city. Soon it's pouring and we start feeling chilly.

"Hopefully it won't get colder than this," Chloe says, her teeth chattering.

"Hopefully," I say. "I didn't bring a coat."

We pass a row of small, bare, red-lit rooms with huge windows. In each one is a lingeried prostitute waiting for a client.

"At least we've got more clothes than them," says Beth.

We cross the same canal further along. Old gabled buildings preside over well-kept flower beds and there's a colourful row of townhouses with coffee shops along the ground floors. We enter one and sit by an open sash window looking out over the canal and its colourful houseboats.

In the 17th century, this city was the leading financial centre of the world. Ships sailed from here to all over the globe: the Baltic, North America, Africa, Indonesia, India, Sri Lanka, Brazil. Overseas trading posts became Dutch colonies. That's all far removed from our experience now, sitting in an unambitious café surrounded by a city of tourists. But the thought of it occupies me.

We order hot chocolate and marijuana – another novelty, buying it openly like this – and spend the afternoon watching rain on the water, enjoying one another's company and getting high.

Phosphor

The next morning we're back at the station and catching a train to Belgium. After a change in Brussels, it's plain sailing to Bordeaux in the French south-west. Hours pass peacefully amid an ever-changing montage of villages and towns, passengers, dreams and skyscapes.

We change in Bordeaux then arrive at a small town called Arcachon. It feels different here, and much warmer. The sun is shining brightly and there's barely a cloud in the sky. The air feels fresh and is fragrant with the scent of grass and warmed stones.

The bus to Cap Ferret is small, old-fashioned and has sand-scratched windows. Our journey takes us in a loop around a large bay: briefly eastward through connecting towns, northward through a tranquil wilderness of green open land, forests and sand dunes, then southward down a peninsula of fishing villages and holiday homes. The man sitting next to us says it's been a haunt of artists and poets since the 1900s.

The bus driver lets us out before the town. We thank him and jump down onto sandy earth. There are no houses and no sounds of traffic at all. It feels remote, almost ghostly. My ears ring. At a solitary shop we buy some baguettes and cheap wine, then with map in hand we set off down a lane towards a forest. Locals greet us; they seem used to foreigners.

The little youth hostel is tucked away amid tall, sweet-smelling pines. It has a kitchen, shower block and general mess room, and outside is an army-style tent with neat rows of camp beds. At the back are freestanding taps and outdoor showers. Washing lines are strung from tree to tree with colourful clothes, some snagging on blackberry bushes.

The smell of coffee must have woken me. People are chatting just outside the tent. Beth's silhouette appears in the doorway.

"Morning, Ally!"

"Hi!" I reply, pulling clean clothes from my rucksack. "How's it going out there?"

"Great! You coming out?"

Outside, a barbecue is underway.

"Ally, meet Arnou and Claude," says Beth in French. "Guys, this is Ally."

"Bonjour," they say, then launch effortlessly into English.

The two guys are deeply tanned with tribal art tattooed over their broad shoulders and biceps. Arnou turns sausages on the grill with a long camping fork, while Chloe and Claude are making French toast. I've wanted a tattoo for months but can't commit to a design. Beth has a Japanese symbol at the top of her arm. I can't remember what it means.

"So you're French, but on holiday *here*," I remark, "in France?"

"But of course," says Claude, amused. "What better country?"

The smell of barbecued sausages is attracting people. Soon there are about fifteen English, Dutch and German travellers, as well as a group of French youngsters.

Later we wander along a forest track to the beach, singing at the top of our voices. Glimpses of the ocean flash between the trees. A sea-salty fragrance moistens the air, birds chatter and swoop from one branch to the other, and the Atlantic whispers loudly, inviting us closer.

We spend the day by the dunes. I hate sunbathing, but this is different. There are no tourists. No hotels. No pop music. In front of us lie vast tracts of sand which flirt in the distance with a turquoise ocean.

In the afternoon we take a walk on the bay side of the promontory. Fishermen are working near the shore and children are collecting buckets of crabs and pulling up nets of tiny fish. Later we cross to the ocean side where a few, faraway sunbathers dot the white sands and surfers catch the waves. Ships sit on the far horizon.

After a mellow day with no sense of time, evening approaches as though suddenly remembering it should. We gaze out to sea, lazing on the dunes, trying to avoid spikey grasses that protrude through the fine white sand. An engorged sun hovers low in the sky, shimmering like liquid fire. Slowly it descends towards the water. I de-cork the wine with a scavenged stick and we take turns swigging it. We seem to have little to say. For a moment, it's as if we don't really know each other at all.

In silence we witness the sun sink, slowly, slowly into the sea. I hug my knees to my chest and feel the loss of its light and warmth. Then I feel agitated, like I should be doing something. The colours of sunset drain from red to mauve. Beth finishes the last of our wine. Stars come out.

On the way back we bump into Arnou and Claude.

"Where are you going?" Arnou asks.

"Back to the hostel," says Chloe.

"We're going to the restaurant in the village," says Claude. "You want to join us? They have great food."

He was right. In a little inn, joined by more travellers, we sit around gingham-dressed tables lit by miniature boat lanterns, sharing delicious fish and a huge platter of thin chips.

The following day passes in similar fashion. When the sun goes down, we stay on the beach a while longer then head off along the shore. Soon we spot a large campfire and make our way over. We come to a group of fellow hostellers playing guitars, dancing jigs in the sand and lying in each other's laps looking up at the black sky. We sit and chat with them. Breezes whisper around us, playing with our hair and rousing the fire.

Afterwards we venture into the darkness, lured by the rhythmic, seductive roar of the ocean. A little way off we make out clusters of human shapes standing at the shore.

"What are they pointing at?" I say as we approach.

"Look at that!" cries Beth.

A blue, luminous glow glimmers in the surf: phosphorescence. Whooping with sudden delight, we fling off our clothes and run headlong into the gleaming, liquid blackness. Up and down the beach, gleeful shrieks pierce the night air as others discover the same magic. We dive in and out of the water, laughing and splashing. We twirl around and around, our fingers skimming the surface and leaving trails of stars in their wake. I scoop up seawater and throw it up to the sky, then gasp in wonder as showers of shimmering sapphires rain down, clinging for a few precious moments to my goosebumped skin.

Back in the tent, in the hours close to dawn, a new blood is coursing through my veins. Lying here in silence, eyes closed, I'm still swimming, swimming, swimming in that ocean with its cascading waves and ethereal constellations. I feel completely at peace. Immersed in all-pervading aliveness. Washed and washed through by some timeless, penetrating presence.

Madrid

The next day, back on a train, we cross the border into northern Spain. Sand is still in our shoes and rucksacks, and our hair is thick and curly from seawater. I look down at my arms and legs and take pleasure in the fact my skin is no longer so white and pasty. Beth and Chloe feel the same.

We're heading for Madrid. Green, undulating landscapes unfold outside our window. I mull over the map in the front of our travel guide.

"I have his number you know," says Beth.

"Whose?" asks Chloe.

"Matt's," says Beth.

"We should give him a call," I say. "Where is he anyway?"

"Said he was headed for Granada," Beth replies.

"Granada?" I say, turning to the index of my book. "I'm looking it up."

"Where *is* Granada?" says Chloe.

"In the south, I think." I flick through some pages then read aloud:

After the Moors invaded Spain in the eighth century, its southern region became the mighty kingdom of Al-Andalus, and the capital of Cordoba was transformed into a centre of unimaginable wealth, sophistication, culture and learning unrivalled anywhere in either the western or Islamic eastern worlds.

I look up from the book. "Have you heard of it?"

"Nope," says Beth.

"Sounds interesting," says Chloe.

I read on about authors, painters and poets who loved Cordoba.

"Read what it says about Granada," says Beth.

"Okay." I clear my throat. *"If you see only one town in Spain, it should be Granada."* I slap the book shut. "Well that was easy."

"Come on!" Chloe laughs. "What else does it say?"

I reopen the book. "Well," I say, skimming down the page, "there's quite a bit about a fortress. But Beth, didn't you say Matt had been brainwashed by some group or something?"

"That's what I heard. I haven't heard anything since though."

"We should go and see what that's about," I say. "Hey, we should go and rescue him."

We disembark at Madrid and find a phone booth to call Matt. Beth taps in his number. The phone rings and rings, then there's a recorded message in Spanish. She hangs up.

"I'd quite like to visit Granada, even if we don't get through to Matt," says Chloe.

"Me too," I say, looking at the departures board.

We have a six hour wait until the next train to Granada. We head out of the station towards the centre of the city. Hardly a soul is on the street and everything looks closed; an unwelcome introduction to siesta time. Roadside billboards announce a temperature of 44 °C and the pavement beneath us is unfamiliarly hot. At some point, when we pause to look at our map, I notice the rubber soles of my gym shoes are leaving slimy patches on the pavement.

We walk along main roads and around huge, grand roundabouts adorned with classical statues. The sun is so dazzling I can barely look up at them. Our rucksacks are heavy and the fumes from the traffic strong. The thought of visiting tourist attractions is unappealing, and the lack of people out and about makes for a lacklustre experience. Five more hours.

We spend the next portion of time wandering from one road to another in search of some activity – other backpackers perhaps – and punctuating our time with buying cold fizzy drinks from the dispensers on the street. Before long we return to the station and its air conditioning.

At the phone booth again, I try getting through to Matt. Eventually, someone answers in English and tells me to hold. I pass Beth the handset.

"Matt!" she exclaims. "Wow! We thought we'd never get through."

There's a pause as Beth listens. Then, "We're in Madrid right now..." Another pause.

Then she turns to us and whispers: "He's invited us to Granada!"

She talks to him some more.

"He'll meet us at the station and we can stay at his flat if we want," she adds.

"Yes!" exclaim Chloe and I together.

"Did you hear that, Matt?" Beth says loudly into the handset. "We'll see you there!"

Granada

Heading south, the vegetation changes as though we're passing from one season to another. Green and lush at first, it's now turning sage and silver, the soil reddening to a rich, burnt sienna. Little by little the land is more arid. But despite the dryness, olive groves thrive as far as the eye can see, their round trees dotting the sloping land like orderly knots on threads. Now and then I notice a farmstead sitting proud on a hill and birds of prey circling and soaring high in the sky. Shepherds herd flocks of sheep.

We arrive at Granada around midday. The shriek of brakes presses a shrill excitement through the air. Outside our window we see people sitting on a bench and a couple standing hand in hand. But no one familiar. We step down onto the platform and into a rush of hot air. Matt's not here, so we walk onto the station concourse, eyes peeled.

"Is that him?" says Chloe, nodding towards someone waiting at the far exit. We keep walking. Then...

"It is!" laughs Beth.

Matt has grown a short beard which makes him look quite different. He's standing with two other guys. We quicken our pace, happy to see him.

"Hello!" says Matt.

"Hellooooo!" we reply.

Matt beams. "Well, this is a surprise," he says with a chuckle.

"Thanks for inviting us," Beth enthuses.

"I'm glad you're actually here!" Chloe says. "We were thinking this'd be a bit hit and miss, then we almost didn't recognise you."

"Well, I'm glad it's all come together," he says.

Matt slowly nods his head, taking in the sight of the three of us, rocking forward onto his toes then back. He seems speechless.

"So..." I say, acknowledging his two friends.

"Ah yes! This is Hamza," says Matt, introducing us to the taller of his friends.

Hamza must be around six foot four. He's broad-shouldered and athletic and is wearing a dark red T-shirt and black jeans. He has a kind face with twinkly brown eyes that crease downwards at the edges. He greets us courteously, his smile revealing large, handsome teeth. His face flushes slightly. We say our hellos.

"And this is Aziz," says Matt. Aziz is almost as tall, but slimmer and wearing a polo shirt and chinos. He faces us squarely, hands on hips as though poised for action of some sort, his eyes examining us with warm intensity. More hellos.

"I think I've met you before, haven't I?" I say, addressing Matt's friends.

"I... don't think so," says Hamza.

I persist in asking where I might have met them. Hamza is from near Norwich and Aziz recently left Cambridge University so it's not impossible our paths might have crossed.

"I'm quite sure we haven't," Hamza says again politely.

"The important thing is you're meeting us now!" adds Aziz.

"Need help with those rucksacks?" says Matt.

Beth giggles at his chivalry while Chloe and I decline the offer, and we all head out of the station, continuing to thank Matt and his friends for meeting us.

Hamza's car is red and titchy. He and Aziz get into the front, while we squeeze our luggage into the boot and ourselves into the back with Matt.

"We'll go straight to the flat, if that's okay?" says Matt. "I'm staying there with Hamza. It's in the old quarter – the Albaicín. I think you'll like it."

Before long we're motoring along the arteries of the town, then through smaller, residential streets.

"So how long have you been here?" Chloe asks, reaching for the car's grab handle.

"About two months," Matt says. "Hamza's an old school friend."

"Are you girls thirsty?" says Aziz, turning back to look at us. "We can stop and get something if you want?"

We tell him we're fine. Hamza asks about our train journey and we tell him about our time in Madrid.

Wooden shutters and brown balconies flash past. The streets become increasingly narrow and I begin to see why Hamza has a tiny car.

Soon he takes a sharp left, and we're driving up, up and

up past a blur of whitewashed walls, ornate doorways and wrought-iron streetlamps. Hamza shifts down to second gear and the engine revs louder. We rumble up even narrower, cobbled lanes, the wheels thudding and shuddering, us gasping as we almost scrape the houses on either side; up and up until Hamza brings the car to an abrupt halt.

"This is it," Matt announces. Hamza yanks on the handbrake.

We get out and haul our rucksacks from the boot. I feel as if I lost my stomach somewhere further back. Hamza leads us up a short alleyway which the car couldn't have fitted through. Its high walls – pitted and dented, with crumbling plaster and brickwork in places – cast a pleasant shade. Cypress trees stand tall behind them, their perfect tips pointing to a clear blue sky. Underfoot are smooth cobblestones laid in a herringbone pattern, and there's a shallow step upwards every five or six paces.

We come out at a sloping little square. Its angles are irregular and its sides comprise frontages of several tall houses, a walled garden and exits to two other alleyways. The sunlight here feels even brighter.

"And this is us," says Matt.

He points to a pretty blue and white sign, mounted high on one of the walls. "Placeta Nevot."

We head across the square to a delightfully traditional, antiquated and limewashed four-storey building. On the upper storeys, glass-panelled, primrose-painted double doors open onto balconies where balustrades guard an array of red, white and pink geraniums so vigorous their pots seem barely to contain them. Adjoining the building to the left are three arches; through them is a densely foliaged garden. To the right is a dilapidated little structure with a sealed-up door and ramshackle roof.

Hamza steps up to the wooden front door, turns the key in the lock and opens it wide. We follow him into a cool interior which smells of fresh plaster and masonry dust, then up a curving stairway of cold, grey marble steps. Barefoot now because of blisters on my heels from Madrid, my feet savour every step. On the second floor, Hamza unlocks another door.

"You can leave your shoes here," he says, slipping out of his leather boat shoes and showing us a footwear rack behind the door. We negotiate the cramped entrance with rucksacks on our backs then follow him down a terracotta-tiled corridor and into a cool and shaded, spacious room.

"So, here we are," says Hamza, crossing the room and opening a set of balcony doors.

Sunlight streams in and illuminates the floating dust.

"Welcome!" he adds, opening his arms and turning to face us.

"Thank you!" we say, offloading our rucksacks by the door. Aziz looks on, smiling.

The room feels clean and fresh and has an aroma of sun-warmed wood. It has whitewashed walls with interesting wall-hangings and a colourful Persian rug which covers most of the floor. In the corner is a wooden desk and chair. There are two bookcases, and along two walls lie dark green divans with propped-up kilim cushions.

"Great, isn't it?" says Matt. "It gets hot in here so we keep the shutters half-closed around now."

"Come check out the view," says Hamza, beckoning us over.

We join him on the balcony, just wide enough for the four of us. To the left, opposite the dilapidated dwelling is a white house, its green-framed windows each mounted with a violet-painted, stone, female face – mythical yet unappealing.

On the far side of the square, nestled in mature palm trees, is a splendid Moorish-style, mauve-painted manor house, replete with Moroccan arched windows. It stands behind a high and crenellated wall, which is lavished with pink-flowering shrubs and creepers that spill over it into the square, partially obscuring its doorway.

"And if you look over there," says Hamza, gesturing to his left through a gap between the neighbouring buildings and over higgledy-piggledy old houses of peeling distemper and mottled roof tiles, "you can just see the Alhambra."

We lean over the balcony and see a section of the great fortress I'd read about on the train. It's an unusual orangey colour. What I can see of it looks impressive and austere. Beautiful. Like no other structure I've seen before.

"Make yourselves at home," says Matt, hovering near the door.

"Thank you!" we say again, going back in to sit on the cushions.

I feel a strong sense of gratitude and can't stop smiling. I hadn't expected such a welcome or such easy-going hospitality. Matt's friends seem totally relaxed, full of nonchalant kindness. After the uncertainty of where we'd stay and who we might meet, arriving here with them is a real relief.

"I'm sorry to say this," Matt adds, "but I need to go straight out to get some food. You can come with me and get a feel of the area if you like?"

"I'd *love* to come!" says Beth, clapping her hands. "Me too," says Chloe. They jump to their feet.

I excuse myself. I still feel carsick. "Is that alright?"

"Of course!" Matt says. "We'll see you in an hour or so."

"Well, it's a pleasure to meet you," says Aziz, also leaving. "I hope to see you some time soon." He turns to Hamza. "Have you still got time to join me?"

"Sure," says Hamza, jingling the car keys in his pocket. In a moment they're all disappearing out the door and down the stairs. I go back to the balcony and watch my friends walk off uphill and out of sight. I admire a blue flowering bush cascading over the wall close by. A couple of swifts dart in front of me then swoop away over the rooftops. I breathe in the view then turn back inside. Lying on the divan, still feeling on the go, I draw my knees up to my chest, glad of some stillness.

Names

I wake with a start. Through bleary eyes I see a man I don't know enter the room. Seeing me, he stops and mutters something in Spanish. I manage a bewildered "Hi", but before I can say more, he's left. I prop myself up, disoriented. I'm half wondering if the man is another flatmate or whether he's an intruder, when I hear a key in the door and friendly voices behind it. I glimpse Hamza's tall frame and bags of groceries disappearing into the kitchen.

"I'll make the coffee!" I hear him shout as Beth and Chloe bound into the room, beaming.

"This is some place, Ally!" Chloe says breathlessly as she and Beth come to sit beside me on the floor. Matt goes to sit on the chair by the desk.

"You should've come!" Beth enthuses. "It's like a maze!"

She turns to Matt. "God, don't you ever get lost?"

"You get to know your way around," he grins.

"Where's your other friend?" I ask, still woozy from my rest.

"Aziz?" Matt replies. "He's gone to help someone. You'll see him later."

"So it's just you and Hamza living here?" Beth asks.

"And a Spanish man called Zayd."

"Ah," I say. "Someone came in when I was asleep."

"And we just bumped into him outside," says Matt. "He's been out of town filming, so we hadn't told him about you."

"Said he was as surprised as you were," Beth adds with a chuckle.

We fall to chatting, telling Matt about our journey. He sits in the chair and listens with amusement. He asks after mutual friends back in Norwich. Soon he comes to join us on the floor. Relaxed and cross-legged, his demeanour emanates a calmness I've not seen in him before.

"So," Beth says tentatively to Matt, glancing furtively at Chloe and I. "We heard you'd been brainwashed by some religious sect. What's that all about?"

"You heard that?" he says, sounding genuinely surprised. "Well, I certainly *haven't* been brainwashed."

He looks straight at us, wide-eyed, then breaks into a broad smile.

"But I *have* become Muslim."

The words mean little to me.

"You noticed my name?" Matt adds, still smiling and looking at us directly.

"I did wonder what Hamza was calling you," Chloe says.

"Rafeek," he pronounces deliberately.

His confidence in what he's saying strikes me. My senses heighten in some intuitive, almost feral way. Without looking at my friends I sense their surprise and it mirrors my own.

"You've changed your *name?*" I say, still absorbing the news.

"Yes."

I try to assimilate the fact, my awareness still vitally immediate and acute. I rewind my thoughts: Beth had said Matt had been brainwashed, but the person sitting with us doesn't come across that way at all.

"So you want us to call you that?" I say, more as a statement than a question.

"If you can, that'd be great," he says.

I study his face, wondering what's going on in his head. He's grown a beard, so he certainly looks different, and it's not just casual stubble or a goatee, but an adult-looking beard with clearly trimmed lines. His appearance is smarter. Something in his eyes is clearer. I recall the last time I saw him, the night we spent doing acid. This is a changed man.

"Well, I'll try and remember," I say casually. "Ra-feek you say?"

"Yes, spelt R-a-f-i-q. The 'q' is a kind of 'k' sound but much further down your throat."

"That's a bit of a strange name isn't it," I say.

Matt smiles. "It means *companion.*"

The sun is now streaming through the windows and catching the side of his face. The light illuminates his right eye, its brown iris appearing translucent, reflective. He holds my gaze, but says nothing. The experience of my recent travels – the sights and sounds, different people, the sense of adventure and newness – it all pales beside this. All eyes are on Matt. He looks down a moment, blushing a little. I think I detect in him a defensiveness. He must sense our scepticism.

"So if Jews follow Moses and have Judaism," I continue, "and Christians follow Jesus and have Christianity – if you're a Muslim, then...”

“Then we have Islam,” Matt says, “as taught by our prophet, Muhammad,” and he adds some unintelligible words at the end of his sentence.

“What’s that you just said?’ Chloe asks.

“Sallallahu alayhi wa sallam,” he says, slower this time. “We say it when we mention the Prophet. It means ‘Allah’s blessings and peace be on him’.”

Silence.

I feel incredibly awkward. I sense Matt feels awkward too. Rather bravely, he goes on to explain how Muslims love and acknowledge all the other prophets and messengers too, including Moses and Jesus, but my attention has diverted to inspecting his expression and demeanour, trying to catch some layer of self-doubt or pretense. For the moment, I find none.

“And this prophet, Muhammad – do you always call him *the* Prophet?”

“Well, it’s one of his names,” says Rafiq. “We also call him the Messenger.”

“I haven’t heard of him before,” I say. “So he lived... when?”

“About fourteen centuries ago,” says Matt. “About 600 years after Jesus.”

He pauses.

“One of his companions said that anyone who saw him was suddenly filled with awe of him, and those who kept his company loved him – sallallahu alayhi wa sallam.”

The room falls silent again. My mind is buzzing. Where do we start? – he’s talking about prophets and messengers. Beth, Chloe and I look at one another and I sense they feel the same. Conferring blessings on a prophet at the mention of just his name is strange to me, but Matt does it without the embarrassment I would surely feel if I were to do the same after mentioning Jesus. It makes me self-conscious on his behalf. At the same time, I'm curious. I don't know one thing about this Muhammad, but I'm touched by Matt's respect for him. I think I even admire it. It has always bothered me when people are disrespectful about God, about Jesus, about holy things.

"The Prophet Muhammad, sallallahu alayhi wa sallam, is a huge part of our lives," Matt continues, "because his whole life is a complete blueprint of behaviour for us. Islam basically means copying his character and actions."

This is *not* the conversation I imagined we'd be having as soon as we arrived. But we're all ears. There's something in the way Matt talks about this prophet. It's not as though he's referring to some myth or legend but to a person he actually knows. I wonder how he has arrived at such a thing.

"Okay, so what *is* Islam?" I ask, watching Matt move back to sit on the divan, observing him more closely for signs of what all this might have done to him.

"Firstly, it's to accept that there are no gods," he says. "There's simply reality – with a capital R. And Muhammad is the Messenger of Reality."

"And by *Reality* you mean...?" Chloe asks hesitantly.

"I mean the source of all creation, of all existence. Of all being and consciousness." Matt is as forthright as ever. "In short – God."

There's another awkward silence. Then Chloe speaks. "So this prophet, Muhammad, is he like the prophets in the Bible?"

"Yep," says Matt. "From the time of Adam, peace be on him, prophets have been sent in every age, to remind people of the true nature of God, as well as how to live in harmony with the world around them."

"So you believe in Adam as well as Jesus?" I ask, wondering if he blesses all the prophets at their mention.

"Like I said, we revere all the prophets and messengers. And part of that is recognising Jesus as one of those prophets, peace be upon him," says Matt. "But not as the son of God."

"Hold on, hold on," I say, starting to laugh – and not because this is particularly funny; it's more of a nervous reaction. "I..." and then I don't really know what to say.

Matt smiles knowingly and there is patience in his expression. Looking at him, I realise it's not his statements themselves that shock me so much as the fact they're coming from such a regular bloke – our friend who wears jeans and plain jumpers and has a short back and sides.

"So you're saying Jesus was a prophet, and not the son of God?" I ask.

"I am," he says. "And he wasn't crucified either."

"Whaaat!" exclaims Beth.

I stare at him.

"Christianity as we know it is built on the crucifixion story. But that didn't happen. And that's not to disparage Jesus in any way, peace be on him."

I want to gasp and question all at once. Plus, he just blessed Jesus. I'm bewildered.

"But you're talking about what millions of people believe!" says Chloe.

"Yes, I am," Matt says, widening his eyes and smiling broadly, almost mischievously.

Chloe looks at me, fazed. I'm quite sure I know how she feels. Of course in one way, Matt's words are outlandish. But they don't *feel* outlandish. And when I think about it – *really* think about it – Jesus as a prophet makes far more sense than him being the son of God.

I'm confronted by the fact that I've always had some

sense of worldview and that part of it comprises what I've been taught about Jesus from a very young age. Whilst I'm totally free to stay with and argue this viewpoint, I can't help feel it is faltering, sagging like the Salvador Dali painting of melting clocks. My body is slightly starting to shake.

Matt clears his throat and glances out of the window. The sky is completely clear. I look carefully at him. His face. His eyes. I'm looking for something that will tell me more about what he has discovered. I hear his new name in my mind and try to make it fit what I see. It's an odd name. In front of me I still see 'Matt'. But if I think of him as Rafiq, the name invites me to see something else.

I look away and around the room. My eyes rest on a picture hanging in the middle of the wall near the desk.

"That's the name of Reality," says Matt.

He gets up and stands beside a framed white canvas. On it appears to be an assemblage of letters painted in black ink. He slowly traces his finger from right to left, pronouncing "Ull...llaaaah".

"What's that you're saying?" asks Beth, her friendly tone edged with disbelief, or perhaps alarm.

"Allah," Matt says. "It's the divine name."

I stare at the word and feel prickles shooting up my spine.

"It's the name Reality has given Itself," Matt adds.

I haven't seen it or heard it before. But the word doesn't feel strange. Or even religious. Its shape and sound intrigue me. It evokes a sense of expanse. I remember this feeling: I'd get it when I talked to my father about outer space, the universe, life after death. The hairs at the nape of my neck are leaping.

"So you're saying that Reality is the same as the Divine, is the same as God, right?" says Beth.

"Yep," says Matt, pausing a moment. "But God in the

Christian sense means something quite different to how Muslims understand it. Christians say that God is three-in-one. We say that Allah is One. And cannot be divided up."

"Okay," says Beth, nodding her head slowly, visibly computing his words.

Like me, it feels as though she's on the verge of laughing, but Matt's earnestness keeps it in check. Plus, I kind of get what he's saying. The Trinity has always seemed a cerebral concept, a curious puzzle whose pieces I can never quite put together.

"And for us," Matt adds, "Allah has no likeness. Whatever you think about Allah, however you perceive Allah to be – Allah is not that."

He pauses. "I've found more clarity using the name 'Allah', rather than 'God'."

There's a pause in our conversation. I hear birds singing outside.

"Did I just see you reading that from right to left?" says Chloe.

"Arabic is read right to left," says Rafiq. He smiles. "You get used to it surprisingly quickly."

Beth points to a large, brass square on the adjacent wall. "And what about that?" she says. On it is etched a maze of parallel and perpendicular lines.

"It's Arabic calligraphy," he replies.

"That's all letters?" says Beth.

"Yep. It says 'No god. Only Allah' repeated all the way around."

"And that?" I ask, pointing to an old photograph above one of the bookcases.

"That's in Makkah," Matt replies, sitting down again by the desk.

We get up and gather around the framed image. "What's

going on there?" I ask, examining a mass of people in concentric circles all dressed in white, and all facing a large, black, cubic edifice.

"They're all praying around the Ka'ba, that black building," replies Matt. "Wherever we are, we pray in the direction of the Ka'ba. It's the House of Allah. So if you're *at* the Ka'ba like they are, you form circles around it."

"And where's Makkah?" I ask.

"In the west of Arabia," Matt replies.

"How many people do you reckon are there?" asks Chloe, peering closer.

"Thousands I guess. But that's an old photo," Matt says, looking over at it. "Nowadays there are way more than that... several million."

"What?" Beth exclaims.

"Every year there are hundreds of thousands more," he adds. "When all those people aren't praying, they're walking anti-clockwise around it. It's part of the rites of Hajj, the pilgrimage."

"But what do you mean by House of Allah?" I ask. "How does 'Allah' have a house?"

Matt laughs. "It's not a house like that. Allah isn't embodied," he says. "There's no old man with white hair and a long beard."

"Thank God for that," I interject. Another image I could never believe.

"It was originally built by the prophet Abraham and his son Ishmael," he says. "It's been rebuilt over the ages."

I never knew Matt well, yet here we are, talking about something so unheard of and unexpected. His certainty is unsettling. It was unsettling at the beginning of this conversation and now it's unsettling on another level, to do with myself: for the first time since my early conversations with Jake in the van, I feel something in me rekindled: an appetite for knowing. Really knowing.

I look at the photograph some more. It's an extraordinary scene. I've never seen or heard about these millions of people who do this. More than that, it seems incongruous I haven't.

On another wall, hanging on a nail, is a kind of wooden necklace. "That's a tasbih," says Matt, taking it down and coming to sit with us cross-legged again on the floor. "It's to help you count your *dhikr*, which is remembering Allah."

His eyes rest on the object in his hands.

"You do it like this," he says, and holding the tasbih with his hands on either knee, he repeats the words: "La ilaha illallah. La ilaha illallah. La ilaha illallah..." and at the beginning of each phrase he moves one bead along with his finger. The words sound alien to me, and the serious look with which Matt pronounces them makes me all the more uncomfortable.

"What are you saying?" I interrupt, feeling I'm saving him from embarrassment.

"It's the same as what's written in that picture," he replies, gesturing to the brass artwork. "No god. Only Allah."

"And why do you say that?" I ask.

"To purify the heart."

"From what?" I ask again.

"From the idea that there are other gods, other sources of power," he replies. "Mainly though, the idea you have of yourself, which amounts to the same thing."

Matt passes me the tasbih and I hold it, feeling the craftsmanship in its smooth, wooden beads. One of them is several centimetres longer with a tassel hanging from its end. Curiosity mitigates my discomfort. I hold the thing to my nose and smell resin. Something makes me think of roses. I ask him what 'tasbih' means.

"A thing of glorification," he says. "But the core meaning of the word might interest you more." Matt beams. "It means *to swim*."

I'm soon kneeling at one of their bookcases. "Have you got a book that describes what Islam is?" I ask.

Matt pulls out a small hardback, a compilation of letters from a Muslim spiritual master to his students. The cover is dark green and faded, the corners worn. I take the book and open it randomly:

Whoever is truly the slave of Allah is not the slave of his passion. He is a wali of Allah.

The word 'slave' disturbs me. I read the sentence aloud.

"You have to put aside slave-trade images for a start," he says, folding his arms. "The point is that if you give yourself whatever you want – if you *give in* to whatever you want – you are slave of your own wants."

He pauses, and with a smile adds, "The Arabic word for slave also means worshipper."

Hamza enters the room. He goes to the desk, opens a drawer and rifles through some papers.

Matt watches him a moment then turns back to us. "All of us are slaves in that we're dependent on Allah. Our hearing, sight and speech, and our knowledge, power, will and life itself are dependent on Allah's attributes. But Allah is not dependent on anything."

I stare at him, going over what he's just said.

Chloe asks what 'wali' means.

"It means friend of Allah," says Matt. "In the sense of being close, or intimate, with Allah. Those people have a strong and rare spirituality."

He means a man of God.

Matt sounds so definite about all this that I wonder if he's met any such people. I want to ask, but I'm starting to feel I'm pestering him. Hamza retrieves an envelope from the desk drawer and starts writing on it. I look down and start flicking through the book, aware that Matt is watching me and that he's probably expecting more questions. I do see more I want to ask about, but what keeps coming to mind is Matt's new name, 'Rafiq'. The more he speaks – and I've never heard him speak like this before – the more I can tell this being Muslim is incredibly real for him. In that sense, I suppose the name change is apt. I'm still not sure about it, but something in me wants to show respect for what he has done.

I flick through to the end of the book he gave me. It contains over two hundred letters, all of them ending with the word 'Peace'.

"Thanks, *Rafiq*," I say, emphasising his name, "but I don't think this is what I'm looking for."

"You're probably right," he says with a rueful smile.

Then Hamza, about to leave the room, swiftly takes the book from my hands, replaces it on the shelf and takes out another. His choice is a slim paperback, new looking. It has the title *Foundations of Islam* in bold, white type.

"It may seem a bit dry," he says. "But it's straightforward." He leaves the room.

I open the book. The layout is like a technical handbook. I turn to the first page and read in big, bold letters: Shahada.

"What does Shahada mean?" I ask Rafiq, who seems acquiescent to a new round of enquiry.

"It means *to bear witness*," he replies, "that there is no god but Allah, and Muhammad is the Messenger of Allah. It's the first foundation of Islam."

Set across the double page are two lists of statements:

1. Allah is One, undivided
2. There is no second with Allah
3. Allah is the Living, the Self-Subsistent
And so on.

I turn the page and read the following two lists – forty statements in all – and all regarding 'Allah'. It's very to the point. I flick through the book and observe subsequent sections on prayer, fasting, wealth tax and pilgrimage. I become engrossed.

"Let's have a look," says Beth, noticing I've gone silent and coming to read over my shoulder. I watch for her reaction.

"Uh-huh," she nods, reading for a short while. "Cool," she says eventually.

I can't gauge if she's interested or not. She goes to the balcony and the room goes quiet. I go back to the Shahada section. It's odd to see such profound statements in numbered lists, but I find myself glued to the pages.

At the same time, I'm reminded of those recent times back home, in the forest, reading about Infinity. As I imagined it, Infinity was an all-encompassing vastness that stretched into the far, expanding depths of the universe. But I'm now seeing flaws in my thinking: I imagined I could 'see' it in my mind, attributing object qualities to it and thus limiting that which cannot be limited. Indeed, my very act of assessing it implies a superiority over the object of assessment – a mistaken undertaking.

Here it says: *Allah is One, undivided.* I like that. Intellectually I understand it, but given my mind can only understand subjects and objects, I intuit that this One is not something to be seen or grasped. It's beyond mind.

Slowly, I read down the list, allowing the words to sink in.

Allah has no first and no last, but is the First and the Last.

Each statement is straightforward and has a clarity that feels scientific. There's no rambling wishy-washiness. I'm surprised by how I 'get' what I'm reading, and how close to home it feels.

No place in Allah's heavens or earth contains Allah.
Rather, Allah is as Allah was before the creation of place.

Nothing in my experience of religious or spiritual writings has been this clear-cut. I wonder why, and read on.

Then there is a fantastic smell of coffee, and Hamza enters the room carrying a tray of cups and saucers and an unusual-looking coffee pot.

"Cool pot," says Beth, her face lighting up.

"Beats instant," Hamza smiles, setting the things out on the floor.

He picks up the octagonal metal pot and pours its dark liquid into our cups, topping it up with hot milk. It's the first time I've had this kind of coffee.

"Interesting read," I say to Hamza, putting the book down. "So I take it you're Muslim too?" I'm sure he is, but I want to know more about him.

"I am," he replies smiling, seeing humour in the fact we both know I'm going to start questioning him. "My siblings and I were all born Muslim."

Hamza has a rugby player's physique; tall with bulky shoulders and thick thighs. He has a handsome face with a short dark beard that has some red in it, a strong brow, high cheekbones and large, brown eyes that twinkle when he smiles, and he often smiles.

"But actually, being Muslim is more like being in your natural state," he says, offering us the sugar then sitting back from the tray.

Beth picks up the coffee pot and studies it.

"In that sense we're all born Muslim," he adds casually.

Hamza seems genuine with his words and unpretentious. I hardly know him, but I feel safe in his presence.

We sip our coffee. It's incredible. Or the whole experience is – I can't work out which. This thing of being Muslim feels so complete for Rafiq and Hamza. The way they talk about it – their manner is so simple and upfront. They clearly believe in God, but it's not religious or toady, not goodie-goodie, not a suit of someone else's clothes, or even a 'belief system'. It's far subtler than that. Their belief seems innate. Inhabited. An intrinsic part of their very being.

I ask Hamza about his parents. He says his mother is from an old English family, his father a Scotsman.

"They became Muslim," he says, "and for several years they spent time in London with another Scotsman – a very special man – inviting people to Islam, and teaching and hosting a growing group of new Muslims."

We listen attentively. Hamza is a couple of years older than us but feels different to guys his age I know. There's an innocence about him. He's self-confident and comfortable in his own skin, but he's modest too. He lowers his eyes a lot. Not in a weird way. And I don't think it's from shyness. Perhaps it's because he's holding himself back, gauging our reaction as he speaks as though wanting to protect what he says from scorn, while wanting us to understand.

He speaks of his parents and the other man with deep respect. I wonder what they're like, and grow ever more aware that this is someone who has had a very different upbringing to me. It interests me. And to think Hamza's family live just a few miles from my family home. I glance at Beth and Chloe. They're looking at him, absorbed.

"Can I show you our family tree?" says Hamza, getting up and going to the bookcase. He pulls out another book. "It's not your usual one."

He comes to kneel next to me, opening the book at the back. "We call this an isnad," he says, pointing to a long list of names in the centre of the page. "It's the authoritative spiritual chain of transmission from our shaykh to his shaykh, then from his shaykh to the shaykh before him, and face to face all the way back to the Prophet himself, sallallahu alayhi wa sallam," and he lightly taps his finger next to the name at the very top: Muhammad, Messenger of Allah.

I take the book in my hands and scan down the list of names. There must be forty of them. I ask after the name at the bottom of the list.

"That's our shaykh," says Hamza.

"Your what?" Chloe asks, coming over to look at the book.

"Our shaykh," says Hamza more clearly, the end of the word 'shaykh' sounding like the end of the Scottish 'loch'. "Our teacher. He's one of the inheritors of the inner wisdom which was transmitted by the Prophet, sallallahu alayhi wa sallam. He's also a reviver of it."

"Wow. So where is he now?" I ask.

"Here, actually," Hamza smiles. "He lives up the hill."

I'm completely intrigued. I can't quite fathom how Rafiq has become a part of all this, and that this guy, Hamza – who seems so like us in many ways – is part of it all too, and grew up with it. I have so many questions. And I keep thinking about this link between these two people in front of me, their shaykh, and the Prophet Muhammad.

I ask what other books he can show me.

"Help yourself," Hamza smiles. "You'll find plenty to keep you busy."

I go straight to the bookcase and start looking, head tilted to one side.

"But you won't find Islam in them," he adds.

"What do you mean?" I ask, looking at him over my shoulder. "You've got loads about it here."

"Islam isn't in books," he says again. "It's with people."

I meet his gaze and realise he's referring to a world of which I know nothing. He turns to Rafiq and says he needs to get back to work.

"The flat next door is being renovated," Rafiq explains. "Hamza's doing the plastering."

"And the owner's coming to check it next week," Hamza says, taking a deep breath and exhaling silently. "Hopefully I'll have it finished by then."

He gets up and leaves the room, reappearing a few minutes later in a grey, misshapen T-shirt. He gives us a wave and heads out the door. I'm disappointed he's gone. There's more I wanted to ask him.

"By the way, there's a conference next week," Rafiq says. "We're expecting people from all over the world."

"Oh, what's it about?" I ask.

"Economics," Rafiq replies. Then he stands up as though wanting to leave the room too. "Are you hungry?" he asks.

We tell him we are, and before we can ask any more questions – I sense he's precluding more questions – he disappears to the kitchen, leaving the three of us in the company of two very inviting bookshelves.

"Is this really happening?" Chloe jokes.

"I know, it's wild isn't it," adds Beth, and any remaining tension dissipates in our good-natured laughter.

Humoured also by the spirit of being rescue-sleuths,

we straight away go to sit by the bookshelves, I suppose searching for something disturbing – proof we need to talk Matt, Rafiq, out of what he's doing here. Beth browses one bookshelf, Chloe and I the other.

"Hey, look at this," says Chloe, pulling out one of the books. "*Indications from Signs*," and she starts flicking through the pages. I look over, noticing and liking how lots of space surrounds the text.

Beth, with her head cocked to the side, starts reading some book titles aloud: "*The Meaning of Man*, *The Book of Strangers*, *The Hundred Steps*..." She utters a little gasp. "I mean..." and she looks at me, her words trailing off.

"Pretty cool stuff, hey," I say.

"You're telling me," Beth says.

Chloe agrees, and there's relief in our consensus.

On the shelves are familiar English classics plus Scottish authors like Scott and Carlyle. German writers – I spot Goethe, Rilke, Schiller. There's Tolstoy and Turgenev. Nietzsche is next to Rollo May, R.D. Laing and other psychologists. Some books are about political theory and finance.

A group of books on the top shelf catch my eye. Neatly aligned, their spines have an exotic script embossed in gold leaf. Below them is a selection of large books with curious titles. *The Muwatta* and *Ash-Shifa* pique my interest. I pull one out with a view to reading the blurb, but '*It's with people*' I hear in my head.

"Found anything?" I ask Beth.

"Yeah," she says. "Have a look at these." She tosses me a small, plastic tub with a bright sticker.

"Energy pills?" I say, turning it in my hand.

"You don't think they're into some weirdo shit do you?" Beth says. "Maybe the brainwashing thing isn't just rumour." She half-grins.

"It doesn't *seem* like they are," says Chloe, holding out her hands as I lob her the tub. Rafiq puts his head around the door to say lunch is ready.

The kitchen, like the rest of the flat, has whitewashed walls and a tiled terracotta floor. Nestled in the corner is a small table and chairs, and opposite is a fireplace. A small window looks onto the neighbour's pitted wall and terrace, and beneath it is a wooden unit housing a gas cooker, some space to chop and slice, and a pot of cooking utensils. It feels hip and cosy.

We sit down around the table set for four. Rafiq says a word I don't understand but which seems to mean *Let's tuck in.* He serves us toasted baguette slices with olive oil on them, then makes a point of squeezing and rubbing a tomato-half over a piece and sprinkling it with salt. "When in Rome..." he quips, and gestures to some pale sliced cheese and fresh basil leaves to layer on top.

"What are those pills in the salon?" asks Beth, hands clasped around her baguette. "The ones with the fluorescent label?"

"Oh, they're Hamza's," Rafiq replies. "For sports and such. His father imports them from America. All sorts of goodies in them – bee pollen, guarana, rain-forest plants..."

"Speaking of which," Beth grins. "Can we score some hash here?"

Rafiq shifts in his chair. "I suppose." He squishes more tomato over his baguette, not looking up. "I don't actually do that anymore."

"Really?"

I'm mildly disappointed. But more than that I can hardly believe it. Rafiq shrugs his shoulders and carries on eating. But on pressing him it turns out that for the last two months he's done no drugs at all. Not even alcohol.

Lookout

Later on, the smell of jasmine fills the warm afternoon air. Rafiq leads us up and up the steep, cobbled slope of the Albaicín, taking turns so often that before I've thought to take note of our route, I've forgotten it.

"So where exactly are we going?" I enquire.

"You'll see," Rafiq replies, his eyes sparkling.

"How do you remember your way?" Beth says. "It's like a warren."

"I told you, you'll get your bearings," Rafiq smiles, looking straight ahead.

I glance at him a moment. I think I'm getting used to his name. And every time I say it, I'm reminded of this thing of him being Muslim.

The street plateaus and opens out onto a spacious thoroughfare. In front of us is a busy outdoor café with white, cramped-together parasols. From it comes the mouth-watering smell of fried fish. We bear right, passing the blank side of an imposing, whitewashed church with a square bell tower, and stone bollards linked by huge chains.

"Here we are," Rafiq announces. "Mirador de San Nicolás."

We walk onto a wide, open-air terrace. Young trees stand proud in the sunshine, and at our feet is a chequered ground of perfectly placed light and dark pebbles bordered by tendril designs. All that however, is just preparation for the view.

"*Mirador* means lookout point," Rafiq says, smiling at our gasps of wonder.

Together we walk towards the view, eyes fixed ahead. Across a valley, rising roughly a kilometre away, is the majestic fortress. It sits along a ridge, enthroned on a vast cloak of foliage. Its walls are reddish orange, ablaze with the sun's setting light, its turrets and battlements offset by pale purple mountains in the distance.

"It just rises out of the rock," Beth says, putting her hands on her head, amazed.

"That's the Alhambra," says Rafiq. "The Muslims built it. It's where the Muslim rulers of this region lived."

We approach the lookout's broad, low-lying wall which drops sharply to a street below. Tourists are taking photos. Lovers are holding hands. Locals are perched on one end of the wall around a couple of guitars. An old lady advertises castanets for sale, snapping them rapidly with skill.

"Muslims were in Spain?" Chloe asks.

"Yep," Rafiq replies. "They established an empire here called Al-Andalus. That's why this area of southern Spain is called Andalusia."

"We read it was a Moorish kingdom," I say.

"The Moors were Muslims," says Rafiq, "and they were here longer than the Christians have been. At one point the empire extended all the way up to France."

I picture a map of Spain and France, my mind's eye colouring in the areas Rafiq speaks of.

All the while, my eyes are roaming the fortress. Its ramparts are at eye level, the sinking sun bestowing upon it deepening hues of orange. I think about the people who built it and ruled from there. They would have lived by the things Rafiq and Hamza have been telling us about.

Below us and below the Alhambra, the city spreads away to the right and blurs into distant plains of dusty browns and violets. A trio of gypsies start singing flamenco close by. They take to strolling back and forth along the terrace, peddling homemade cassettes. We too walk, enjoying the warm, mellow ambience. More and more people arrive for the sunset, bringing more conversation, music and laughter. Swifts flit this way and that, disappearing then reappearing from amid the rooftops and alleyways and the great, open sky. There's a sense of excitement in the air, an almost tangible quality of togetherness.

Soon, evening breezes pick up.

"I need to be heading back, if you don't mind," Rafiq says eventually.

After a lingering look we return to the labyrinth and head downhill. In what seems like little time we are back at the flat. Rafiq disappears into the bathroom then emerges moments later with wet face and hair.

"So, I'm leaving now," he says. "See you in a couple of hours. Make yourselves at home." With that he slips on his sandals and disappears out the door.

"Wow, we're definitely in the best part of town," Chloe

says, going to sit on the divan. "Let's go to that Mirador place again tomorrow."

She pauses a moment.

"Matt seems okay, don't you think?"

"Yeah, I reckon," says Beth, stepping out onto the balcony. "He seems pretty sane."

"I'm used to him rolling his eyes when he hears someone spouting crap," Chloe says. "So, I guess I hadn't been *too* worried about him."

"Looks like our rescue plan might not be needed," I grin.

"I'm kinda disappointed about that," Beth adds mischievously.

"Well, let's see," adds Chloe. "We've only just arrived. Let's give it some time."

Beth sits down amid the pots of geraniums. Arms around knees, she rolls a cigarette. Chloe goes to take a second look at the photograph of the Ka'ba then opens her rucksack to dig out her sketch pad.

I rummage in my rucksack for my shampoo and razor, looking forward to using the bathroom while the guys are out. "I'm having a shower, okay?"

"Okay!" Beth calls out, puffing smoke rings into the little square. "Leave me some hot water."

Revealed

Two hours later, Rafiq is back with Hamza and two friends. One of them is Zayd, the 'intruder' from yesterday. The other is Aziz who met us at the train station. He lives further up the Albaicín.

Zayd rustles up some pasta and tomato sauce as effortlessly as I would make a piece of toast. But unlike my cooking, Zayd's food is restaurant quality, replete with fresh basil and oregano, green olives and grated parmesan on top, plus a side basket of sliced baguette, fresh from the local bakery. We eat from two platters set out on the floor, one for the boys, one for us girls. The fact these guys actually cook, eat 'real' food and eat it together feels quite novel. Wholesome. More than that, there feels something of wisdom in it.

I ask Zayd about being Muslim. He says his parents

became Muslim years ago in the north-east of Spain. But it wasn't until he came to the Muslim community in Granada that he discovered Islam for himself. He's now at a film school downtown. Two years older than us, he has thick, longish, wavy hair, a Roman nose and unusually blue eyes for a Spaniard. He's suave and has impeccable manners. I smile to myself – he reminds me of James Bond, without the lechery. His English, although accented, is really good and entirely without the usual 'kind of like' fillers. I ask how he learnt it.

"Simply by spending time with our shaykh," he says casually. "He ignored the fact I didn't speak English, and talked. I went from not speaking one word to, well, I hope my English doesn't offend you."

"What exactly do you mean by *our shaykh*," Beth asks.

"Well, he's our teacher," Zayd says. "An extraordinary one. A master."

I look carefully at him for signs he might be hiding something, but I don't sense anything dubious. In fact, he's so relaxed, I start wondering if it's my own lens of scepticism that I should be doubting. When the meal is finished we start helping to clear the table. Hamza stops us. "You're our guests," he says simply, gathering up the cutlery.

Beth looks at me and grins. "If you say so."

The guys take everything to the kitchen. I hear them chatting and the clinking, clanking of washing up. We get up and go to relax on the divan.

"They're quite together on the home front aren't they?" Beth grins.

Rafiq walks back into the room grinning.

"I heard that."

Beth laughs. "Hey, I didn't mean it in a bad way."

"Yeah, I'm impressed actually," says Chloe.

Rafiq shrugs his shoulders. "Well, the Prophet, sallallahu alayhi wa sallam, spent some of his time working at home too."

His comment completely changes the tone.

"He'd help tidy up, wash clothes, make bread, mend his own shoes, bring goods home from the market – nothing wrong with that."

"True," I say, wondering what to say next and feeling that same curiosity and awkwardness coming over me.

Rafiq sits down. On the far wall are the bookcases.

"So, if Christians have the Bible," I ask, "what do Muslims have?"

"The Qur'an," Rafiq says. "Although they're not really equivalent."

"How come?" says Chloe.

"The Qur'an isn't a collection of reports. It's entirely the speech of Allah."

He gets up and takes a large book from the top shelf of the bookcase by the window. Bound in reddish-brown leather, it has gold embossing on its cover and spine. He takes a cushion from the far side of the room, places it on the floor between us then rests the book on top.

"Qur'an means 'recitation'. And this here is a mus-haf, which means 'copy', because it's a written copy of the Qur'an, of the Words of Allah."

He then says something under his breath and carefully opens the book.

"What did you say just then?" I ask, recognising the word.

"I said *Bismillah*," Rafiq says. "It means 'In the Name of Allah'."

"Ah, that's what you guys say before you eat, right?" says Beth.

"Yep," says Rafiq, "and before we do anything, really."

I remember the men who helped us in Amsterdam. They had said the same word, like an echo forward in time. My attention returns to the book. I look at its opened pages. Rafiq points out some decorated writing and says that it's the title of one of the surahs, or chapters. I reach to touch the page.

"No," he says, reaching his hand toward mine. "Sorry Ally, you can't touch the letters."

"No?"

"Only if you're Muslim. And in a state of purification."

"Purification?" I repeat, jarred.

I look at Beth and Chloe to check their response. They look a bit shocked. But my reaction soon turns to elation. If this really *is* the word of God, then the prohibition is entirely fitting. I look up at Rafiq's face. He half smiles, and I sense now real empathy, where before, back home, there was something more laissez-faire.

"None of it has been altered since the time it was revealed," Rafiq adds. "Not one dot. Original copies still exist."

"What do you mean – *revealed?*" Beth asks.

"Allah sent down the Qur'an on the Angel Jibril – or Gabriel – who transmitted it to the Prophet Muhammad, the Messenger of Allah, sallallahu alayhi wa sallam. In turn he recited it to his family and Companions, who memorised it and also wrote it down on animal skins and pieces of paper. After the death of the Messenger of Allah, it was collated into book form," he says.

At the back of my mind is a question on repeat: *what IS this that Rafiq has found?* I study the script before us. It's beautiful. Unlike anything I've seen. Bows, arches and half loops are embellished by dots, circles and tiny diagonal lines. I look at what may be a phrase, then more closely at a cluster of shapes I'm guessing is a word. Out of the blue, the man on the bench in Norwich comes to mind.

My gaze rests on one particular form, a letter perhaps.

"These are actually God's words?" I remark, mostly to myself.

Rafiq looks at me directly. "The Word of Allah exists perpetually outside of time and space. But like I said, when it descends into our worldly realm it takes on a recited form, which when written down looks like that." He gestures to the book in front of us. "So, yes."

"Wow," says Beth.

Rafiq closes the book and puts it back on the shelf. He clears his throat as though to change the subject.

Aziz puts his head around the door and says he hopes to visit us tomorrow afternoon. "It's no accident you're here," he adds, half-joking, half-serious.

Rafiq turns to the three of us. "So I hope you'll be comfortable? We'll knock before coming in so don't worry about any more intruders," he grins.

"It's more than comfortable," Beth says. "Thank you so much."

"Sleep well then." He leaves the room, closing the door behind him.

"Right then!" says Beth grinning broadly, looking at Chloe and I with hands on hips. "I wonder how this'll all pan out?"

"I know, it's weird," I reply, going to fetch my rucksack. "But it's also kind of interesting."

"Yeah. Well done for arranging it, Beth," says Chloe.

I pull out my sleeping bag and unfurl it on the carpet.

"It's kind of Rafiq to let us stay," she adds.

"Who told you he'd been brainwashed?" I ask.

"A mutual friend," says Beth. "But it was over a few beers."

Chloe unrolls her camping mat. "Can you pass me that cushion?"

I throw a couple of cushions her way. Then, "Shush a minute," I whisper. "Do you hear that?"

"What?" whispers Beth, standing still as a statue. Just audible is the sound of a man's voice. Not talking or singing, but somewhere in between.

"Must be one of the guys," says Chloe.

Soon there is the sound of several voices. A kind of chanting. Then it stops. We look at one another.

We take turns brushing our teeth in the kitchen sink, not wanting to hog the bathroom. Soon we're zipping ourselves into sleeping bags. Midnight has come and gone, but the temperature is still hovering in the mid 30°s. We unzip our bags and lie on top. We toss and turn, share comments about being too hot and clammy, and giggle infectiously.

Eventually I settle on my back, spreading my limbs out starfish-style. I think how wonderful this place is, and how different, how wonderfully different my experience of it is from how I'd imagined it back on that train, reading to my friends about Granada from my travel guide.

Worship

I wake up to sounds of running water and footsteps. It's still dark. I look around. A glimmer of light seeps towards me through a gap in one of the shutters. I turn to Beth, then Chloe. They're asleep. Then I hear the same chanting coming again from one of the other rooms. I listen, ears pricked, holding my breath. After a while it stops. I look around the room at the pictures. My eyes rest on the canvas with the divine Name. After a while I fall back to sleep.

"Morning!" calls Rafiq, knocking on the door. "Breakfast's on the go."

It's late morning. We convene with Hamza and Rafiq in the kitchen, the coolest part of the house. Zayd is out. Squeezed around the kitchen table, we eat hunks of bread dipped in a big plate of olive oil and honey – it's delicious and another thing I've never had before.

Aziz arrives and comes in to greet us. He's in a pale blue, short-sleeved shirt and beige longish shorts, and he's glowing from an early morning run in the hills. He goes straight to the stove and sets about making coffee. I take another piece of bread.

"You know," Aziz says, turning away from the stove and leaning back on his hands to face us directly, "Allah has made the human situation easy to understand."

We all look up from our breakfast except Rafiq, whose face flickers with knowing amusement.

"What are you *talking* about?" says Beth, chewing some bread.

"Does it make any sense that life should be an incomprehensible mystery?"

We stare at him and munch.

"Of course not!" Aziz continues, his eyes alive and intense.

"The human situation?" says Beth, stifling a laugh. "You make it sound so serious."

"You want me to make light of it?" he says quickly, his smile fading, his face acutely alert.

Aziz is certainly blunt. Yet it's paired with a gentle, almost hesitant tone which is altogether endearing, and goes some way to offset his out-of-the-blue statements. Still, Beth blushes. The coffee pot splutters and burbles loudly, like a polite cough in the conversation. Aziz sets it on the table and we help ourselves.

"We're designed to worship, whether we like it or not," he says, sitting down with us.

Am I? I think to myself.

"Everyone worships something," says Aziz. "In the

Qur'an, Allah says: '*I only created jinn and man to worship Me.*' So worshipping Allah is our purpose. It's what we're for."

"Maybe it's what *you're* for," I say, expecting a riposte, but it doesn't come. Then I feel a bit rude. I smile, hoping to make up for it.

Aziz looks away but my eyes stay on him, wondering at the changing expressions that cross his face: widening eyes, an eyebrow that rises and falls, the suggestion of a smile, as though all sorts of thoughts are coming at him and he's deciding which one to voice, or whether to voice any at all.

I take another sip of coffee and wait for what he might say, glancing at him while he stays silent. His eyes are grey green, expressive and slope upwards at the corners, and his eyebrows are wide. His hair is mousey and parted on the side, and his skin is fair and smooth, clean shaven but for the semblance of a goatee. In fact, it doesn't look like he can grow a full beard yet.

Chloe starts chatting with Rafiq. Still I'm waiting for Aziz to speak. Then what I sensed rising comes to the surface.

"Allah says in the Qur'an," Aziz says, "that *everything* prostrates to Allah – the sun, the moon and the stars, the mountains, the trees, all the animals – because all of creation is submitted to being that which it is. A cat doesn't wag its tail like a dog, just as a dog doesn't hunt by night. Their obedience to Allah is their being entirely what they are."

Aziz looks at me carefully. I feel he's daring himself to continue.

"But we are different," he goes on. "Although our physicality is in total submission to Allah's laws of physics, we've been given a consciousness which sets us apart from all other living creatures – one in which we have the experience of choice. It's a different ball game. Our choosing to worship Allah is our opportunity to experience ourselves in our fullness, because that is our divinely designated purpose."

Chloe shuffles in her chair.

If I'm to really get what he's saying, I'll have to ask him to repeat himself, but I'm reluctant to put myself in a position where I'll have to strongly disagree and potentially offend him as well as Rafiq. We got here only yesterday and I don't want to blight their hospitality.

"What are jinn?" Beth asks.

"They're beings made from smokeless fire," Aziz says. "They inhabit our world but we can't see them. The Qur'an was revealed for them too."

I glance at Rafiq.

"Are they like us?" asks Chloe. "Do they look like us?"

Aziz sips his coffee, looking to the table.

Hamza answers: "They're like us in that they have a choice to obey or disobey Allah. Some people I know have seen them."

"Ghosts?" asks Chloe.

"I don't know about that," Hamza says.

Then Aziz speaks deliberately: "If you don't worship Allah, then you're not fulfilling your purpose."

He pauses.

"You're not fully who you *are*."

His eyes glance at each one of us, as though to gauge our attention. "Just as deafness denies you your hearing, so lack of worship denies you knowledge, since you don't know who you are, why you are here, what you are here for and therefore what existence is for, and because of that you won't be able to confront your life."

The little kitchen is silent. The tension is electric.

Rafiq clears his throat. "Didn't you say we were taking them out this morning?" he asks Hamza.

"Or confront your death," concludes Aziz.

"We hadn't planned on such a long breakfast," replies Hamza, nodding at Aziz.

"Oh," says Aziz, looking contritely at his watch. "Apologies," he says. "You should get going else you'll burn to a cinder out there."

He clears his throat and looks at the guys.

"But maybe wait a bit, so we can pray together beforehand?"

"Sure, let's do that," says Rafiq. He turns to us. "Hope you don't mind waiting a bit?"

"Bloody hell," I exclaim. "You lot pray all the time!"

"Five times a day," Rafiq corrects, playing it down.

"Five!" I exclaim. "And you do them all? Every day?"

"Of course," he says, humoured.

I try not to appear flabbergasted. "When you feel like it, or...?"

"Not exactly," says Rafiq, finishing his coffee.

"I think we heard you last night," says Chloe. "Praying, I mean."

"Probably," says Rafiq.

We look at him quizzically.

"So, the first prayer is from first light until sunrise," he says. "Then the second is at midday when the sun is just past its highest point in the sky, the third is in the mid-afternoon, the fourth just after sunset, and the last – the one you heard – is during the first third of the night, starting when the redness of the sunset has left the sky."

Aziz gets up. "I'll get ready and wait for you chaps in the other room."

He nods at us, excusing himself. Hamza joins him. Now it's just us girls and Rafiq and the remains of our breakfast.

"So, Rafiq," says Beth, cocking her head to one side, "all this praying makes you feel good, right?"

Rafiq pauses. I can tell he doesn't like the question.

"It's not really about how I *feel*," he says. "But it does feel right." He shrugs. "Deep down, *I* feel right."

"In what way?" says Beth.

"Well," he says slowly, his eyes glancing up at the ceiling. "It's like..." and I sense he's trying to get to the essence of it. He looks back at Beth. "It's like I have a new awareness. I mean, I've always persevered in things – school, work, whatever – but they've always been things driven from a very in-my-head place. A few months ago I'd *never* have thought I'd be persisting in prayer but here I am, doing it, being it, and it's been amazing because..." he shakes his head and lets out a little gasp. "Because..."

Then he smiles broadly with a chuckle.

"I can't explain it really. I guess I'm more aware of my place in the world. Tuned in to it, you could say; tuned in to where the sun is in the sky, and even the shadows it casts – when they stretch to twice your height it's time for the mid-afternoon prayer – and then," he glances up again, then back at the three of us, "and then in doing the prayer it's like I'm bringing myself back to centre. I'm kind of roping myself in from all my goings-on in the world and surrendering myself in the face of it all. Not in the sense of being defeated or like a victim – it's the opposite of that actually – it's more to do with submitting myself to the knowledge that I'm a created being and Allah is the Creator, and we've come from Allah and we're going back to Allah, and so I'm handing over this whole business of being 'me' to Allah, and..."

He lets out a little gasp. His face has flushed and I can tell this isn't altogether easy for him, but also that it's really important for him to express.

"Go on," I say.

"Well, when I prostrate, I'm putting my head below my

heart. I'm subordinating my mind to my heart because my heart has a knowing that's beyond my mind. It just... *knows*."

He pauses, his breathing more steady.

"And in that sense I'm going beyond myself. I'm tuning in to the source of who I am, as well as the source of the sun and its light and its shadows and... well," he looks directly at me, his eyes clear and bright: "To the source of everything."

"What if it's cloudy?" I ask.

Rafiq grins and shakes his head. "I knew you'd ask that. Then you estimate it. But just being aware of those prayer times every day, every week, every month, and how they change as the daylight hours change – it gives you an inner rhythm."

"So you've really been getting up at the crack of dawn to *pray*? Every day?" says Chloe.

Rafiq holds her gaze. I can't tell if he's embarrassed by the admission or annoyed at our continual questioning and incredulity.

"You think it's totally strange, don't you," he says.

"Strange? Ha!" I reply. "Well it's... it's *unusual* you'll have to admit."

Rafiq nods, starting to clear the table. "I thought that too when I arrived here." He smiles, seeming to recall it. "But it feels so obvious and natural now. You've heard the dawn chorus, haven't you. The birds?"

"Of course."

"And you've seen how they fly?"

I say nothing.

"That's their worship, Ally."

"That's *poetic*," I say, teasing.

Rafiq ignores my remark. "Just as, say, the oscillating of the quartz stone is its worship."

The idea intrigues me and I want to argue. "Then you'd

have to say," I suggest, "that the whole universe is in worship as everything is comprised of oscillating waves of energy."

"Exactly, Ally. Ex-act-ly."

I cross my arms.

"All of creation is glorifying Allah," says Rafiq. "We just don't understand its language."

I think of the lime tree back in Norwich. Rafiq gets up and stacks the crockery at the sink. Beth and Chloe smile at one another, quietly enjoying the exchange.

"I suppose it's a different point of view," I remark glibly, belying the fact I'm quite taken by it.

Rafiq looks back at me, eyes alive.

"But..." I clasp my hands to the sides of my head, "five times a day?"

"I know, I know," Rafiq says.

He washes his hands at the tap, dries them, then comes to sit down.

"It's easy to get caught up in things," he says. "But the prayer releases you from that, from your self-involvement. The day revolves around it instead of around you. Not in an oppressive way but... it's like resting points that illuminate the day, purify the day, and purify the things in yourself that aren't really acting from a true place. After the prayer, everything feels kind of new again. You start afresh."

I look at him, trying to imagine what that must be like. I'm not sure I *can* imagine it.

Rafiq leans back on his chair and lets out a laugh. "All a bit deep for breakfast."

"No, it's okay," I say. "It's just..." My mind turns over his words. "It's just a lot to take in."

Zayd appears at the doorway. "Hello everyone," he says. "Are you joining us, Rafiq?"

"Yep," replies Rafiq, jumping up.

Their footsteps disappear down the corridor. I stretch out my arms and breathe in deeply.

"Well!" I say to my friends with a little laugh.

"Yeah!" grins Beth.

Chloe lets out an emphatic sigh and smiles at me.

We look at one another with a mix of amusement, wonder and disbelief. Chloe gets up and starts the washing up. I want to talk more with her and Beth about all this but it seems we've had our fill of words for the while. We don't get further than listening out for more strange sounds and whispering our amazement at what Rafiq and his friends do. Soon we hear them reciting. We've heard it several times now. Then Rafiq appears in the doorway.

"Shall we go?" he says.

Alhambra

Antiquated houses rise high on either side, tempering the sound of our voices and blinkering a blue-violet sky. Walking downhill, our footsteps blend with an acoustic guitar from a nearby window, then a dog barking. Further, and we pass through a lively enclave of Moroccan tea shops and North African clothing, crockery and knick-knack boutiques. I want to stop and browse, but Hamza keeps a purposeful gait.

At the bottom of the hill I hear the hum of traffic. We turn left onto a shaded street of small restaurants and tapas bars, joining posses of youngsters laughing loudly, arms draped around one another. Motorcyclists hoot and weave precariously through us all. Soon we come out into another square, but this one is huge, busy and bright.

"Plaza Nueva," announces Rafiq.

I shield my eyes from the sun, taking in the spectacle. Cafés nestle beneath grand, neoclassic and baroque buildings, their tables, chairs, parasols and awnings encroaching into the square, which teems with bustling locals, tourists, hippies and pigeons. We cross to the other side and pass a spattering of souvenir shops, postcard stands, 'I love Granada' T-shirts and Spanish flags hanging motionless in the soaring heat. Craft outlets sell leather and ceramic wares and again I want to stop, but we continue.

We take a steep, quiet lane up the far side of the valley we saw from the Mirador and break into a sweat. Passing through an arched gateway, we continue upwards into a spacious and sprawling grove of trees, a woodland into another world. On either side of the lane rises a music of clear, running water, tinkling and babbling down channels of neatly laid stones. The shade gifts us the ease of looking upwards, and between thick tree trunks that rise on slopes ahead, we glimpse the towering majesty of russet-red walls.

"What we're about to see," says Hamza, "is the last of all the palaces built by the Muslims in Spain during their 700-year rule."

The Alhambra. Ahead to our left is a lofty archway set within a metres-thick wall. People are queuing for tickets and chatting. We get in line. When it's our turn, Hamza goes up to the booth, pays for us all before we can protest, and walks off through the archway.

"Come on then," says Rafiq, walking off too.

We follow them out into a large and open, sandy, baking-hot square.

"So, there're basically four parts," says Hamza, pointing with his whole hand: "The old fort is just there, Charles V's palace is next to it and then there are the Moorish palaces." He looks around. "We can explore the gardens too if you want," he adds.

I shrug my shoulders. "Let's go!"

First we visit the old fort. It's clearly the oldest part of the whole complex and comprises bold, angular towers, walls and ramparts. The smell of stone is acute in the hot dry air. We walk along the parapets, exulting in the views and marvelling at the treetops on the valley shoulder below. Beth, Chloe and I prance around, feeling on top of the world.

A little way off, Hamza and Rafiq are at a wall looking out onto the whole of Granada. We join them. Opposite at eye level, we spot the Mirador de San Nicolás and its visitors looking back at us.

Next we visit Charles V's palace, a grand, square building with completely different architecture – Italian Renaissance. It has rectangular and circular windows, and there are decorative pediments, pillars and stone statues on each of its four sides. The whole thing looks a little out of place.

"Some say it was designed by a student of Michelangelo," says Hamza. "When the Catholics re-conquered Granada, they built it to stamp a Christian identity here."

Inside is a huge, round, open-air patio. Two stories of marble columns encircle it. Its floor is a lake of grey marble. People are standing on opposite sides calling out and giggling, and we wonder why. Then we realise the acoustics are those of a whispering gallery and we're soon joining in the experimentation, sharing mischievous exclamations and brief operatic impersonations.

The next part of the complex is the Nasrid Palaces. We cross a marbled, enclosed courtyard and step through a doorway into a shaded, high-ceilinged room. People are whispering and pointing. Reaching for their cameras. Shaking their heads. Slowly, my eyes adjust to an emerging world of pillars, mosaics and arched windows. From floor to waist height are glossy, geometric tiles, and above is the most exquisitely patterned stucco, the like of which I've never seen. I come to a standstill, my eyes drawn to endless ornamental patterns, motifs and running borders carved into rich cream and pale umber plaster, its tones deeply warm and natural.

We walk on slowly, feasting our eyes on a series of sumptuous rooms and courtyards – all without furniture, yet furnished entirely with this immaculate craftsmanship.

Then I think of the brass bangle on my upper arm. "Hey look," I say to Chloe and Beth, taking it off and holding it out in front of us. Its Celtic knotwork bears a striking resemblance to what I'm seeing all around me. But more intriguing is what I notice above it: finely worked, cursive lettering wrapped around the upper parts of each and every wall. I can't stop staring, marvelling.

Hamza comes to stand next to us. "All verses from the Qur'an," he says, stepping forward for a closer look.

Rafiq joins him. Arms folded across chests, they confer with one another, deciphering words.

"You see that segment up there?" Rafiq calls out to us, his voice not raised but clearly audible above the tourists' whispers. "It says: *La Ghalib illallah*. You see how it goes all around the room?"

We walk over, looking to where he's pointing.

"What does it mean?" asks Chloe.

"It means, *No victor, but Allah*. You'll find it all over the palace."

I wait to see if he'll say more but he simply stands there, relaxed. Looking.

His silence leaves me to my thoughts. No one triumphs, no one wins, no one achieves success – except by Allah. I start seeing the phrase everywhere.

Eventually we move on, following Hamza and Rafiq

through royal rooms with filigreed walls and white marble floors. Some have vaulted ceilings bearing extraordinary honeycomb structures which taper downwards like stalactites. We amble through shaded courtyards and alluring passageways, pausing to point and stare; past countless arches, trickling fountains – one guarded by a circle of stone lions – and dark, still-water pools.

"Imagine the sultans seeing their palace ogled at by tourists," Chloe remarks.

"It's had worse," says Hamza. "Napoleon blew parts of it up."

We leave the palaces and go outside. The temperature is overwhelming and must be pushing a hundred. I rub the back of my neck, aching from all the looking up. We head towards the hills and an area called the Generalife, squinting in the sun's glare. I ask which general it was named after.

Hamza smiles. "It's actually from the Arabic, Jannat al-'Arif. It means *the Gnostic's Garden*."

Around us are flowerbeds, colonnades and pavilions. I imagine a wise man drawing inspiration from it all, pausing now and then to contemplate life's meanings. We keep walking – away from the buildings and facing towards the hills – gravitating to trickling waterways and fountains where water splashes onto paving stones, cooling the air. The heat is overpowering. It's become a struggle to take it all in. My eyes, too dazzled by the sun's roar, are now only half open, with the effect I'm half in the gardens and half in my interior landscape, roaming my thoughts, which keep returning to Rafiq's new life here.

I look over my shoulder. He and Hamza are behind us, deep in conversation. I stop and watch them a while. A wave of affection comes over me, and I feel as though I've known them far longer than these two days.

"Ah!" Chloe sighs loudly. "I'm knackered!"

"Me too!" says Beth. "I mean, it's amazing but..."

We turn around and wait for the guys.

"We can go if you like?" suggests Rafiq, catching up with us and handing Chloe his bottle of water.

It's an easy stroll back down to the big square and an easier one into an ice cream parlour. By the time we're heading back to the flat it's six or seven o'clock in the evening.

"Welcome back," says Zayd, greeting us at the door. With bare and swollen feet, we pad into the salon. "How was it?" he asks.

"Amazing," gushes Beth. "You've been up there too, right?" she asks, sitting down and rubbing her feet.

"I have," he half-smiles.

Then I remember I didn't follow up his mention of their shaykh. I want to. We sit down and I'm about to ask him when Hamza enters the room and asks him and Rafiq if they're ready to go.

"Where are you going *now*?" I ask.

"To the weird," Rafiq replies. "See you later, okay? We'll be gone a few hours."

He closes the salon door.

"They're going to the what?" says Beth.

"I'm sure he said *weird*," says Chloe, as the door to the flat closes.

"We'll have to ask later," I say.

With the guys out, the flat feels suddenly empty. I reach for my rolling tobacco.

"So, what shall we do now?" says Beth, a rascally look in her eyes.

Chloe shrugs her shoulders. I put down my tobacco.

"We're going out!" I say, getting to my feet.

Hollow

The sky has ripened to warm orange. Sparrows and other birds have begun their dusk-attuned melodies, enriched by the amphitheatre of our little square. We wend our way down through the maze with a skip in our step, the air warm and smelling of sunbaked clay and fried olive oil.

"Rafiq's friends seem pretty cool," says Chloe.

"I think so too," I say. "Safe to say, Aziz is pretty unique." We laugh.

"Don't you think there's something kind of different about them?" says Beth.

"Like what?" I ask.

"I don't know," she says. "They're just..." and she lets out a laugh, "I don't know."

I think about Hamza and his parents, the uncommon

life they have led. I wonder about the special man Hamza mentioned. Soon we're at Plaza Nueva.

"What do you think about everything they've been saying?" I ask.

"Yeah, it's interesting," says Beth. "It's not like I agree with it all, but hey, Rafiq seems pretty cool with it."

"Yeah," says Chloe, almost ambivalently.

The cafés are full and playing music. Gelled-hair waiters rush between the tables. Taxis and minibuses rumble this way and that, unsettling the birdlife, and the dimming sky contrasts with the glare of lamps and lights from the street. I want to talk more about the guys and everything they've been saying. But words don't come. It agitates me.

"Let's head that way," I say, looking down a wide street.

Away from the old quarter we head downtown. Hills are silhouetted behind. The city is buzzing and I'm ready for its urban, restless energy. We spot plenty of backpackers and feel a tribal affinity with them. We say "Hi," wave a hand, smile. Like us, they're wandering. Looking around. Taking it all in.

We begin to chat about where we'll be travelling next. Cities are mentioned, possibilities aired. Leaving Granada suddenly becomes a reality I wasn't really thinking about. I feel a pit in my stomach. All of a sudden, leaving just for the sake of moving on seems horribly empty. I try pushing the sentiment away.

It's dark now. The streets are four lanes wide, the pavements generous. Plenty of room for crowds to mill around. We explore areas away from the bustle, stumbling on alleyways and bars where DJs spin hip hop, ska and a booming bass of dub-reggae mixes. A smell of ganja hangs in the air, whetting my appetite. The clientele looks cool too, inviting in a familiar way, but somehow not inspiring enough for us to join them.

We keep walking. I feel I'm looking for something. And that hollow feeling at the thought of leaving doesn't go away.

Back at Plaza Nueva, we stop at a kiosk to buy crisps and fizzy drinks. We go to sit on a stone bench. I lift the ring pull on my can, toss it in the bin and take a sip. I realise I haven't thought of going into a bar for a beer. We look around, sharing simple observations. But not much more. I think of Rafiq, Hamza and the others.

"Hey look," says Chloe, pointing to a poster advertising Flamenco. "We should go."

"Yeah," says Beth, opening her crisps and munching clumps of them.

Something feels odd between us. I roll a cigarette, half-trying to work it out.

"Do you think the guys will be back at the flat?" Beth says.

I'm relieved she's asked. It feels like we're killing time until seeing them again.

Hajj Abdullah

Today is our third day in Granada but it feels like our tenth. Afternoon finds us striding up the Albaicín with Hamza to visit one of his friends.

"So who is he, this friend of yours?" Beth enquires.

"His name's Hajj Abdullah," replies Hamza. "He's been a student of the shaykh since the early 70s. You'll like him. And he loves to talk."

"He has a long name," I say.

"There are people with longer ones."

"I don't mean that badly," I add quickly.

Hamza looks at me. "When someone's been on Hajj, the pilgrimage, they're called by the title of Hajj as mark of respect. Hajja, if you're a woman."

We turn off and contour along a lane.

"And Abdullah?" I ask. "What does that mean?"

"Slave of Allah," says Hamza matter-of-factly.

"You what?" Chloe laughs nervously.

"Abdullah means *Slave of Allah*," Hamza says again.

"That's an unusual name," I remark, wanting to say something complimentary but imagining how strange it would be to call him by those English words. I say nothing.

Hamza half-smiles. "I get you might not get it."

"Well..." I start, but I'm thinking of that book Matt showed me, wondering what it means to be in service not of oneself but of Allah.

"It's also one of the names of the Prophet," Hamza adds.

"Like a middle name or something?" says Beth.

"Partly. The Prophet's father was called Abdullah, so part of his name comprises 'son of Abdullah'. But he's called Abdullah too. It's completely who he was."

I wait for more.

"He has many names actually," Hamza goes on. "Nabiy Muhammad is Arabic for the Prophet Muhammad. Rasulullah means the Messenger of Allah. Then there's Ahmad, the Highly Praised. Mustafa, the Chosen One."

He pauses a moment.

"I know a recitation where two hundred names are mentioned," he says.

"Two hundred?"

Hamza glances at me, seeming to measure my interest. "Yes. The Trustworthy, the Guide, the Reminder. Piercing Star. Abundant Rain. The Friend..." He says something under his breath. I imagine it's that blessing phrase.

A group of lively girls are walking towards us. They quieten a moment, staring at Hamza. I notice their Spanish tanned skin. Long legs. I glance at Hamza who briefly looks at them then looks away. When they pass us I hear them giggling and whispering. I look back over my shoulder and two of them are doing the same. Hamza clears his throat.

"So tell us," says Beth. "Who's this shaykh you guys talk about?"

Hamza looks at her a moment. "Remember that special man I mentioned, who my parents met?"

"The Scotsman?"

"That's the one," says Hamza.

"Zayd said he's your teacher," says Chloe.

"And he used the word 'master'," I add.

"Um-hmm," says Hamza.

He's either thinking what to say or reluctant to say it.

"So what's he like?" I ask.

"That's not easy to explain," he says smiling. Then a more serious look comes to his face.

"Basically he's a man of Allah. A great man of Allah."

He takes a deep breath, unhurried.

"He just sees the whole of you. And sees right through you too. It's like he has X-ray vision – you can't hide anything."

"What would you want to hide?" I ask.

Hamza lets out a little laugh. Then he pauses in thought. "The false things in oneself, I guess."

I can't imagine Hamza harbouring any falsity.

We turn into a tiny alley and climb five narrow steps to a white stone house with a dark green door, ajar.

"Allahu akbar," Hamza calls through it. He clears his throat and again calls though the door. "Hajj Abdullah?"

"Come in, come in," an American voice answers.

The door opens wide and there stands a man who exudes warmth and diffidence.

"Hellooo!" he says, appearing genuinely delighted. "*As-Salamu alaykum!*"

"Wa 'alaykum salam Hajj," replies Hamza.

We step inside a small, lime-white hallway. Our host, a mass of nervous energy and bottled-up delight, looks from us to Hamza and back again. He must be in his mid-forties, slim built with wiry muscles – hard not to notice since he's dressed only in a white vest, Marlon Brando style, and long shorts. His skin is tanned and supple.

"So," he drawls in a Boston accent. "You're the backpackers, hmm?"

Hamza introduces the three of us by name.

"Fantastic!" he enthuses. "Come, make yourselves at home." He shows us into the salon. "Excuse the mess. I'm working on the final draft of my book and can't seem to concentrate on much else."

I glance around. A large desk is piled high in papers and several books as well as a typewriter and a pair of reading glasses. Apart from this, the living area is clean and tidy. There is a whole wall dedicated to bookshelves.

"I haven't met a writer before," I remark.

"Ha! Well, it's a bone of contention," he chuckles. "My day job is construction engineering but I try to balance the two things, you know? I'm writing something about America at the moment. Have you folks read any American writers? Whitman or Faulkner? Pound?"

Beth mentions the Jack Kerouac novel she's reading and how she'll be doing American Studies at university.

"American Studies? You must be joking!" he gasps. "The country's finished!" He throws his hands in the air. "Self-imploding! Just a matter of time." Then he motions to chairs around a coffee table. "Please, sit down."

His flat is small, furnished tastefully to the minimum and there's an abundance of natural light. He edges around the desk.

"Genocide!" he mutters under his breath, unnecessarily rearranging a couple of the piles. He looks up at us. "That's what the US was built on. Sustained of course by prisons and slavery." He sits down at his desk and leans against the back of his chair.

He begins to expound on the Native American nations – how they were "systematically wiped out in a genocide for which Congress has never made amends, while urging Germany and even Switzerland to pay up for their part in the genocide of the Jews."

He shakes his head, looking us in the eyes.

"Meanwhile the remnant of original Americans live enclosed in reservations – read *zoos*," he parodies his own accent. "Blighted by endemic diabetes resulting from state-granted diets of white flour and sugar. Three hundred languages wiped out! And for what? The price of the dollar, that's what. And you know what's written on those greenbacks?"

He leans forward with both hands extended on the desk in front of him. "'Ex pluribus, unum,'" he says to effect. "You know what that means?"

"From many, one?" I offer self-consciously.

Hajj Abdullah slaps his palm on the desk. "Exactly! And that's democracy for you." He leans back, satisfied. "Want some coffee?"

His eyes sparkle. They are slightly bulbous. A prominent nose gives away Italian roots. His charisma is wired; a male Patti Smith-like poet. He seems almost as young as us.

He lets out a little chuckle and gets to his feet, nodding to Hamza to join him. In the adjacent kitchen they start fixing some coffee. We hear Hajj Abdullah ask Hamza how his work on the flat is coming along. His tone his fatherly. Chloe and I go to the window and look out onto the rooftops, glimpsing the plains of the city through the gaps. A young woman opposite is watering geraniums on her balcony. Her water spills down the side of the wall. The sky is blue and open. I feel open too.

"Here we are," says Hajj Abdullah, carrying a tray to the table. He sits down and invites us to join him. "Bismillah. Sugar?"

"Who's the man in the photograph?" asks Beth, pointing to a framed black and white photo hanging close to the door.

"That's our shaykh," he replies.

He glances at the picture for a moment then runs his hand over his short beard. The photograph is of a man sitting cross-legged on the floor. He is wrapped in a dark, heavy cloak and robe, eyes lowered, and his head is swathed in white material, a bit like a small turban, itself covered mostly by the hood of his garment. His face is thin with a neat beard.

"It's quite an old photo now," Hajj Abdullah explains. "Taken in the early seventies. This is a much newer one..." and he reaches to turn a framed colour photograph towards us which stands at the edge of his desk.

"The same man?" I ask, looking back at the image on the wall.

Hajj Abdullah nods. The three of us examine the more recent image. It is of an older gentleman. Composed, he sits on the side of a cast-ashore rowing boat, hands crossed, with reading glasses in one hand. Pine trees surround him, and to the right is the shore of a lake. He gazes directly, his look at once intelligent and distinguished. His smile conveys contentment and a subtle mirth. He wears a Scottish kilt and a maroon fez which looks not at an inch out of place.

"Hamza mentioned you've known the shaykh a long time?"

"Ha! I wouldn't say I *know* him," he remarks, amused. "But yes, I've moved in his company for quite a while now, quite a while."

"So you can tell us what a shaykh is?"

Hajj Abdullah lowers his gaze a moment. He leans forward a little.

"Essentially he's a guide. A guide on the path to Allah. Because he has travelled that path to Allah and has arrived."

He pauses to observe our reaction, narrowing his eyes as though willing us to pay attention, or perhaps to understand. Then he adds: "He has reached the goal."

"The goal being...?" says Chloe slowly.

"You mean he's enlightened?" Beth says eagerly.

Hajj Abdullah leans back again. "I don't use that word. It's tossed around like a beach ball these days."

He looks at Hamza then back at us.

"But this path to Allah you talk about?" starts Beth.

"...is not some out-there abstract concept," Hajj Abdullah interjects. "To quote our shaykh: *It's a coming out from the safe place of existence into the alien existence of search.*"

"Cool!" says Beth with a tone of glee.

"And I will add to that," says Hajj Abdullah, unaffected, "that it's a journey you take with people who want the same thing."

"So how does a shaykh figure in that?" asks Chloe.

"Now you're talkin'!" he chuckles, repositioning himself in his chair. "The shaykh helps us recognise things – *deeply* recognise things – in ourselves as well as out in the world. As the Sufis say: he who knows his self, knows his Lord – knows Allah."

We look at him, waiting for more.

"You've barely touched your coffee," he says suddenly. "Sorry, I'm holding you hostage by talking." He motions towards our cups. "Bismillah, bismillah!"

I drink the coffee in one go.

"It's interesting what you say," I start, not knowing how to go on but wanting to.

"You'll find plenty to interest you here, that's for sure!" Hajj Abdullah chuckles then runs his hand down over his beard again, eyes moving quickly between us.

I believe him. My gaze rests on the photograph in front of us. I turn again to look at the black and white one behind us. The two images make such different impressions: one outward looking, the other, inward.

"I like the old photograph," Beth says, pointing to the one on the wall. "He really looks like a shaykh in that picture."

Hajj Abdullah frowns. "For me it's the other way around," he says, leaning back in his chair and throwing a glance to Hamza who says nothing. Hajj Abdullah looks at me, a touch of rebelliousness in his gaze.

"Well," Chloe comments, putting her cup and saucer back on the tray, "he must be a really good teacher if you've stuck around so long."

Hajj Abdullah doesn't reply immediately. "Yes, well," he says, again running his hand over his beard, "he's simply the sanest human being I've ever met."

And with that he turns the photograph on his desk away.

Prayer

The next day we take our first siesta. When I awake in the afternoon I feel groggy and strange. Now I'm standing at the balcony, refreshed and ready for part two of the day.

Our little square has also come back to life. People are passing from one end to the other. Opera from a nearby house saturates the air with sound. Tiny gold flowers on my dress glint in the sunshine.

Rafiq enters the salon and tells us he'll be going out for a couple of hours. "Feel free to make your own plans," he says casually.

He and his friends leave the flat at this time every day, and I don't think they're off just to hang out. I ask him about it.

"I was going to explain that," he says. "We all gather for

Maghrib, which is the sunset Prayer, then we stay on for the weird."

"The *weird?*"

Rafiq splutters into laughter. "No, Ally!" He regains his composure. "W-i-r-d. The Wird. *Miftah al-Wird* – the Key to the Source. It's something we recite."

"Oh. Do you have to do it?" Chloe enquires.

"No," he smiles.

Beth takes the words from my mouth: "Can we come along?"

"Sure," says Rafiq. "We'll be leaving in ten minutes."

"Leaving to where did you say?" I ask.

"The *zawiya*," he says. "It's where the shaykh lives, higher up in the Albaicín." Then he goes to his room.

We turn to each other and wonder what to wear.

"Maybe you could find something covering your arms and legs a bit more?" suggests Hamza in the kitchen. "And the women usually cover their heads," he adds.

"Really?" says Chloe.

Hamza blushes. "Please don't feel you have to," he says, seeming to back-pedal.

"No, it's fine, we will," I say, feeling game and wanting to respect our friends' ways.

We return to the salon and rummage through our rucksacks.

"What can we stick on our heads?" Beth mutters, rifling through her stuff.

I go into the bathroom and close the door, take off my little dress and put on something else. Then I take the dress and try tying it around my head. It knots easily at the nape of my neck, and I wrap the ends back to the top of my head, tucking the material snugly so it stays. I look in the mirror, turning my head side to side and adjusting some creases. It looks quite nice. I find my friends in the kitchen.

"Ta-daaah!" I declare, striking a pose. "What d'you think?"

"That's inventive," Rafiq grins. I'm sure he's laughing with me, but I suddenly feel self-conscious. In fact, I'm so used to having my hair all about me that this is disconcerting. Beth appears in the doorway and my inhibitions recede.

"Where did you find that?" I laugh. "You look fantastic!"

An elegant head-wrap has transformed her into an African queen. "This ol' thang?" she says. "It's a tablecloth I found under a table. Oh... you don't mind do you Rafiq?"

Rafiq waves his hand. Then Chloe joins us. She's found some sort of navy bandana, gypsy-style.

Aziz shows up in the doorway. He's speechless for a moment.

"Looks like you're ready to go," he says, eyes glinting. "Shall we?"

Sunset is nigh as we step into the square. Making our way uphill, the sound of opera recedes, and in its place, growing more distinct, is the chitter and trill of birdsong. Conversations drift from balconies and blend with laughter, indistinct rock music and the clanging of cooking pots. A voice somewhere erupts into an argument that fizzles out as quickly as it began. Bougainvillea hangs over walls and spills into streets and alleyways in shocking pinks and oranges. After a few minutes, the hill levels out and we pass a small bakery to our right. A little in front is a high, pockmarked wall, its soft orange stone contrasting with the surrounding lime-white and offering a dark, arched entrance.

"See that?" Rafiq says, looking up at it. "It's a remnant of eleventh century fortifications. *Arco de las Pesas* it's called."

"Archway of the Weights," adds Hamza.

We enter it: half gateway, half right-angled tunnel.

"The king's inspectors would come here to see that the merchants' scales were all in order," says Aziz seriously, his voice echoing slightly.

We come out at a quiet, peaceful square called Plaza Larga. It's roughly six houses long and four wide. At either end is a tree swaying gently, providing dappled shade for people sitting underneath. Red bricks pattern the ground and are bordered by cobblestone strips. We pass a tiny stationer on our right then a glass-fronted café clad with elegant Moorish-style columns and arches on our left. We skirt around the tables of an open-fronted bar towards a grocery shop, then head up a slim pedestrian thoroughfare no more than three metres wide – you could lean over the balcony and pass your neighbour opposite a baguette. The walkway is beautifully kept. Cobbles are swept, attractive wrought iron guards every window, and a plethora of flowers spill down from balconies.

"Ah, that smell of jasmine again," I say, breathing in deeply.

"A companion of the Prophet," says Aziz, "said that he hadn't smelled amber, musk or anything more fragrant than the smell of the Messenger of Allah, sallallahu alayhi wa sallam."

I glance at him, wondering what it's like for these things to come so readily to mind.

"Nearly there," he adds with barely contained delight.

At another plateau, we cross a wider street. In a wall opposite I notice a small statue of Jesus or perhaps some saint nestled high up in an alcove. Its paint is chipped and its face half-crumbled. Close by, Spanish youngsters in denims and aviator sunglasses strut their stuff. Scooters and small cars seem all in a hurry, disturbing the otherwise peaceful neighbourhood with hoots and honks.

"So," Aziz continues, slowing his pace as we continue uphill. "We sit separately by the way. The men and the women. But I'm sure you'll be well taken care of."

"Separately?" My heart sinks. I thought we'd be with them. I turn to Beth and Chloe. They also look put out.

The street narrows again and we arrive at a traditional white house with an open door. Other people are arriving and they briefly greet us, appearing intent on entering rather than socialising. Our friends go in. I turn to Chloe and Beth, make a *here goes* face, and we step inside a cool, spacious atrium.

A water fountain is in the centre. Geometric tiles adorn the walls and large pots of glossy-leaved plants stand in clusters beside them. Tucked in the far corner are a small garden table and chairs.

Aziz affords us a moment to admire it. "Shall we see you afterwards?" he says. "We can meet up outside."

We follow Aziz through a passageway to a kind of anteroom. Ahead is a huge, wooden door with an enormous brass handle. I imagine opening it onto a hoard of treasure. On our right, a group of men are removing their shoes and going through a double doorway into a large room. I see Aziz joining them, and he catches my eye and nods towards a group of women converging at an entrance further along. Beth, Chloe and I head towards them, glancing at one other in anticipation. We copy the women by placing our shoes on shelves. Warily, I wonder whether to walk in unannounced, then a woman puts her hand on my arm, saying something I don't understand. She is short and elderly, and her blouse generously covers her ample bosom. Gently but firmly, she leads me with Beth and Chloe to a little washroom.

"*Wudu?*" she enquires. I shrug my shoulders and smile defensively. "Wudu!" she repeats, eyes shining. I don't understand. She says something in Spanish, motioning towards a row of small taps set low along the wall. I turn to Beth and Chloe who are watching for my response. The woman takes off her headscarf and rolls up her sleeves. She looks at me, tilting her head to suggest I should do the same. I take off my head-dress and pull up my sleeves.

"*Bis-mil-lah!*" she declares, and holding both her hands under the running water she rubs one hand with the other. "Tres veces," her gravelly voice commands. I watch, understanding 'three times'. I bend down and copy her, stealing a glance at her tanned face. She shows no awkwardness.

The woman cups some water in her right hand and rinses her mouth, then sniffs a little water up her nose and snorts it out. We copy her. Face. Forearms. Rubbing with water, everything three times. Head, ears and finally the feet. She waits for us to catch up, then points her index finger into the air and says something else I don't understand. I raise my finger and smile self-consciously.

"*Ash-hadu....!*" she says again, and waits while we repeat it. Then: "*Ash-hadu an la ilaha illallah.*" We say it. "*Wa ash-hadu anna Muhammad ar-Rasulullah.*" We copy. The woman grunts in affirmation then passes us a towel.

"Ven conmigo," the woman beckons. 'Come with me.'

Her face is lit like a beacon. We fumble to put on our headdresses. I feel refreshed. She takes my hand in hers – her grip strong, her skin soft – and leads us out of the washroom. Beth and Chloe are at my side but I feel suddenly aware of how separate we are.

We enter the large room. It's furnished only with a sand-coloured, natural-fibre carpet and divided in two by a sheer white curtain hanging in the middle. The walls are white. At each end are full wooden bookcases. People pour in from the two entrances. Women sit against wooden panelling that runs dado height around the room. Some of them are chatting in whispers. Some sit in contemplation. Some look up and smile, nodding their heads in welcome.

The old woman lets go of my hand and bids us sit. Then she walks away. I make my way to the far side of the room, gravitating to a pair of women sitting near the corner. They look up at me, and a sensation of familiarity comes over me like that at the train station when I first met Hamza and Aziz. Beth and Chloe join me and we sit down beside them.

"Hello," says one of the women in a hushed voice. She leans in towards us. "I think we heard about you. You're the backpackers aren't you? I'm Qudra. This is Aneesa."

Qudra holds my gaze with pale green eyes; a spot of brown in one of them, a hint of mischief in both. Whispering, we take turns to introduce ourselves and tell them how we got to be in Granada. They listen attentively, casting looks at each other.

Qudra tells us she's from the south of England. Aneesa, round-faced, glowing skin, is from Vancouver. I reckon they're in their mid-forties. I find myself wondering where I might have met them before. I ask how they came to be here. Aneesa leans forward and begins to reply, but then a soaring, penetrating call silences everyone. Those still standing sit, and soon everyone is quietly sitting facing the front of the men's section. After each phrase of the call, a ripple of words passes under the people's breath. I look around at the women. They appear alert, waiting. Then another call prompts everyone to their feet. As I'm watching them, Aneesa pulls my arm and whispers loudly, "Come with us."

Before I understand what's happening, I'm on my feet joining a long line of women in front of the curtain. I lose Beth and Chloe and wonder if they too are in it. I stand shoulder to shoulder with Aneesa and someone else. A voice says something from the front. Women on my either side raise their hands towards their ears, palms facing forwards. I notice the men doing the same in front. I don't know what they're doing. They then lower their hands to their sides. I do the same and wonder what Beth and Chloe are thinking.

Everyone stands still, looking forwards and down. I do the same. The air feels charged. A man at the front starts reciting something. Then, following his lead – and with long pauses between – we bow, stand again, go down and put our foreheads on the floor, sit, put our foreheads on the floor again, stand up, then do that all over again, several times.

A memory surfaces. As a young child I said prayers before going to sleep. I'm surprised at how clearly I now recall it. I'd perfume my wrists and neck with my special violet-flower water, put on my long dressing gown with its Chinese fastenings, then kneel beside my bed, forearms resting on my duvet, hands pressed together. It didn't matter if I was happy or sad. There was always an underlying sense of something sacred. I'd talk to God. Ask. Then climb into bed.

When I was seven, my ritual was influenced by women I saw in a Japanese period drama on TV. Their grace enthralled me and I'd practise emulating their distinctive poise, their decisive, conscious movements. It seemed right when approaching God.

I come back to the present. We're in a sitting position now. Pristine energy surrounds us. Part of me feels reconnected to the past and to those times of intuiting the presence of the Divine. A deep shudder passes through my heart. Then there is the subtle thrill of this new and unknown situation. I keep thinking, *"Who are these people?"* but my question finds no ground. Instead, the anticipation of whatever might come next jitters in my stomach. I wonder whether, if I were to let go of that, I might perceive something quite sublime.

The prayer finishes. Supplicating hands are raised. There's a short recitation I recognise from the flat, then people stand and start praying separately. I spot Beth and Chloe, apart.

Qudra finds me and tells me they're going to do the Wird. Again, we face the front of the room in neat, cross-legged rows. There are no dimmed lights. No candles or ambient music. Beth and Chloe are a little way down the line. Through the curtain I make out about fifty men. I try to spot our friends, then decide not to look. I look down at the floor and feel the presence of the whole room. I recall Rafiq saying, "the Key to the Source." Then I think how all this is what he also encountered on his arrival here a couple of months back.

The Wird begins. It's like a spirited plainsong. More monotone than melodious. It has an energetic rawness. As it goes on, the pitch is raised, invigorating it. After a while, my legs are aching. Then the repetition of a particular phrase beginning with a strongly breathed 'H' distracts me from physical discomfort. It unnerves me. Like a short brief roar, there's something primal about it. I wonder what it means.

Other phrases come. They affect me physically, their sounds lingering around my heart and solar plexus. I feel a pulse in the base of my spine. The top of my head tingles. I cross my legs the other way. I wonder how long this will all continue. Then there's a marked change. The tempo slows right down. Clipped phrases are pronounced with emphatic clarity. I notice the silences between them. Cavernous and potent. Full of energy. Like wound-up springs. Then in one long, drawn-out breath, the word 'Allah' is sung out until the very last bit of breath has left the lungs.

For a moment there is silence.

Then the word, or rather the Name, is repeated quickly,

its ending expressed like the thud of a drum, urgency in its rhythm. Then silence again.

More recitation ensues. That too ends. Or has it? Hands are in supplication again, a man at the front saying things in Spanish, his words echoed by a chorus of 'Amin'. Then it ends. The women next to me smooth their hands over their faces. Everyone relaxes and starts moving, getting up or talking quietly with one another. I glance over at Beth and Chloe. They're staring right back at me.

I get up and go to sit with them but before we can confer, women start converging to welcome us. A petite, tanned, attractive woman sits herself down squarely in front of us. She's wearing a well-tailored, cream silk blouse and a long, fox-coloured chamois leather skirt. There's something about her which kindles my interest.

"Hello," she says melodiously in an American accent. "I'm Nuriya."

The turquoise colours of her headscarf match her unusually wide and liquid green eyes, her glowing skin wrinkling attractively around them as she smiles. We introduce ourselves. She seems delighted to meet us and completely focused on each one of us. I ask what her name means.

"It means *luminous*," she says. "Beautiful, no?"

She's well named.

"We're staying with a man called Rafiq," Beth says. "Do you know him?"

Nuriya's face lights up. "Ah, so you're the friends he mentioned? Fantastic!"

Her English is fluent but something in it suggests an extraction I can't place. I mention it.

"I *am* American!" she laughs. "But I've lived here for twenty years, so my English strays sometimes."

She looks warmly at the three of us. "So, what are your plans here?" she asks.

"We don't really have any," says Beth, shrugging her shoulders with a little laugh.

"We're just visiting for a few days," I add, "then heading off to Italy."

"Well, I'm here to help if you need anything. You know about the conference, no?"

"Yeah, Rafiq mentioned something about it," Beth says. I had forgotten.

"Well, you should go to it," she says matter-of-factly. "You should definitely go to it." She smiles with infectious warmth. "How about you come to my house tomorrow for coffee? We can talk properly then."

I feel an immediate connection with her. It seems she's taken to organising us. But I like it. And I think I want to go to that conference.

"Ask Rafiq to walk you over to mine tomorrow," she says. "You're just a few minutes away."

We thank her and I want to know more about her but she says goodbye, gets up and walks purposefully towards the door, her skirt swishing left to right like a pendulum. She looks back over her shoulder. "Hasta mañana!" she calls out softly, her perfume lingering in the air.

Enough

It's almost dark. Rafiq, Aziz and Hamza are waiting outside. When I see them, a vivid, lucid image comes to me: a torrent of water gushing between them and myself, and if I don't jump over to their side I'll be swept away.

"So how was it, being in there?" asks Aziz.

"In-ter-est-ing," says Beth, leaving the word hanging.

"We'd never have guessed that's what you were up to every evening," Chloe adds, and we laugh.

We start walking downhill, a new warmth between us. The sunless street hosts a spectrum of greys. Streetlamps illuminate our faces. Beth and Chloe whip off their head-regalia and shake out their hair. It's great to be outside, together, stretching our legs. Part of me feels quiet and reflective, yet incredibly elated, like I want to skip, sing and do cartwheels.

"What was that repeated phrase with the strong 'Ha' sound?" I ask Aziz.

"*Hasbunallahu wa ni'amal-Wakil?*" Aziz replies. "It means 'Allah is enough for us, and the best of guardians'." He looks at me studiously.

"I think that was the one," I say. "It stood out."

We come to the glass-fronted café – Casa Pasteles – and go in. At the far end are a group of men I recognise from the Wird. Aziz waves to them then places his hand on his heart. They return his greeting in the same manner. We go up to the counter and Hamza asks what we'd like to drink, suggesting something we haven't heard of.

"Horchata," he repeats. "It's a mix of milk and tiger nuts."

I say yes because I like the sound of tigers. I'm expecting Hamza to ask what we thought of the gathering, but he doesn't. He sets about drawing chairs to a table by the window and making sure there's space for us all. We sit down to the best view over the square. But Aziz ignores what's outside and turns to me.

"You were asking about *Allah is enough for us*," he says, purpose in his voice.

"I was," I say, still euphoric.

"It can be about provision," Aziz says. "That you'll have whatever you need. When you're worried about something or fearful, or you're flagging and feel you just want to give up, then *hasbunallah*. Allah *is* enough."

"So it's about being detached from things and not getting stressed out by them?" I say.

"How very Zen of you," says Aziz. "I see it more to do with the destiny. That you know how everything coming your way was decreed at the beginning of time, and your turning to Allah – your reliance on Allah – is your reflection of that knowledge and a deepening of it. Part of wisdom is to recognise the Provider in the provision."

He pauses.

"But the secret of this is concealed. So every form of provision is accompanied by the existence of the means."

"How do you mean?" I say.

"I mean the ways our needs are met. The means disguise Allah. We get food by earning money, shopping and cooking – that's the way we get it, but in reality our meals aren't ultimately originated by those means."

I try to assimilate his words. I'm not sure I understand.

"Of course, the means have to exist," Aziz continues, looking at me. "But we want to see beyond them, which is why we do things like reciting the Wird. We remind ourselves that Allah is enough for us, but you only really start to know that when you stop looking at the means. So we sit still, look down and stop gawping at whatever or whomever might distract us."

I think back to my experience of the Wird and wonder how those around me experienced it.

Aziz continues: "If you want to know the Provider, you have to see the means for what they really are, which is that they are, every single detail of them, entirely dependent on Allah. Saying 'Allah is enough for us' is our acknowledgment of that. And saying it regularly is a vehicle that can take us from mental understanding to true knowing. Once you have this knowledge, your life changes completely."

His eyes search mine. Mine search his. Then coffees and horchatas arrive and Aziz settles back in his chair.

Chloe speaks. "We met some interesting women tonight."

"Yeah," Beth effuses. "I've never seen so many different kinds of people in one room."

"I wish I could speak Spanish," adds Chloe.

"You'll pick it up," says Rafiq.

I sip my horchata – thick, proteinous, ivory liquid – through a fat black straw.

"It's a bit like rice milk and almonds, don't you think?" I remark.

"With a ton of sugar," Beth adds.

I sip some more, still trying to place the flavour. Aziz's words have affected me. I feel overwhelmed.

"Wow," I sigh, looking at Rafiq and his friends. "There's just so much to take in here. The architecture, the culture, and the women I just met – it's all so beautiful. I feel..."

"Ally," Aziz interrupts, eyes wide and unblinking. "You see that beauty because it's all in you."

"Ha-ha Aziz, very flattering," I say.

Aziz leans back in retreat, cheeks flushing. I realise he didn't mean that as a compliment and I feel suddenly abashed.

Quickly I continue: "You say that, but what about all the ugly things in the world: the hatred, the wars – I see all that too, you know."

"Of course you do," he says, leaning forward again. "The whole cosmos is you in miniature. Whatever you recognise, you do so because you have it latent in you."

I don't reply.

"I get that," Beth pipes up, reaching to take another sip of her drink.

"What *are* tiger nuts exactly?" Chloe asks.

"They're actually a kind of tuber," says Hamza, who seems relieved to change the subject. "One of the oldest cultivated plants in Ancient Egypt. At some point they were introduced to Spain where they're grown like rice. Mostly in Alboraya I think."

"Alboraya?" Beth repeats. "Ah, I think that's where my

friend lives. Near Valencia?"

"Could be."

"We're heading there next," I add. "Valencia. When we leave Granada."

As soon as the words leave my lips I regret saying them. I don't want to give the impression we've had enough and want to leave because I don't feel that way at all. Hamza nods and looks to Chloe and Beth, then at Aziz who says nothing. Rafiq smiles and clears his throat, looking quickly at each one of us.

The horchatas are too rich to finish. We step into the square through throngs of jovial people and past waiters serving paellas, pastas and drinks. A man and a woman, Flamenco dancers, are performing in the middle of the square. They strut and swoosh, their impassioned gestures embodying the music. We stay and watch. It's impossible to tell whether they're following the musicians or the musicians are following them. Rip-roaring acoustic guitars spangle the air with music that pings and peals. Hands clap. Feet tap in snatched rhythms, as though the very beats of the music are in danger of being stolen and there's no time to lose, and all of it compounded with whoops of delight from the crowd. The dancer's dress flies this way and that, her eyes made up like Cleopatra, haughty and alluring, her movements keeping perfect time with her tight-trousered, tuxedoed partner, a puffed-up bird in ritual courtship.

I turn to Rafiq. "Thanks for letting us come tonight. It's quite special – your community I mean."

He smiles knowingly. "Ally, you have no idea."

Alastu bi-Rabbikum

"I see you survived," says Zayd back at the flat, walking into the salon with a glass of water.

He's unhurried and at ease, and there's a look of intense interest in his eyes.

"Just about," says Beth, grinning.

"But I think I embarrassed myself," I say, clasping my hands to my face. "I told some of the women I was sure I'd met them before. They probably think I'm nuts."

"They wouldn't think that," says Zayd. He goes to the balcony. "I'm sure they were delighted to meet you." He turns to look at the view.

"You probably have met them before," Aziz pipes up, coming to sit at the far side of the room.

"No," I say. "I asked them."

"But I'm talking about something else," says Aziz, a delighted look inhabiting his face again. "I'm talking about before the creation of the world."

Beth, Chloe and I look at each other. Here he goes again. I settle my gaze on his, ready to spar. I sense he knows we know he's going to launch into something brazenly didactic, and it seems to amuse him. His eyes sparkle. A smile plays at the edges of his mouth. Perhaps he's waiting for one of us to say something. We don't.

"May I go on?" he asks genuinely.

"Sure. Of course," we say, agitated.

"I was going to explain that before the creation of time, Allah brought the spirits of the whole human race together. A pre-primordial meeting of souls. So Ally, your déjà vu sense of *knowing* us shouldn't come as a surprise. It's all there inside you."

"You're saying we existed in a world before this one?" Beth asks.

"Yes." says Aziz. "But the important bit is this: when Allah gathered all of us in our essential, spirit form, He said to us: *Alastu bi-Rabbikum?* – which means 'Am I not your Lord?' and every one of us said, 'Yes'."

"So you're saying," says Beth, "that every human being who's ever walked or will ever walk the face of this planet has acknowledged God?"

"I'm saying exactly that," Aziz says, trying not to smile broadly. "And I'm saying that in sensing you've met so many of us before, you're recognising your reflections. The Prophet, sallallahu alayhi wa sallam, told how the believers are a mirror of one another."

"I don't *exactly* remember being asked anything *before the beginning of time*," says Beth, poking fun.

Aziz raises his eyebrows, saying nothing.

"Do you remember it?" I ask Aziz. "Is that how you became a Muslim?"

He pauses to consider, lowering his eyes. "Of course, I can't say I remember in the usual way we remember. But in my heart of hearts – yes." He looks up at us. "I do remember. There's something in me that says, 'Yes,' and is perpetually saying, 'Yes,' and I can't forget it or deny it."

"But how do you know that happened?" asks Chloe. "That bringing together of all the souls?"

"Qur'an," says Zayd simply, coming in from the balcony.

"Indeed," Aziz continues. "And it's that Divine question which sets in motion this urgent, unquenchable desire to know, to get back to, to reconnect with what happened."

"You what?" asks Beth, bemused.

"We're not just our physical, mental and emotional selves," says Aziz jubilantly. "There's something else." His face radiates delight. "Deep in our cells, we have the vibrational memory of *Am I not your Lord?* And we also have the answer. Think about it: when we're here, we want to go there. When we've got this, we want that. We're never content. But this restlessness, this movement inside us we can't get rid of is how we are made."

"But *why* should we never be content?" I ask.

"Because we would forget the question," Aziz says. "Our restlessness is our opportunity to find out about ourselves."

Zayd speaks up: "And when we truly find out about ourselves, we find out about Allah."

He lingers a moment, studying us. "Excuse me," he says, "I'm going to start supper."

I watch him leave the room. I want to know what he means: finding out about Allah.

Beth clears her throat. "I don't mean to be rude," she says to Aziz. "But what if I told you I just don't *believe* all that?"

Aziz's jaw goes slack, his mouth agape. "Then I'd tell you the fundamental distinction within the human species is between those who recognise and accept Allah, and those who don't. Forget nationality, race, gender or age: you submit to the reality of Allah, or you don't."

"That's a tad narrow, don't you think?" says Beth, smiling at him defiantly.

"I happen to think it's rather broad," says Aziz. He draws in a deep breath. "Anyway, who's hungry?"

He excuses himself and joins Zayd in the kitchen.

"Bloody hell!" laughs Beth.

"Yeah, he's quite something," says Chloe.

Whatever the case, I'm glad of a break from all this deep talk. Plus, I'm hungry. Chatting and cooking sounds travel up the passageway. Hamza enters the room and smiles.

"Has Aziz been talking to you?"

"Talking *at* us, more like," Chloe laughs.

Hamza goes to the balcony. All the while, Rafiq has been sitting by the desk, his forearm pressed around the back of his chair.

"Is this what you went through when you arrived here?" I ask him.

Rafiq chuckles, exchanging a knowing look with Hamza. "They just told me to have a shower, then I said my Shahada in front of everyone and was Muslim. Questions came later."

"*What?*" I say.

"Yep."

"But..."

"It's different for everyone," says Rafiq. "Some people realise and accept it years down the line. For others it's immediate."

I look back at Hamza. "But you grew up Muslim, didn't you? Did you automatically accept all this?"

Hamza comes in from the balcony and stands near Rafiq. "It was a mixture of things. And still is." He puts his hands in his pockets, taking an audible breath. "There's a part of me that wonders if I would've become Muslim had I not been brought up in it. In a way I envy people who discover it for themselves."

"Well, I reckon Rafiq's right," says Beth with a tone of finality. "It's different for everyone."

Zayd appears at the doorway. "Supper's nearly ready."

"We'll lend a hand," says Chloe, getting to her feet with Beth and heading to the kitchen.

For a moment I stay in the room, thinking about what Hamza said. I appreciate his honesty. But what Zayd said earlier has stayed with me: that when we discover the truth about ourselves, we discover Allah. I mull it over. What does that *mean?*

Then the words *Am I not your Lord* come to me and I enter the sense of being asked something from beyond, searching in myself for an authentic response. I incline to 'yes'. But not in the context of my Lord being 'Allah' or of being a Muslim, rather in the more general sense of believing – no, *knowing* – there to be a great, all-powerful, all-knowing Presence, far greater than myself and anything the universe contains.

A deep part of me is engaged with all these reflections and ruminations. At the same time, I feel irritated by it all, wanting just to talk about 'normal' stuff and have a good time.

I realise I'm still wearing my dress on my head. I hadn't minded wearing it at all, but I take it off now and run my hands through my hair, enjoying its curliness from being twisted up.

"Smells great," says Hamza in the kitchen, peering over Rafiq's shoulder as he slices grilled peppers.

Zayd drains the pasta. Beth gets plates. I grab some cutlery and Chloe puts glasses on a tray and fills a jug of water. We take everything to the salon and lay out a tablecloth.

"Bismillah," says Zayd as he serves each plate.

Each time he says it, I think of the question Aziz told us about – *Am I not your Lord?* I don't hear the question itself. But I feel its presence. It's a familiar feeling.

"Bismillah!" says Zayd, and we tuck in to the colourful meal. Vegetables here are amazingly tasty. Fried onions, tomatoes, grilled peppers and aubergines mingle with pasta, salt and olive oil.

Eating together is an event in itself. Joyful. I make a mental note to learn how to cook properly. But I know all this isn't just about the food.

Love

I'm still awake. It's too hot. I get up and go to the kitchen for a glass of water. In the half-light, I find Hamza waiting for the kettle to boil.

"Can't sleep either?" he remarks.

"What time is it?" I reply wearily.

"Getting on for three, I think." The kettle starts whistling. "I'm making chamomile tea. Want some? Might help you sleep."

"Alright."

Hamza puts teabags into a couple of mugs and adds the boiling water. Its aroma wafts towards me.

"Honey?" he asks, drizzling some into his mug.

"Please."

Hamza hands me the drink. "Bismillah, here you go." He

looks nowhere in particular. "Hope that helps. See you in the morning."

"Goodnight," I reply.

Hamza leaves the kitchen. The door to his room clicks shut. None of the guys have tried anything on with Beth, Chloe or me. Their hospitality seems more genuine because of it.

I feel my way back along a dark corridor to the salon. Beth and Chloe are sleeping. The room is dimly lit by a streetlamp outside. I settle on my makeshift bed and pick up my drink. It smells of apple blossoms and dried grass. I take a sip and am taken back to times in the van. I start thinking of Jake and wonder what he's up to. I flick through memories of woodlands. Forests. And empty north Norfolk beaches, where the sands stretch half a mile beyond the dunes before slipping, like a letter into an envelope, into the sea.

I take another sip and think of my mother in her kitchen writing letters to overseas friends on her humming, electric typewriter. I think of my brother, doing voluntary work now in Zambia.

I look around the room, colourless in the darkness, its objects given sense by my daytime memory of them. Aziz's words emerge in my mind. They're provocative, but they don't offend me. He has something I can't quite put my finger on. I try to unpick what exactly is making me think about it.

I glance around the room. In the darkness I make out the photograph of the Ka'ba. A black square in a blur of white. I think of all those people walking round and around it and imagine bees humming at a hive. My mind drifts.

Love. That's it. That's what Aziz has. An overwhelming absorption in what he's saying. But not 'all you need is love'. Not 'make love, not war'. Not 'peace, love and harmony'. It's what is always bubbling inside him, and it's always something to do with Allah, and this prophet, Muhammad.

I begin to think about that name. 'Allah'. In the last couple of years I've moved away from saying 'God'. God as Heavenly Father was too up in the clouds, so I had a phase when Earth Mother felt more grounded. Lately I've preferred more ambiguous vocabulary: Supreme Being. Great Spirit. Both are neither up nor down but conveniently somewhere else. Then there is 'Intent'. But all those names seem to have certain colours and associations.

The name Allah carries no such baggage. To me, it has a clear, transparent quality. At the same time, it's not that either. I turn to look at the image of the name hanging on the wall. I can barely see its shape but I keep on looking at it. I think of Rafiq's words from when we first arrived here: "Whatever you think about Allah, Allah is not that."

Once when I was a child, I took a necklace from my mother's jewellery box. It was a string of pastel blue, multifaceted beads the size of pearls. Some opaque, some translucent, and joined at the ends by a diamanté clasp. I was admiring it in the half-light of a rain-pounded window upstairs on the landing next to the piano, when it came apart in my hands, the beads clinking against one another as they fell to the carpet. I scooped some of them up and rolled them around in my palms, mesmerised by their appearance, their blueness a pool of myriad hues, ethereal against the dark and stormy sky.

Then, for what was probably just a few seconds, I myself became also those beads which I held. As I looked on, suspended in a moment that seemed void of time, there was no end of me and no beginning of beads, just a gentle, steady, all-pervading, emanating and radiating presence of forms whose essence seemed something like love. It felt completely natural. Not unusual. And afterwards it made me think of God.

I look away from the name on the wall and bring to mind how our friends pronounce it: "All*aaah*." It's another language, yet it feels immediate and present. Not foreign. I whisper it into the room. Then I finish my drink and lie down, waiting for the chamomile to take effect.

Guidance

"Morning, Ally," yawns Beth, stretching out. "How did you sleep?"

"Hmm? I don't feel I really did," I mutter, trying to open my eyes.

"Why didn't you wake me up?" Beth says, poking my arm. "I could have kept you company."

Chloe stirs. I sit up, aware of sounds in the kitchen.

"Chloe, wake up," I say, prodding her. "The guys are up."

It's around nine. We roll up our sleeping bags and stack them with our pillows in the corner of the room. By the time we're taking turns in the shower the guys have all left, and by the time we've had our breakfast we're starting to wonder how to get to Nuriya's house. All we can do is wait for Rafiq to return.

"Shall we do a quick reading in the meantime?" I suggest to Chloe.

"Sure," she says brightly. I fetch the Tarot cards and set them out on the floor. I turn over each card.

"Wow, it's almost the same," Chloe says. "And the other day I had the Blasted Tower too."

"Which means...?" asks Beth.

"The destruction of illusions and delusions," I reply with mock-serious tone.

"Freaky," Beth delights.

"Let's do mine," Chloe says.

I collect the cards, shuffle them, then place them out. Chloe turns up her cards. We look at each other.

"That's weird," Beth says flatly.

"Looks like we're in for a spiritual rollercoaster," I joke.

"Okay, my turn," says Beth.

She shuffles, lays down her set, then turns them up.

"That's *really* weird," Beth repeats, staring at the cards.

The front door opens and closes. Hamza walks into the room. "What game is that?" he asks casually, putting his keys in his trouser pocket.

"It's not a game," says Beth. "It's the Tarot."

"Tarot?" says Hamza. "How can you be doing that?"

"Quite easily," replies Beth with a big grin.

"It's so odd," I say. "The cards are saying..."

"They're not saying anything," Hamza says flatly. "They're bits of card."

He throws them a disparaging look and walks across the room towards the balcony.

"Are you telling us off?" I say, my cheeks blushing, unsure of the line we seem to be crossing.

Hamza doesn't reply, which isn't like him.

I continue awkwardly: "It's not like we believe in 'bits of card'."

I watch him close one of the shutters.

"But it's pretty freaky that for the last weeks I've been getting practically the same reading every time."

Silence.

"Don't you think?"

"Bit of a contradiction, isn't it?" he says, turning to face me. "Saying you don't believe in them while talking about what they're saying."

He goes to the other balcony and looks out onto the square.

"It's no big deal." I mutter, feeling gutted.

Hamza faces me again, something softer in his countenance, his eyes large in the shady room. "You can't turn to those things for guidance."

Chloe picks up the cards, knocks them into a neat pile and puts them quietly back into their box.

"If our lives are predestined, why shouldn't we try to take a look at what's coming?" I protest.

"What, to avoid it?" Hamza says. "And because some cards told you?"

"Well maybe to accept it," I reply.

Hamza doesn't answer. I hear a door open and close. Rafiq enters the room. "Hi everyone. Ready to go?"

"Definitely!" We reply, jumping to our feet.

"Everything okay?" he says, looking between us and Hamza.

I explain the cards.

"Oh!" Rafiq laughs. "You won't be needing those now."

Lustre

We head uphill into the sun-bleached maze. Breaking from our familiar route to Plaza Larga, we turn right onto an undulating lane then down some wide and curving steps. Three huge huskies doze on the warm cobbles and we stop to admire them. They lift their heads a moment, their moonstone eyes squinting in the strong morning sun.

Descending further, we arrive at a narrow street with high, whitewashed walls. A little way along, Rafiq stops at a large wooden door with metal studs and ornate hinges the length of my forearm. Beside it is mounted a white tile with *Carmen de l'Agua* painted in blue cursive letters. He presses the buzzer. The door clicks ajar.

"Right," he says, stepping away. "I'll see you later."

"You're not coming in?"

"No," he grins. "I think this is a women's exclusive. I'm off to see Aziz."

We reluctantly say goodbye. "Say 'hi' from us."

"Will do." He raises his hand and briskly walks away.

We look at one another. Then I push open the heavy door and we step through its threshold.

"Oh my *God*," gasps Beth.

Inside is a landscape of trees and shrubs and a heady scent of blossom. Nearby are hanging vines of passion flowers, white with purple-stamen centres. A turquoise swimming pool nestles in the corner to our left, and beside it are walls bedecked with bright orange and red bougainvillea. On our either side stand square stone pots of bay made into topiaries, and to our right are terraced flowerbeds and petite pathways which seem to whisper '*this way, this way!*'

"It's the Secret Garden," Chloe whispers loudly.

We start down stone steps following the natural slope of the grounds, amble through a small grove of lemon trees and come to a grand, white house with large wooden shutters. We approach the front door. It opens, and there stands Nuriya, radiant, warm and welcoming.

"You made it," she laughs with open arms. "I'm so glad." She kisses us on both cheeks. "Come on in!"

We step straight into what appears to be the heart of the house. A huge panelled window looks out onto a perfect view of the Alhambra. Paintings adorn the walls. A Persian rug lies on a lacquered, quarry-tiled floor, and beneath the window stands a long dining table with a large jug of giant daisies.

"Wow, you wake up to this view every day," I say, going to the window.

Nuriya's face lights up, and she joyfully exclaims something foreign-sounding with the word 'Allah' in it, then saying, "Allah has been very generous to us."

Calligraphy hanging on the wall catches my eye. I go to take a better look. The outside of the picture has a repeated floral design and the inside is what I imagine to be Arabic script.

"What does that say?"

Nuriya reads it out then tells us the meaning: "*Call to the Truth. Abolish taxes. Repress injustice.* It's the motto of the Murabitun, the Muslims who ruled here."

"They must've been popular," Beth grins.

Nuriya smiles. "Well, their people enjoyed fair governance."

"What's the canvas made of?" I ask.

"Leather," Nuriya replies, enjoying my interest. "Touch it."

I run my fingers over its textured surface. "I love these earthy colours."

"They're painted on in washes after the tooling."

She comes to stand beside me.

"I'll show you how it's done some time."

"You made that?" says Chloe.

"Sure did. I make bags and briefcases, wallets, book covers... you name it. I've been fortunate to have a *maestro* – you know, a teacher – who's one of the very last traditional leather-workers of Andalusia."

Nuriya takes us along a passageway and outside onto a terrace. Some women are sitting around a large, white table and at the sight of us they extend cheery welcomes.

Nuriya excuses herself to fetch drinks. Her guests introduce themselves. Bilqis is English, Firdaws and Hafsa Spanish. We sit down, and I start asking the meaning of their names.

"She was the Queen of Sheba," says Bilqis, her accent indefinable but well spoken.

"Do you know the story about her?"

We don't.

"Ah, I love her story!" Bilqis says happily.

"She and her people were sun worshippers. But at some point in her reign, the king of the neighbouring lands, Solomon – who was also a prophet – wrote to invite her to submit to worship of God. Allah. They shared some correspondence – she's noted for her diplomacy – then she decided to go and visit him. Over the course of her stay she experienced various extraordinary things which made her realise how in worshipping the sun, she'd actually wronged herself."

Bilqis is dressed in summer couture. She's around fifty and has impossibly milky, radiant skin. She expresses herself with gracious, slender hands, like a ballerina dancing. The shape of her eyes makes me think of Genghis Khan.

"Where's that story from?" asks Chloe.

"From Qur'an," she says. "Where we're told she then submitted to Allah, the Lord of all the Worlds."

She pauses a moment.

"Interesting isn't it," she addresses her companions, "how we're told she'd wronged herself. Not a sun god or any other god, or Allah even, but *herself.*"

"My name is one of the gardens of Paradise," Firdaws continues. Her face suggests Moroccan descent. Her dark, shining eyes are lined with navy kohl and her teeth just protrude over her full lips.

"And mine is *young lioness,*" says Hafsa carefully, her Spanish accent strong.

The other women laugh gently, as though acknowledging some trait or temper they are familiar with.

All Rafiq's friends seem to know what their names mean. I watch the women as they talk. Knowing the meaning of their names lends them another aspect. It makes me want to know more about them.

"But enough about us," Firdaws says, clasping her hands. "We want to know about *you*!"

Beth explains how we came to be in Granada. The rumour about Rafiq's brainwashing amuses them. They ask if we've seen the sights then enquire after Rafiq and his companions. I mention the Tarot episode.

"Hamza was so disapproving," I say, still irritated.

Bilqis looks sympathetic. "The occult can be so tantalising," she says. "But it's one of the lower sciences. What might interest you is one of the things which blew me away when I became Muslim – the science of the angels."

"You believe in angels?" I ask.

"It sounds odd doesn't it," she says. "But to understand them you have to put harp-playing cherubs aside."

Her look is direct and intelligent.

"There's an angelic component in everything that happens. In fact, there's nothing in existence which isn't imbued with an angelic presence."

Normally, I might have written off anyone saying these things. But there's something in the way she explains it that doesn't put me off. She also seems entirely unconcerned as to whether we believe her or not, which lends her words all the more credibility.

"Even in our greeting," she goes on, "when we say As-Salamu alaykum – Peace be upon you – we use the plural form of 'you' since we're also addressing the angelic presence accompanying you."

"...not least of which are the Noble Recorders," adds Firdaws. "The angels at your right and left shoulder, recording everything you do."

Nuriya reappears with drinks and a plate of ground

almond sweets.

"So you'd say there are angels here with us right now?" Chloe asks.

"Of course," replies Bilqis.

"And," adds Firdaws, "if you visit your fellow Muslim in the way of Allah, just as we're visiting Hajja Nuriya here, then you're accompanied by seventy thousand angels which remain with your host." She puts her hand on Chloe's shoulder and grins at Nuriya: "So please come to my house next time."

We pass the morning getting to know the women and listening to their stories. They're a generation older than us. But it doesn't feel that way. Bilqis travelled the world, toured with theatre groups and lived in a tepee for seven years in the Yukon before meeting Muslims. Nuriya travelled up and down the west coast of California following the Stones, the Doors and Jimi Hendrix. But they don't seem to have settled into the comfortable traffic of middle-age. Their youthful searching seems internalised to a deeper, inner highway.

"It's time for the midday Prayer," says Firdaws, glancing up at the sky. Bilqis checks her watch.

"Excuse us," says Nuriya, clearing the table. "We'll be back out in a while."

With a laden tray she disappears after her companions into the house, her flip-flops clicking like castanets.

"Let's go in too," says Beth, getting to her feet and stretching her limbs.

It's silent inside the house. We wonder where the women have gone.

"Ah, I hear them," Chloe whispers, treading quietly in the direction of a sunken room. "Down there."

We tiptoe down polished steps into a refreshingly cool salon. The women are at the far end facing away from us in various positions of bowing, standing and prostrating, long garments swathed around them. We sit down some way behind them and wait.

A bookcase stretches from floor to ceiling along the length of one wall, stopping short at a group of healthy-looking plants in earthenware pots. I notice a large stereo system and a huge CD collection. Dark brown leather sofas with brass studs are arranged in a C-shape facing the Alhambra.

All the while there are the sounds of praying. The billowing of a linen skirt. A tinkling bracelet. Bare feet moving against carpet fibres. Whispers. An impression of consonants. I sense a steady luminosity and an almost tangible lustre in the air around us.

One by one the women finish praying. Then a door slams somewhere and we hear children's voices.

"Los niños!" Nuriya says, getting to her feet. "Back from school already."

We follow Nuriya up the steps. Her four children crowd around her, speaking a mix of Spanish and American, eager to share stories of their morning. They each greet us with an *hola!* then make off in every direction, bringing the house and garden to life.

Challenge

We've now spent six whole days in Granada. Our interrail tickets are slowly running out, so we need to get moving if we are to visit Italy.

It's a warm and sunny morning as we make our way to the payphones in Plaza Nueva to call Beth's Valencia friend. No reply. Beth thinks she must be down at the beach. But she could have taken off for a few days. Or might not be in Spain at all. By lunchtime we've almost given up. Then she answers.

"Yeah, it's totally cool for you guys to come and stay," she says.

Afterwards, walking back up the Albaicín, I feel uneasy. I've grown attached to our new friends. Plus, there's another thing: the conference. It's just four days away, and Rafiq and other friends of his have been talking about it. I'd love to attend. Then again, four days is a long time to wait when travelling and the others are eager to get going.

The remainder of the day passes swiftly. Rafiq and Hamza prepare a farewell supper. Zayd is here. Aziz too.

"So you're really leaving?" asks Zayd as we're finishing the pasta. "I was hoping to show you the documentary I've been working on."

"The unknown beckons," Beth grins.

Rafiq enquires politely of our route. Chloe mentions train times. Aziz is pointedly quiet.

At some point Hamza brings in some crème caramel and we eat it slowly. I'm about to get up and make coffee for us all when Aziz clears his throat and speaks up: "Don't get on that train tomorrow," he says, his tone urgent. "You've tasted something here, you know it. If you leave, all this will become a curious memory. A dream."

The three of us exchange awkward looks.

"We've already arranged things with my friend," counters Beth. "She's expecting us."

"Forget about your arrangements," Aziz says. "What's important is happening right here. Right now. You think you stumbled on all of us here but it was no accident. In fact, everything in your life has been set up for you to experience this very moment."

We look at one another again and I feel my insides tightening.

"The so-called moment of truth isn't accompanied by lightning bolts, fireworks or an angel bonking you on the head with jingle bells," he says. "Or is that what you're waiting for?" His eyes flit from one of us to the other.

Beth blushes. Chloe looks confused.

I want to respond but nothing comes. I want to go. But I also want to stay. Aziz looks disturbed by our silence.

I expect a barbed comment, but his face softens, his eyes full of concern. He lifts his palms upwards.

"You're being offered the Garden," he says. "Take it."

Stars

Twelve hours later, we're on a train heading north-east across the Iberian Peninsula to the Mediterranean coast. Rolling hills of olive groves dominate the landscape. Mirages levitate off the dry earth, their watery illusions shimmering in the near distance. It's chilly inside our air-conditioned carriage. Goosebumps stand proud on my arms and legs. I cross my forearms over my waist.

The movement of the train lulls me in and out of sleep. In the clickety-clack I start hearing sounds of dhikr. *La ilaha illallah, la ilaha illallah, la ilaha illallah.* At first I dismiss it as rhythmic coincidence. But having heard it, I can't unhear it. And it's so clear. I submit to its sound, hearing it as a song of departure, expecting it to fade along with my experiences of Granada.

My thoughts slip away to meeting Rafiq at the station. I recall our conversations in the flat. The Wird. The smell of jasmine in the Albaicín. Then those women, each and every one bearing some quality that impressed me.

My breathing becomes shallow. I wish I could relax, feel at ease, look forward to our next adventure. I consciously exhale, trying to let it all go, *willing* myself to let it all go. But the further we get from Granada, the more uneasy I become. Eventually, I fall asleep.

It takes eight hours to reach Valencia. When we arrive, we catch a bus to a place called Gandia. Awaiting us is an attractive, plump, blonde-bobbed young woman with a wiry boyfriend standing beside a small, shiny blue car. Lara is warm and friendly. Her boyfriend is a bit distant. We pile into the car, exchanging excited pleasantries. The boyfriend sticks a Metallica cassette into the tape player, turns the volume right up, and thumping his foot down on the accelerator he drives off at speed.

When we come to a stop, we've arrived at the very edge of a beach. The boyfriend revs the car onto the cusp of the dunes, its front wheels sinking in the dry sand. With ringing ears, we get out and stretch, bodies still stiff from the train journey. Before us is the ocean. The tide is in. A thin band of coastline extends as far as we can see and sunbathers fleck the ivory sand.

In front of us is a circular, thatched beach bar. Lara and her boyfriend make a beeline for it, pulling stools from beneath the counter as though they were at home. Trashy pop music thuds and pulses. People in bright, skimpy clothing are standing around sipping beer and cocktails garnished with paper umbrellas and impaled fruit. Mirrors behind the bar reflect the customers, some of whom are checking their appearance while waiting to be served. I exhale slowly, puffing out my cheeks.

We order drinks and chat for a bit, then with plastic cups in hand we walk midway to the shore and sit down on the sand. I look out to sea, gutted. I breathe in the beauty of the view, hoping it will displace the discomfort in my chest. It *is* beautiful here. The ocean extends in ripples of glistening aquamarine, the crest of each wave sparkling in the late afternoon sun. It's still hot. I sip my drink.

Lara's house is several miles inland, up a steep little road that bends like stacked hairpins this way and that. Nestled on a hillside is a village whose whitewashed houses are packed together along narrow, twisting streets and prettied up with sprawling roses, pots of geraniums and shrubs ablaze with bright orange flowers. Palm trees grow in clusters near huge spiky-tongued plants. Locals are out and about. Some look our way and raise a hand.

The boyfriend parks the car alongside Lara's house. We get out and admire the view. With the hill at our back, huge swathes of agricultural land lie below us. Most of it is orange groves, a novel sight which spreads out towards the coastline like a green gingham cloth. In the distance, the sea glimmers with flashes of sunlight, a thousand mirror signals for all to see.

Lara takes the keys from her bag and goes up the steps to her front door. We follow, sandy shoed.

Later, lying in bed, I go over the day. I feel so out of place. Like I shouldn't be here. I turn to face the wall and try not to think about it.

The next day is just beach and day. Hot and long. I'm not cut out for this. I try to convince myself I'm having a good time. At least I'm getting a tan. How do people lie in the sun like this for so long? I saw two women lying on the beach for nearly five hours.

By late afternoon I'm glad to be getting back into the car and its deafening music.

"You've really caught the sun," Chloe remarks as we walk up Lara's steps.

"You can tell already?" I reply anxiously, reaching to feel my shoulders. "Agh, I could fry an egg on this skin."

"Omelette for supper?" Beth grins.

The others open beers and lounge around. I retreat upstairs to examine my sunburn and slather it in after-sun. Dusk is coming. I go downstairs and pitch in with making supper.

Lara says the house belonged to her mother who recently passed away, and that she's come here to feel close to her. Suddenly I feel we're imposing and I say so. But Lara says she's glad to have us and that her mum would have wanted us to stay.

Later, something sparks my curiosity. Out of the far window is a view to the top of the hill and what looks like an old fortress. I ask Lara about it. She tells me it's a fortress built by the Moors.

"You can walk up there," she says casually. "Only takes ten minutes, and the view's spectacular this time of day."

She walks over to the kitchen table and knocks out a cigarette from a box of twenty. She lights it and draws deeply, looking vaguely out of the window in the direction of the old ruin.

"It's not private property," she adds, exhaling. A faraway look comes over her. I wonder if she used to go there with her mother.

"Can we go up before it gets dark?" I ask. But before she

can answer I have a better idea: "Could we sleep there?"

"Don't see why not," Lara replies. "It's probably bloody uncomfortable though."

I don't care. I turn to Beth. "Why not?" she replies with a big grin.

"Chloe?" I call out. She's ensconced on the sofa flicking through an English magazine. "Wanna come?"

"Not really," she says, looking up a moment. "You go ahead."

Beth and I excuse ourselves, grab our packs, and hurry out in the hope of reaching the ruin before sunset. We follow the village road towards the hill, and when it forks we continue straight upwards along a stony, overgrown path. Shrubs thrive miraculously here and there amid the arid soil, some smaller bushes flecking our surrounds with vivid yellow.

The derelict fortress comes into full view. Heavily weathered, two square towers stand at either end of a high wall with vertical slits. A tree pokes out of the top, its branches swaying in the breeze and catching at the masonry. We make our way around rocks and stone debris, scratching our legs on the scrub. We find a small path and hasten our step, our laughter mingling with the occasional sound of a cricket. At our backs the sun is near to setting and casts a deep orange glow on the ruin's sandstone blocks. Our shadows stretch tall before us. We play at jumping on them.

As we get closer, an archway at ground level becomes apparent and offers an entry point. We clamber through. Inside, the ruin's original layout is discernible from tumbledown interior walls. The upper floor is long gone. But remnants of its edges cling to the sides of the walls, precariously accessible by stone staircases. Whole doorways remain, as well as some kind of cistern in the centre. Crumbled bricks and stones lay strewn across the dusty ground. Weeds grow in nooks and cavities. Every detail bears testimony to the age and neglect of the place. We throw down our rucksacks and start clambering about, hearts pumping faster with a sense of reverence and trespass.

We find an archway just wide enough for the two of us and which looks out to the sea. We squat in its warm, craggy threshold. With a sense of achievement and relief, we watch the sun dip into the vast, watery horizon. The light fades. The air cools. As dusk yields to nightfall, there's little to do except change out of our clothes and settle down for the night. Beth and I choose spots a few metres apart and close to walls that still radiate the warmth of the day. We get into our sleeping bags and lie down, our hair like nests in the dust of old. Cricket song fills the air.

"Can't get earthier than this," Beth sighs contentedly.

I agree. My shoulder blades poke into the ground, aggravating my sunburn. But I don't mind. I love the wildness. We chat about this and that. We take some clothes from our packs to use as pillows. Soon, the walls and towers have relinquished their form and colour to the darkness. My eyes refocus into the depths of the sky. One by one the stars come out and before long the dimming firmament has transformed into a shimmering cloak of jewels sparkling silently in the blackness.

"Oh, I forgot!" Beth says quietly, breaking the silence. "Lara gave me something." She reaches to her pack and extracts a candle, twisting it into the warm earth between us. In seconds a flickering glow outdoes the starlight, obliging shadows to dance unsteadily on walls close by.

"Bit spooky isn't it?" Beth whispers.

"Why are you whispering?" I whisper back, and we laugh out loud, eager to stave off the eeriness. "I suppose it is," I say, turning onto my side to face Beth and the small, bright flame.

"Chloe should've come," says Beth.

"Yep," I reply, wondering how she's getting on with Lara and her boyfriend.

Beth turns onto her back. "Lara said pottery from the Bronze Age has been found here." She scrunches her fingers in the brick-dust beside her. "Think of all the people who've slept here."

I turn and stare into the darkness.

"Romans... Christians..." Beth mutters. "Then the Moors." She pauses. "Okay if I blow out the candle?"

"Hm-mmm..." My voice trails off. Sounds of the night envelop us. A couple of birds bill and coo. The high-pitched whine of a mosquito threatens nearby. Chilled breezes swish through grasses in the walls.

"Do you think those Moors were like our friends in Granada?" I ask, turning my head from the sky to look at my friend.

"Beth?"

Her eyes are closed.

I look back into the darkness, my eyes resuming their wandering of the stars. I imagine the peoples of the past but their forms are superseded by more recent impressions: seeing the copy of the Qur'an, the old lady teaching us wudu, being pulled up to join the prayer. I recall my meetings with all those people in Granada. I feel as though they inhabit a kind of parallel universe. I've been living life in my carefree, spontaneous world, but something about the way they are is truly different. Daring. What they do, the way they live, the way they *are* – in one way it feels quite radical. In another it feels deeply natural. Purposeful. It's as if they're all moving somewhere, like a train that won't wait.

I close my eyes and hope for sleep. I feel the pulse in my neck and my body against the hard ground, but those people in Granada feel closer. I'm breathing their air, and with every breath there comes something of their spirit into my bloodstream. I breathe out long and hard, willing it away.

That night I have a vivid dream. A man robed in white is beckoning me towards him.

Return

The warm sun of morning falls on my face and wakes me. By the light in the sky I reckon it's a couple of hours after dawn. I'm surprised to have slept so long. I stretch out my limbs and feel the cool earth on the backs of my hands. I turn to Beth. She's rubbing her eyes. We push down our damp sleeping bags.

"That was incredible," says Beth, yawning.

I shake the grit from my hair and admire our surroundings.

"Shame Chloe missed it," I say.

We get up and amble to the archway. The stones are cold and damp. I recall my thoughts from last night and wonder how to express them. Somehow I can't. Then I decide not to. Sitting opposite one another, still bleary eyed and a bit dreamy, we pass some time quietly rolling tobacco and admiring the landscape: Lara's village below, the citrus groves, the hills, the colours of the far off sea. Beth expects Chloe to come up and join us. We linger where we are, half-waiting, half-enjoying our sense of being on top of the world. My burning tobacco hisses and crackles. It contrasts with the silence of scenery below.

Hunger eventually sends us back down to the house. Inside, the kitchen clock says it's ten to eight. I find Chloe and say hi, then head to the bathroom for a wash. The walls are emerald green and around the bath and basin are all sorts of seashells. Perhaps Lara's mother collected them. I wonder what she was like. Brunette, I imagine. With a love of warmth.

I splash cold water on my face and peer in the mirror at my tanned and freckled self. I think about Lara's grief, intuiting a landscape I cannot know, yet know so intimately in myself.

My reflection lasts just a moment, but it's enough to reconnect to that child place in me. That private, chasmic realm. I sense the silence of its years. And though it has kept a part of me secluded and sacred, it has always been here, present.

I splash my face again, the water bringing me to the here and now and causing my hands and face to tingle. I feel the beating of my heart. The pulse of blood through the arteries in my neck. The hair on my head beginning to prickle. I notice my lungs rising and falling. Breathing in. Breathing out. I'm aware of how the skin on my shoulders, back and thighs feels tight and aglow from sunburn.

Here I am – so alive – beside these shells which seem to straddle life and death. I observe my eyes, brighter now, a searching look in them. Besides the billow and swell of my thoughts I feel I'm hearing my body speak, and that in its subtle movements I'm listening to the preciousness of life.

It reminds me how, at any moment, life can be taken away. I know that so well. My heart beats even stronger and I feel a shock of urgency: I mustn't waste this life. I don't *want* to waste it.

I start wondering about the life of the next world. Will I get my reward in heaven? Will I even experience heaven? Then I think of my dream, of the radiant man in white.

Downstairs, we eat toasted baguette with olive oil, sliced tomato and primrose-coloured cheese. Chloe and Beth tell Lara where we're headed next. I sit and listen, watching Lara's affirming responses, indifferent to her snippets of advice.

"I'm thinking about going back for the conference," I blurt out.

"You what?" says Beth.

"You know, the conference in Granada."

"Yeah, I know what you mean. But why?"

"I just feel I've got to go back. Just for the two days. What do you think?"

"I think we're on our way to Florence, that's what I think!" says Beth, aghast.

"And I'm really looking forward to that but, I don't know, something's telling me I should go back first."

"Back to what? What for?" Beth looks as though she's going to burst out laughing but doesn't. Chloe says nothing. They both stare at me.

"I want to know more about the politics and economics side of things." I try to explain more, but my reasoning limply trails off.

"Look, we're already in Valencia," Beth persists. "Florence is much nearer from here and it's one of the most beautiful cities in the world. How can you not want to go there?"

"I *do* want to go there," I reply. "But there's something

in Granada."

"Of course there's something!" Beth laughs. "And there'll be something wherever you go, and that something right now is called *Firenze*!"

She gets up to fetch her tobacco then comes to sit beside me, offering me some. She lights her cigarette and takes a deep drag.

"So the conference might be interesting," she says, "but it'll be over on Sunday evening, and then what?"

She exhales a trio of smoke rings and stares at me. I have to force myself to meet her gaze.

"Then our timing for the rest of our journey will be scuppered, that's what. We won't make it to Italy at all."

"It's not just the conference," I say, searching for words. "It's... aaah!" I fling my hands in the air, mortified at trying to convince my friends to change their plans. I get up and pour a glass of water. Beth and Chloe exchange inaudible words. I go and sit at the table again.

"Look Ally, don't worry," says Chloe. "We had a fantastic time with Rafiq and all that, but we'll have a fantastic time in Italy too." She looks at me in her reasonable, even-keeled kind of way.

"I'm not worried. But... I'll be worried if I don't go back to Granada."

Silence.

I take a sip of water.

"Hey, why don't I go back, you two go ahead, and we'll rendezvous in Italy in a few days' time?"

"No way!" exclaims Beth. "We're not going without you!"

"I second that," adds Chloe.

"Look, it's Thursday today," I say soberly, and with sudden clarity I put forward a plan: "We can be in Granada tonight. The conference is over the weekend. And we can be on a train to Italy on the Monday where I promise you two can decide on *everything*."

Beth frowns and drags deeply again on her cigarette. She taps it, watching the ash fall into the ashtray. I look at Chloe, feeling almost guilty because I know she'll concede.

"I don't mind," Chloe says with a casual shrug of the shoulder. "We could go back I suppose, hey Beth?"

Beth eyes me for a prolonged moment.

"Okay Ally," she says, some sparkle returning to her demeanour. "I hope it's worth it."

"It will be," I tell her. "I know it will be."

PART III

Providence

We try calling the guys' flat in Granada but no one answers. The conference is imminent so we don't want to wait around – Lara and her boyfriend take us straight down to the train station. I hug Lara goodbye and tell her I hope she'll be okay. I think of the seashells in her bathroom and feel a pang of sadness. But also hope.

The train journey is long. Back in Granada, still no one answers the phone. We set out on the main road towards the old quarter and eventually find our way to Plaza Nueva and another payphone. I dial the number. Twice. Then...

"No way!" Chloe exclaims.

On the far side of the square, walking in our direction, are Rafiq, Hamza and Aziz.

"Wow!" Beth laughs.

Just the sight of them confirms my intention to return. Something in their camaraderie makes them stand out from the crowd.

We grab our rucksacks, excited, and meet them in the middle of the square. I feel so relieved. I explain why we decided to come back, mindful of my enthusiasm and turning to Beth and Chloe with an apologetic expression.

"Well," Aziz says matter-of-factly, "Providence is with you." He seems entirely confident.

Chloe and Beth chat happily with our friends and my concerns at having pulled them back to Granada are allayed for now.

"So what are *you* up to?" Beth asks the guys.

"Busy receiving conference guests," says Rafiq, slightly brusque.

I suddenly wonder if we can fit in with their arrangements. I'd assumed we would go straight back to their flat. Or at least hang out with them.

Hamza courteously steps in: "How about I take you up to Hajja Nuriya's for the while? She'll be happy to see you, and we can meet up later when we're done?"

The walk up the Albaicín is effortless. Hamza tells us about other guests arriving from Malaysia and Switzerland.

"Aziz and I are taking them to their accommodation," he says.

"We're hosting several hundred people all in all," Aziz adds.

"Wow," says Chloe. "I've hardly noticed any hotels in the Albaicín. Are they all staying downtown?"

Hamza laughs. "I think most of them are staying with us, with our community."

"That's a lot of work," Beth exclaims. "Are you all okay

with that?"

"We're greedy for the *baraka*," grins Aziz.

"He means we're greedy for the blessings that come with having guests," says Hamza.

"Hopefully you'll meet some of them," says Rafiq.

"You should join us for supper," adds Aziz. "I'm inviting myself too." He looks at me with a faux-sheepish grin. "Hope you don't mind Hamza?" he adds with a chuckle.

"Zayd's cooking tonight," Hamza smiles. "I'll let him know."

Leaf

Nuriya's face lights up. "Come on in!" she exclaims. "You're just in time for lunch."

Her table is beautifully set with baskets of bread, a tray bake with melted cheese and a platter of chicken. Her children go to and fro with cutlery and glasses. I haven't seen such helpful children. Her husband, Hajj Abdulmalik, appears from the salon where he's hosting a group of men. He's tall and tanned, distinguished looking, and is wearing a thin brown cardigan over a pale pink shirt.

"Ah. You must be the English girls," he says slowly, with a heavy accent.

There's a playfulness in his eyes. I feel he's about to say *'what shall we do with you!'* Nuriya hands him a platter of food. He looks at it for a moment then smiles ruefully at his wife.

"I believe you've been too generous with our meat," and he picks up some of the chicken legs and puts them carefully on our platter on the table. He turns to us, his manner commanding and intelligent.

"The Prophet, sallallahu alayhi wa sallam, taught us not to make our stomachs graveyards of animals."

I'm struck by the image and caught off guard by his mention of the Prophet. He wasn't so much expressing an opinion, as telling us how it is. I think I'd feel affronted but for the fact I agree with him. He thanks his wife and returns with his diminished serving to his guests.

"We're hosting Indian and Zulu guests from South Africa today," says Nuriya, putting a tall pepper grinder on the table.

"Zulu?" I go quietly to the top of the salon steps and peer down into the room. Beth joins me. I see four black men, three wearing colourful, loose tunics and smart, brimless hats, the other in a western shirt and trousers. Of the three Indian gentlemen, one stands out because of his white hair and neat white beard that contrasts beautifully with his skin. They sit composed in front of the platter of food, two of them with their right knees drawn to their chests.

"Pssss," says Nuriya, beckoning us away with a chuckle.

"Sorry," I say sheepishly.

We go to sit down and I notice a riding crop hanging off one of the chairs.

"I went riding in the Alpujarras this morning," she explains, joining us at the table. "A bit crazy since there's so much going on right now but," she winks at me, "I *had* to go." I had been wondering about her jodhpurs.

After the meal, Nuriya excuses herself for a siesta. We hang out in her salon. Half an hour later she reappears, looking at us with delight.

"Are you girls up for a walk?"

The Albaicín is starting to feel like home. I know where to buy bread, banana juice and tobacco, where to have the best coffee, tapas and ice-cream, and if I were blindfolded I could more or less guess my location by the smells of spices in the Moroccan quarter, bar food near the Mirador or cigarette ends in the backstreets towards town.

Soon we're at Plaza Larga. The square is empty and the cobblestones strewn with the first leaves of autumn. It's coming to the end of siesta time and Casa Pasteles and the neighbouring shops are getting ready to reopen.

"Allah!" exclaims Nuriya all of a sudden, exuberantly throwing her arms up.

Sitting at a table in the centre of the square are some girls our age. There's an audible buzz of excitement as they jump to their feet and greet Nuriya with bear hugs, exclamations and glowing faces.

"I wasn't sure if you were coming!" Nuriya says.

The girls introduce themselves and we sit down.

"I've known these girls all their lives," says Nuriya with a look of pride.

The girls – five of them, Caucasian, from Switzerland, Germany, England and Ireland – look affectionately at Nuriya as she asks about their studies, their families and who else they know is travelling to the conference. A waiter arrives with our drinks.

One girl, Mishka, makes a special effort with us. She has large, almond eyes that look kind even when she's not smiling, and a cheeky laugh. Another is Hamza's sister. The resemblance is obvious: she's beautiful with long dark eyelashes, noble-looking. Her presence is gentle and self-assured.

We talk a while and I find myself wanting to find something in common with them. We talk about school, music, even drugs – they've never taken any – but it seems we share no particular interests. They have an air of naivety, or perhaps innocence, which intrigues me. It's something in their manner. How they talk. How they listen. They seem cut from another cloth.

"Hey, there's Aziz and Rafiq," says Beth rising to her feet. "Over here!" she calls, waving.

They approach, and Aziz greets us with a swooping gesture of his hand to his heart, saying 'As-Salamu alaykum' to us all.

We return his greeting and listen to Aziz and Nuriya talk about the guests they are hosting. Nuriya then gets to her feet. "How about you come back to mine for a while?" she says to the girls. She turns to us with a big smile. "I'll leave you to catch up, okay? But I'll see you soon."

We say goodbye and watch as she and the girls leave the square, their lively talk audible even after they've disappeared from sight. Aziz and Rafiq sit down. Now that they've seen to their guests they are more relaxed. We chat about our time in Valencia.

"Where's Hamza?" I ask.

"On another airport-run," Aziz says. "He's meeting us here once he's dropped the guests at the flat."

"You've got conference guests too?" I ask.

"Yes. Here to play the bagpipes."

"Bagpipes?" exclaims Beth, turning to me with a giggle. Rafiq looks away and smiles.

"Well, it's good we met you here," Aziz says. "Hamza wants to take you up into the hills."

"Really?" I say. "Is he coming soon?"

"Should be. Assuming the plane was on time."

Aziz looks at his watch then turns to us. His face is alert and clear, his chest noticeably rising and falling with his breathing, and trembling slightly. He places his hands squarely on the arms of his chair.

"So," he says with familiar gravitas. "You came back."

His intense gaze is reassuring now that I'm used to it.

"I hope this time you..."

And then he stops mid-sentence, staring, because out of the blue, a leaf is floating down right in front of us. It lands in the centre of our table. It's the size perhaps of my hand, quite green with brown curled-up edges.

"No leaf falls without Allah's decree," he says, pointing up his index finger.

He looks at me directly, with unnerving, unwavering certainty.

I want to respond, but his words ricochet inside me, overriding any idea of what I might say in response. I look back at him in silence. For a drawn-out moment no one says anything. I feel caught off guard – not only by him but by myself: his words seem to have bypassed some inner barrier and struck me at my core. He's speaking the truth. I *know* it. I feel I'm looking into a mirror that is reflecting some unarticulated part of my own being. Still I say nothing.

Then the moment passes and my insides are recoiling at his gaze, rendering me self-conscious and compelled to look away.

Rafiq breaks the silence. "Well, I'm glad to see you all back."

"But you never really left, did you?" says Aziz, his persistence allowing no escape.

I smile and shrug my shoulders, conscious of what my friends might be thinking. I stay quiet while Beth launches into an account of how I just *had* to come back for the conference, and how if everything had gone to plan, "we'd probably be eating spaghetti Bolognese somewhere between

Bologna and the Leaning Tower of Pisa."

She's joking of course, but it makes me uncomfortable. I hope for her and Chloe's sake that the days ahead will have been worth coming back for.

"Where's Hamza got to?" mutters Aziz, tapping the sides of his chair and looking around the square. He turns to us. "I've got a class at five, you see. Would you excuse me? Rafiq, I'll see you after the Wird, inshallah."

He gets up and goes to pay the bill. I watch to see if he'll turn back to us but he doesn't. He walks purposefully out of the square.

"Inshallah?" says Beth.

"If Allah wills," Rafiq says.

Another awkward pause.

"So where are the pipers from?" I ask Rafiq.

"Just outside Glasgow."

"I wouldn't have put bagpipes and a Muslim conference together," I say.

"Well the shaykh *is* Scottish, remember," he replies. "He loves the bagpipes."

He looks at me a moment.

"Islam isn't a culture," he adds. "It's a filter for culture. It lets the good things through and keeps out the bad."

A gust of wind blows through the trees, sending more leaves to the ground.

"Ah!" says Beth suddenly. "There's Hamza!"

We look to see Hamza jogging towards us. Catching his breath, he says hi, takes a chair and plonks it down beside us.

"Sorry to keep you waiting," he says to Rafiq, wiping sweat from his forehead and sitting down. "So much traffic coming into town." He turns to us, "You all alright?"

"Aziz was here a minute ago," I say. "He said you were planning a trip to the hills."

"That's right. How about it?" he says energetically, raking his fingers through his damp hair.

"You're not too tired?" I ask.

"Hey, I'd like to take you," he replies, still breathing hard. "Rafiq?"

"I'm in."

Hamza jumps up. "Then I'll just get a drink of water and we'll be off."

Alive

After twenty minutes of walking uphill, we have left
the traditional houses of the Albaicín far behind and a
mountainous landscape stretches out before us. Ahead, the
opposite sides of the valley converge like the prow of a ship.
Houses sweep downwards and away below us, and if I look
behind me I see them undulate along the valley floor past the
Generalife and Alhambra and up over the other side of the
valley: a tessellated wave of roofs flowing to flatter terrains
where the city proper sprawls into a blur of arid plains. A
smell of parched vegetation hangs in the air. There's a whiff
of wood smoke. Hot rubber. Cooking.

The houses here are smaller and increasingly embedded
into the rocky scarp of the hillside. Soon they resemble
caverns. Thick blankets and worn, faded rugs hang at their

entrances in lieu of doors.

"Look at that one!" says Beth, stopping to admire one with particularly colourful fabric and a pretty street lamp mounted beside it.

A dog pads alongside us for a while. Soon it loses interest and sits panting in the middle of the road.

"The rock around here is a mix of clay and pebbles," says Hamza. "Soft enough to excavate but stable enough for the cave walls to hold their weight."

"Quite the expert aren't you," Chloe smiles.

"I'm replastering that flat. I've got masonry coming out of my ears."

Cave houses stretch around the neck of the hillside like beads on a necklace. Old women sit on chairs outside some of them, evoking postcards for sale on street corners in the town. Tanned, weathered faces. Silver hair drawn up into buns. Black blouses with embroidered shawls draped around plump shoulders. They stare at us as we amble past, returning our greetings in coarse, gravelly voices.

"Over there is the Sierra Nevada," says Rafiq, pointing ahead. "The highest mountains in Spain. You can ski there."

A donkey trots past pulling a cart with a man on it. From the reins swing bright pink and red tassels, and rusty discs jingling like a tambourine.

"He looked like a gypsy," I say quietly.

"He is," Hamza replies, glancing back at the man. "They've quite a presence here."

We continue in silence. The afternoon sun wanes, ripening to a rich gold.

"I think it's here," Hamza mutters. "Yep..."

He scrambles up a crevasse between two little houses and onto a scrubby, slim track. I look back to Beth and Chloe and they acknowledge my delight. The track levels out and we follow its jagged contour around the hillside. Giant cacti cling to the edges of small cliffs. The occasional barking of dogs ricochet around the valley. I see and hear blackbirds singing, their song sweet in the dry, clear air. Soon we're passing makeshift dwellings with chicken-wire fences. Hens scratch at parched, gritty earth. A tethered goat strains to munch leathery scrub. I see women tending children. A man in his thirties hangs washing. Other men the same age are collecting firewood. They have long, unruly hair and grown-out beards. I catch some of them speaking German.

"Nearly there," says Rafiq, looking ahead.

The air feels cooler when we reach a tract of flat land. Brushwood grows all around, with gorse brightening the landscape with rich yellow flowers and scenting the air with a heady, coconut perfume.

"We can stop here for Maghrib," says Hamza, going to a patch of bare earth and kicking some stones to the side. "When the sun disappears completely, it's time," he adds.

I go to stand with Beth and Chloe. We take in our surroundings, waiting to see what the guys will do next. The sun, enlarged and rippling, is just touching the horizon. We stand still. Not speaking. Watching it slip out of sight. Hamza goes a little way off and kneels down on the ground. I hear him say 'Bismillah' and see him patting the earth with the palms of his hands then rubbing them vigorously over his face and forearms.

"He's doing *tayammum*," Rafiq explains. "It's how we purify ourselves for the prayer when there's no water around."

Rafiq goes to join him. Hamza raises his finger and says something. He stands up, brushes himself off and waits for Rafiq to finish. Without a word, they go to stand shoulder to shoulder, facing the mountains.

I watch them a while, then look away. Beth and Chloe

have wandered a little way off together. I see Chloe rubbing some stones side to side with her foot. Beth, hands on her head, is taking in the views.

I turn back to the guys. Part of me says I shouldn't be watching them. But something in their movements is so compelling. I feel a beauty I can't quite place. They're prostrating now, their foreheads on the dusty earth. I consider how they are facing that black, cubic Ka'ba – not visible to the eye, but known, deduced from the sun's westerly position in the landscape. They draw back and stand up again. I wonder about all those Muslims I don't know. They too will have been watching for this sunset. They too must now be standing in prayer. I imagine how in different parts of the world, some might be doing the midday prayer. Or the afternoon one. Others might be getting up at the first glimmer of dawn. After a few more minutes, Hamza and Rafiq are reciting familiar phrases then shaking hands.

"What's that you recite after the prayer?" I ask Hamza afterwards.

"It's the prayer on the Prophet," he says, dusting off his trousers. "It means asking for Allah's blessings and peace on the Prophet, his family and companions." He catches my eye a moment as he dusts off his hands.

The blaze of sunset is paling. High overhead, wisps of florescent cloud still streak the sky with oranges and pinks, but their brightness is diminishing by the minute. Breezes rustle through the shrubs and grasses, bringing the scent of evening. I feel an invigorating chill and rub my upper arms. We look out across the landscape to a dimming view. Houses, hills and a dusky Alhambra are fading to indistinct shapes and shadows.

"It's getting cold," says Chloe.

"Shall we go?" suggests Rafiq.

I look around for Beth and spot her a little way off. Her back is turned. I pick my way over prickly grasses, trying to avoid the thorny bushes that tug at my clothes.

"Beth?"

I go to stand at her side. Her head is tilted back, eyes closed.

"I'm just drinking it in," she half whispers.

I wait for her to open her eyes, her face luminous in the half-light. But she doesn't. I go to stand beside her, facing the same direction. I know how she feels. The atmosphere around us is alive. Sentient. For a moment I'm just absorbing it. Breathing it in. If we were back home we'd have given ourselves over to that familiar maenadic state and danced and roared with delight, but I resist it and instead let it well up inside.

Back with the others, we more or less retrace our route. Stars gradually appear. I count eight or nine. Minutes later there are too many to number.

"I don't think I've ever seen so many," says Chloe.

We stop a moment to look.

"The Prophet said his companions are like stars," says Hamza, gazing upwards. "Follow any one of them and you'll be guided."

Beth looks at Hamza. "But don't you feel that no matter what you do, nothing will come close to that time when the Prophet and his companions were alive?"

"Not really," says Hamza. "People are essentially the same now as they were then."

"Yes but... so much time has passed since then," says Beth. "Surely it's become lost?"

"No," says Hamza, still looking upwards. "It's not lost."

He pauses, as though savouring something within him. "We have a connection with them that has nothing to do with time."

"How do you mean?" I ask.

Hamza looks at me a prolonged moment. "How they lived and what they lived for is still alive."

Then he looks up to the sky again, shy of his words perhaps. I watch him. He shakes his head gently, a look of strength and wonder in his face.

I look up at the stars. The same stars the Prophet and his companions would have seen.

"Let's go," says Hamza, glancing around. "I'm not sure it's safe here at night."

Continuing downhill we cover ground twice as fast, soon finding the gap between the cave houses then following the winding road downhill into the familiar streets of the Albaicín. There's a calm and amiable feeling between us. We can talk or we can walk in silence, and both feel comfortable. Natural. Beth comes to walk beside me.

"You okay, Ally?"

"Yes," I reply with a sigh, opening my arms as though embracing the whole world. "You?"

"Yeah. Hungry though."

I put my arm around her shoulder and wonder whether for Beth, being here with these people is just another experience to add to her list, or whether she's affected by them like I am. I hope it's the latter because I really want to talk it over with her – and there's so much to talk about. Maybe she's thinking the same? Something prevents me from asking.

Paella

Tonight we're a full house at the guys' flat. Hajj Abdullah has just arrived, Aziz is on his way back from helping more conference guests, and the bagpipers – John and Duncan – are relaxing on the divans. I'd expected a pair of stout, red-faced old gentlemen, but they are fresh-faced students in denim shorts and flip-flops.

"You don't have to be middle-aged to appreciate the pipes," says Duncan in a thick Glaswegian accent.

I think I've offended him. Hamza gets up to let in Aziz, who is laden with magdalenas from the bakery. My attention reverts to the guests. John tells us about their piping at summer gigs and festivals. I tell them how we came to be in Granada and how we are staying longer than expected.

"Uh-huh," says John.

I mention the Muslim community here, how intriguing it is.

"Right," says Duncan.

I expect them to start asking questions about it like we did. But they don't.

"Here we are folks," says Zayd, entering the room with Aziz carrying two large platters between them and setting them down on the floor. "Some Spanish culture for you."

Before us are two mounds of bright yellow rice and colourful vegetables, with shrimps, prawns and calamari rings.

"We might not finish it all," Zayd says.

"The Prophet said to fill your stomach a third with food, a third with water and to leave the remaining third empty," says Aziz. "Sallallahu alayhi wa sallam."

Chloe and I speculate about how big a third of our stomach is.

I'm glad I'm vegetarian as it precludes eating the purple baby squid. Beth and Chloe tease me for being fussy.

"How do you make the rice so yellow?" asks Beth, pushing tentacles around her edge of the platter.

"See those scarlet threads?" replies Zayd from the other end of the table. "Stamens from the crocus flower – saffron."

Afterwards, Rafiq serves us sliced oranges sprinkled with sugar and cinnamon. Hamza chats with the pipers about Scotland. Beth and I talk to Hajj Abdullah. I tell him I intend to study English literature and philosophy at university. We discover a mutual appreciation of Shakespeare. As we're talking I become conscious of my exposed legs – a novel awareness – and pull my dress over my knees. It keeps riding up however. And I keep pulling it down.

"How's your writing coming along?" I ask, eager to know more about him.

"I'm putting it on hold until my guests have gone," he says, smoothing his hand over his beard. "Ask me this time next week and maybe I'll have a more interesting answer."

We'll be gone by then, I think to myself.

"So what can we expect at the conference tomorrow?" Chloe asks.

"Well firstly, a hot car journey to Seville," says Hajj Abdullah.

"Does it only concern Muslims?" I ask gingerly.

"No!" says Rafiq, smiling.

"Only everyone and everything on the planet," says Hajj Abdullah. His eyes dart between us girls and Rafiq. "You'll find out tomorrow. I'm just not the best one to explain it."

"I don't know much about economics," I remark to Rafiq.

"Now's your time," he replies.

Reminder and Renewal

Hajj Abdullah was right about the journey. It's long and hot and we arrive in Seville thirsty.

We approach the steps of a smart, glossy-looking building and converge with a colourful throng of attendees, relishing their medley of languages and accents. Malay people acknowledge us with smiles and dipping nods of the head. Behind us, an exuberant boom of African-Americans grabs our attention. Some of them are dressed in baseball jackets, caps turned back to front, and we strike up a conversation with them. An elegant and beautiful young woman comes to our side, her skin dark and flawless, making me conscious of my freckles. I mention our car ride.

"I hear you, sister," she says, as though she's known me for ages. "We're just getting over jetlag."

The sequins on her blouse catch the sunlight.

"Where're you from?" asks Beth.

"Atlanta. You know Georgia?" Her intonation rises attractively at the end of her sentence.

"My geography's a bit sketchy," I say. "But sounds like you've got a southern accent?"

"Sure have. And these here are my brothers and sisters from Charleston." She turns to a group behind her and waves. You know Charleston?"

"No," I say, curious. "Is that... in Georgia too?"

"South Carolina, US of A. You should come visit us sometime – see how the Deen is spreading. It's *wildfire*."

"See how what, sorry?"

"The Deen. The way of life. The life transaction."

"She means *Islam*," says a towering man beside her with a deep, rich voice. He must be pushing seven foot tall. He smiles at me, nodding his head.

I'm struck how these African Americans are Muslim. More and more, I'm wondering how come I've never been exposed to any Muslims at all.

We enter through tall glass entrance doors into a spacious, high-ceilinged lobby. There's a murmur of hushed voices and the clicking of heels echoing off marble. We file into the auditorium.

"There're so many people," Beth whispers.

We look for empty seats next to each other and eventually spot some to the upper right. The auditorium is modern-looking, sleek, and smells of freshly vacuumed carpets. The stage is empty but for a long table with small microphones. Three black women catch my eye with their flamboyant puffed sleeves and huge shiny headdresses. Men in white robes take up a section near the front. Another group in dark red fezes sits close by. On either side of us are perfumed

Spanish women, well dressed in silk blouses and Jackie O-style jackets. They greet us warmly. A hush descends as three men ascend the staircase to the right of the podium and take their seats at the table.

"I think that's the shaykh in the middle," I whisper to Beth.

"Yeah, I reckon," she says excitedly. "I recognise him from the photographs."

"Si," says the woman next to me. "That is the shaykh."

I study this man whom Rafiq, Hamza and their friends have spoken of so highly. He is wearing a cream linen blazer, a pale blue shirt and a navy tie. I imagine he's in his early sixties. He has a long face framed by large eyebrows that protrude like hoods over his eyes. His nose is prominent though not large. His silver beard is short and neat and comes to a point just below his chin. Although he is sitting down, he has the appearance of being tall. He looks out into the auditorium with a keen expression, surveying the audience.

"Who are the other men?" I whisper to the woman.

She leans in towards me. "The man on the left is a scholar and translator from England."

The man is fair-skinned with a kind, open face. He looks middle-aged, although there are hardly any lines on his face. He has a trimmed beard and thick, greying hair combed neatly to one side. He appears slightly nervous, organising his papers in front of him and pausing a moment to adjust his glasses. His clothes are neat and a little old-fashioned. Perhaps a bit hot for this climate.

"The other man is an economist," the woman says.

This man is much younger, Mediterranean looking with thick curly hair, a bit outgrown, and a hooked nose. He's wearing a navy suit with cufflinked sleeves just protruding from his jacket. His tie is a little on the wonk.

The woman smiles. "You will enjoy listening to him."

More people enter and search for seats. Then a young man standing at the far right of the podium recites something. I wonder if it is from the Qur'an. Everyone is quiet, the atmosphere charged. The recitation ends and the young man sits down.

The shaykh then leans towards us. He puts his forearms on the table.

"As-Salamu alaykum."

His voice is firm and authoritative. Clearly audible in the silence.

"Welcome."

The people sitting either side of him are motionless. He smiles broadly, pausing a moment. Then he tells us we will be hearing talks about the current political situation of the Muslims. He speaks about the restoration of something called 'Zakat'. His English is refined. There is something of old nobility in him. He smiles again. I sense in him a depth of joy.

The grey-haired scholar gives the first talk. He has a certainty in his voice as well as a slight stammer – it lends him a courageous quality – but I understand little of what he says. It concerns individuals and Muslim groups I've never heard of. When it finishes, Chloe and Beth raise their eyebrows at me and shrug their shoulders. As we walk out for refreshments I feel a bit tired but mostly full of dread that the whole morning will be similarly unintelligible, and that Beth and Chloe will be upset we're not eating pizza in Naples.

We get a coffee and stand awkwardly holding our cups and saucers. The woman who was sitting next to me approaches.

"Si, si, it was a lot to take in," she smiles sympathetically.

A bell rings signalling the next talk, and she takes our

empty cups from us and places them on a table. Back in the auditorium, there is a beautifully woody, resinous fragrance like nothing I've smelt before.

Hushed silence. A youth appears at the side of the podium and introduces the Mediterranean looking man. This man clears his throat and says some Arabic phrases. Then he pauses for some seconds, looking out at us almost provocatively.

"Religion is dead," he announces in a strong Spanish accent.

There is another pause. The auditorium is silent.

"We are allowed to question God..."

He looks at us keenly.

"...But we may not question the interest rates."

Now I'm wide awake.

"The age of the philosophers has been replaced by the age of the economists. Financiers are now the people who say how society has to be run. They are the dictators. An unelected, hereditary oligarchy."

The speaker is not smiling. His eyes are on fire.

"If you look for religion today, then capitalism is what you will find. Its system of usury exists all over the globe, preached by an atheist priesthood who tout their sacrament of paper money and debt in their temples of the bank and stock exchange."

I look at Beth and Chloe. They're looking at him with faces alive and attentive. I feel my body relax.

He continues: "But Allah says in the Qur'an: *'Allah has permitted trade and forbidden usury.'* What is usury? Usury is the taking of interest. The taking of *any* interest. And it is more than that. Usury not only destroys trade but it corrupts the foundations and fabric of society. The Muslims are all too familiar with this. The Ottoman and Moghul empires were smashed not by armies but by the introduction of paper money and the plague of banking."

His face becomes stern.

"Money created from nothing is an act of violence. An assault on freedom. It taxes everyone who uses it. As long as we accept this tax, we shall continue to be bled, and we will never comprehend the nature or extent of our subjugation."

He talks on, and it's riveting. No tedium at all. More than that, his words make sense to me.

"The financiers are like Pharaoh's magicians," he says. "They have created the appearance of value in paper and electronic money. But when that is faced with true value in the form of gold and silver currency, it is shown up as the illusion it is: worthless paper and digits in cyberspace."

He leans forward, hands on table. I notice a large signet ring on his right hand.

"Undoing this is not voluntary work for a Sunday afternoon," he says. "To establish Zakat is obligatory. We have no choice. Zakat is a pillar of Islam, and thus a pillar of society. Without it we have an impeded movement of wealth. Without it, we have no Islam."

He pauses.

"So this is the fight of today. This is how our fight must be defined. Not on physical battlefields. But against the degradation this usurious system imposes on us every day."

He leans back, smiling as though he were friends with us all. Perhaps he is. Then he reaches into his blazer pocket, pulls out a coin and holds it out in front of him.

"This is the gold dinar. This is *real* wealth!" he calls out. "This is the weapon of the Muslims. This is victory."

The gold glints in the glare of the spotlights. I wonder which of these people made it. He slips it back into his pocket.

"The coin speaks for itself. It is real money. And Zakat has to be paid using it, as ordered by our Messenger. Our way puts people on a path where they must work together and collaborate in the creation of a new society. We do it *not* because we are rebels or revolutionaries, but because we love and obey Allah and His Messenger, sallallahu alayhi wa sallam."

The words *sallallahu alayhi wa sallam* ripple through the audience. The speaker surveys us all, beaming, and I feel the atmosphere shift from passion to something serene.

"This is a spiritual journey," he continues. "But make no mistake – we do not worship coins. We worship Allah. And the power of the gold dinar is in our submitting to Allah alone, because He has ordered Zakat, and Zakat is assessed and paid in gold."

He motions to the shaykh seated beside him.

"This is what our shaykh has been instructing us to do. This is our responsibility," he says. "And this is our future. We have to seek out others who also want this future and we have to come together. The times will get worse, but we can be the element which will transform the base metal of extreme capitalism into the rich, pure gold of the Deen of Islam. Whoever wants to join us in this, you must come forward. I welcome you. Above all, we are at your service. As-Salamu alaykum."

Someone stands up and calls out, "Allahu akbar!" A handful of people repeat the exclamation like an echo. We look around, bemused. The voice calls out again and lots of people rise to their feet repeating 'Allahu akbar!' in one voice. Again the call is sent up and the chorus fills the hall with such magnitude, I wonder what will happen next. But then the people sit down. Quiet ensues.

The shaykh leans towards his microphone. His eyes roam

the auditorium, collecting us all in his gaze.

"The Muslims are people of reminder and renewal," he says, his voice much slower and deeper than the last speaker's. "They are the bringers of the good news and the warning."

There is a searching look in his expression. Then he smiles, appearing completely comfortable to pause a moment.

He goes on: "They are the transmitters of the map for the future upon which destinies will be played out, until it all folds up and returns from where it came – to Allah, exalted above everything that can be attributed to Him."

He looks over the whole audience, his gaze piercing. I feel something huge coming from him. I'm almost frightened of what he might say next, but eager to hear it. I feel the whole audience is expectant of his next words, but he simply turns to the speakers and thanks them, greets the audience once more and declares the end of the morning session. He sits back and signals to the youth at the side of the podium, who announces lunch, further meetings in private groups and the afternoon talks.

The lights in the auditorium come back on. I watch the shaykh and his two companions leave the podium. They make their way to the space between the stage and the front row of seating, where they are surrounded by a group of well-dressed young men. One of them kisses the shaykh's hand. The woman next to me smiles and puts her hand on my arm. She gestures for us to get up, then she accompanies us out of the building to the gardens at the back where people are gathering. She goes to talk to a friend.

"Well, what next?" Beth laughs.

"Right!" Chloe exclaims.

We spot Rafiq and our friends with a group of other men, young and old, at the far side of the gardens. They all look so smart, many of them handsome. But something beyond appearances touches me. I perceive a deep and genuine affection they have for one another. I see it in the way they look at each other, how they interact.

Then I notice everyone turning towards the doors of the building. The shaykh is walking out, accompanied by the second speaker and some other men. He walks purposefully, leaning forward a little. They seem to be walking in our direction and I feel my heart beating faster, unprepared for an encounter.

"I don't like this whole *leader* thing, Ally," whispers Beth at my shoulder as we watch on. Then the shaykh and his group veer away, passing through the gardens towards an exit. "It does my head in."

Her words make me uneasy. We watch as they make their way to a shiny black car at the roadside, climb in and drive away.

Chloe turns to me. "Can we go now?" she says.

"Go where?" I reply, watching the car disappear from view.

"Back to Granada?" she says anxiously.

"You don't want to stay and hang out?" Beth suggests. A group of exotic foreigners has caught her eye.

"We can do that back in Granada, can't we?" Chloe looks at her watch. "It's only two o'clock."

Beth shrugs her shoulders. "I don't mind," she says casually. "We can go if you want."

"It's fine with me," I say, aware of how they've both accommodated me. "Let's see if we can catch a lift with someone."

"It doesn't look like anyone's leaving now," Chloe replies. "Let's get a taxi."

"A taxi?" Beth scoffs. "It'll cost a bomb! Why on earth do you..."

"I'll pay," says Chloe, her tone urgent.

Seeing my surprise, her expression softens.

"Sorry guys," she adds. "It's just... I just want to leave now, okay?"

Chloe seems spooked and I don't understand it. For me, coming here has made everything the guys have been saying more real. They don't just gather and recite things, they're engaged in doing something about society's troubles. They have a plan. Maybe that's what scares Chloe. Or maybe she's just had her fill of talk.

"Okay, okay," I say. "Let's go."

We head to the road where the shaykh departed. Yellow taxis are queueing at the curb. We approach one, negotiate the fare back to Granada – three days' earnings at the chocolate factory – and get in. The cab smells of tobacco smoke and strong air freshener. We pull away and Chloe's mood immediately brightens.

I decide not to probe her reasons for leaving. I open my window a few inches, glad of the rush of air on my face. I twist my hair behind me to stop it whipping my eyes.

Seville recedes behind us. But the words I heard there stay with me.

The Muslims are people of reminder and renewal. Bringers of good news and a warning.

I examine the experience in my mind, mulling over this thing that Rafiq has taken on. It's a spiritual path. But it's a worldly one too. Law. Economic transaction. Social responsibility. Justice. It's the whole package. And I like politics. Not necessarily party politics, but the idea of being part of something that can effect positive change.

A memory comes to mind from when I was studying A-level politics. A friend had made a thoughtless remark, and it prompted our teacher to pounce towards him, grip either side of his desk with knuckles turning white and proclaim:

"*Think* for yourself! Don't just copy your parents!"

That scene is still vivid in my mind.

Our teacher had grown up in Belfast amid the Troubles, so he knew about politics, especially tribal politics. Through him I gained another window onto the world – and it was stimulating. Meaningful. By the end of the course I was fired up and ready for action. For what exactly I didn't know. But it seemed just a matter of time.

I wonder now what that teacher would make of this conference, of these people minting coins and declaring economic war on bankers. They seem far removed from political party intrigues and debate. Most significant of all, what was spoken about didn't seem to come from personal opinion. It came from another source.

The drive to Granada is long. I'm thirsty and wish I'd picked up one of the mineral waters they were giving away outside the auditorium. Chloe has fallen asleep. Beth is making a roll-up in the front. The taxi driver is smoking an unfiltered cigarette. I gaze onto olive grove hills, my eyelids heavy.

"Hey, there's another one," says Beth, waking me up and pointing towards a black, metal bull silhouette standing high on a bare hillside.

"Half-way there," says the driver in Spanish.

I try to think about Italy and our next destinations – Florence, Rome, Pisa – but in my mind's eye I'm back in the auditorium. I'm recalling all those different, fascinating people. Then there is the shaykh sitting at that conference table, leaning towards me, eyes seeing.

"The Muslims are people of reminder and renewal."

Simple

Rafiq and the others arrive back at the flat several hours after us.

"You left early," remarks Aziz. "Everything alright?"

"Yeah, fine thanks," says Beth. "We had a good time." She looks at me and grins. "What we could understand of it."

Chloe seems happy to see the guys again, but she's exceptionally quiet. I hope she'll open up about what happened earlier on.

"Hey, when everyone stood up and started saying... what was it?" says Beth, starting to laugh. "We wondered what on earth was going on."

"Allahu akbar," says Rafiq, smiling.

"It means Allah is greater, doesn't it?" says Chloe, coming out of herself. "Remember Beth, Hamza was mentioning it when we visited Hajj Abdullah."

"That's it," says Beth, clicking her fingers.

"It's a bit of an odd expression, don't you think?" says Chloe. "I'd have thought you'd be saying 'Allah is greatest'."

"It's not correct to say that," says Aziz soberly.

"But..."

"Because Allah is not a thing," says Aziz. "So Allah cannot be the greatest of all things. Allah is the bringer of things into being and therefore always greater than whatever greatness can be ascribed to the things of this world."

"Hmm," she says, mulling it over.

"I hadn't heard of usury before," I say. "But the way that man was talking about it, I can't quite understand how I hadn't."

"Because it's become the norm," says Aziz.

"I think I came across it in history," says Beth thoughtfully, "when we were studying the Reformation? But I'm sure we were taught about *excessive* interest."

"That's the lie that let it in," says Aziz. "It's *any* interest. So paper money is usury because it's made out of practically nothing, then given a value."

"Aha..." says Beth, sounding unsure.

"Don't get hung up on the money aspect alone," says Aziz. "Usury concerns the whole of trade, not just the nature of its currency. It basically all boils down to inequity in the transaction."

"Sounds like it's worth a conference in itself," says Chloe, coming to life again.

"True," says Aziz. "Why do you think the rich are getting richer and the poor are getting poorer? We need to know about these things. The *root* of these things."

I'm realising I don't know about these things at all, but I'm starting to get a feel for the magnitude of them.

"I got a bit stuck on the Zakat thing," I say tentatively.

"In what way," says Rafiq. "You got it's a kind of tax?" His puts his hands on his hips, poised to do something.

"But that's exactly what I don't get," says Beth. "You want to tax people?"

Aziz comes to sit down. Rafiq decides to join us.

"It's 2.5% of your unused wealth," says Aziz. "It's taken yearly and distributed to people in need."

"A kind of welfare system?" I say.

"That's right," says Rafiq. "And a safeguard against hoarding wealth."

"Which means there can be a healthy circulation of money within communities," Aziz adds. "And countries."

He pauses.

"But it has another dimension. Allah says in the Qur'an: *Take Zakat from their wealth to purify and cleanse them.*' And Allah also says: *Anything you give as Zakat, seeking the Face of Allah, you will get back twice as much.*'"

"The Face of Allah?" Chloe says.

"It's an expression," says Aziz. "It doesn't literally mean Allah has a face like us. It means you want to witness Reality directly."

Beth speaks up: "But don't you think having your money taken off you in the hope of spiritual enlightenment is a tad idealistic?"

"No," says Aziz.

"Or socialist?" she continues. "I don't want to work my arse off to have my earnings swiped out of my hands..."

"Of course not," Aziz interjects. "But Zakat isn't paid on your income, only your *unused* wealth, your long-term savings, and you have to own more than twenty gold dinars-worth before you pay a penny – and that's a fair amount of money."

"If you say so!" say Beth. "I'm not exactly used to thinking in terms of gold coins."

"You got me there," says Aziz. "So look at this way – think how much tax we pay without realising it: V.A.T. nearly 20%. Income tax up to 40%. Inheritance tax up to 40% too. And that's just the start. But there aren't any such taxes in Islam."

"None at all?" I say.

"Just the annual 2.5% off your unused wealth."

The straightforwardness of it is astonishing. But almost too good to be true. Too easy. Aziz reads my thoughts.

"Bear in mind we're talking about a de-centralised system, where money is collected locally and distributed locally. For it to be effective, people have to know who's in need and who's not, and with a bit of imagination you can see how that builds and maintains bonds within communities."

I start imagining it. Then my mind wanders.

"But how do you pay for the other needs of society? Roads, hospitals, education?" says Chloe.

Aziz smiles. "Awqaf."

"What's that?" she says.

"Basically, it's a perpetual foundation. I mean, the Christians had them too."

"That man, the shaykh," I start. "How come he's talking about all this financial stuff?"

Aziz grins. "You mean he should be sitting in holy solitude in some back-of-beyond temple?"

"Well, I did kind of imagine him being above everyday goings-on and whatnot."

"Ally, his having something to say about current affairs is congruous with being a true shaykh."

He says it as though it were obvious. We look at him in silence.

"So you look to him for political instruction?" I say.

For a moment Aziz frowns. He looks as though he's

about to say something. No words come.

Beth speaks. "Hajj Abdullah described him as a spiritual guide, and that you need someone like him to show you the way on your spiritual path?"

Aziz looks at Beth, then at me, then back at Beth. "He's both of those things," he says. "But he's not a guru."

"He seems like one," says Beth. "He seems to be in charge of things, wouldn't you say? I mean, I don't mean that in a bad way, but..."

Then Aziz interjects: "A guru will say, 'You need me.' But a shaykh will say, 'You need Allah'."

His words land with me. They bring relief. I wonder whether Beth saw a guru leaving the conference building today. I appreciate her aversion if she did. But that is not what I saw. What remains for me is curiosity as to who that man is. And all of what he said.

"By the way," Aziz adds, "you're witnessing history in the making."

"How come?" says Beth.

"The minting of gold and silver – inshallah it'll be the end of banking as we know it." Unabashed delight inhabits his face. "And Islamic banking for that matter."

"You *don't* want Islamic banking?" asks Beth, sitting up.

"No!" he says. "It has nothing to do with Islam. It's an *Islamising* of banking, which is an atheist practice. It's no better than an Islamic brothel."

"But banking and paper money are used all over the world," I protest, almost sorry for him in his enthusiasm for the impossible. "How are you going to..."

"We're not intimidated by the apparent power of the present system, Ally."

"You make it sound so simple," I remark.

Aziz smiles broadly. "Because it is."

Coin

Evening. We've been invited to a post-conference 'do'. The venue is close to the bottom of Cuesta del Chapiz, a steep, arterial road bordering the Albaicín and close to the river. It's easy to find. The entrance is flanked by two huge metal-studded doors and mediaeval-style strap hinges, like a gateway to a castle. We go in.

A stately paved area stretches towards a manor house. All along it are groups of guests standing in conversation. To our left, lamp posts stand proud of a row of mature cypress trees, their soft glow illuminating linen-clad tables set with jugs of sparkling punch and neat rows of glasses. Bats flit above us, just visible against the indigo sky. Suited young men are serving soft drinks to the guests, while waiters weave through the gathering offering trays of canapés and petits fours. Ice clinks.

Beth laughs nervously. "Not sure I like the look of this," she says.

Not so long ago we were getting stoned in a backstreet café. Now we're moving amid a community of well-heeled, healthy-living and politically sophisticated adults. Like Beth I feel uneasy. But something stops me agreeing with her out loud. Maybe I'm still too curious to cast aspersions.

Chloe however, is charmed. Eyes alive, she observes the spectacle with a look of wonder.

"How about we say hi to the people we know then leave?" I say.

"Okay," says Beth quietly.

We walk through the gathering. People greet us and nod kindly.

"Wow, look over there," Chloe exclaims, pointing to a floodlit Alhambra across the valley.

"Hola!" trills a voice behind us. Nuriya. She pinches my waist playfully. "How are you all?" she asks.

"I feel a bit weird to be honest," I say.

"Why?" she laughs. "It's an occasion to celebrate."

"Celebrate?" I respond limply.

"Yes! Look what I've got..." She puts her hand into a pouch and takes out a silver coin, just smaller than a two-pence piece. "The first coins have been minted – bismillah!" she says, handing it to me.

"It's so light," Beth remarks.

"Cool," adds Chloe, leaning in.

Nuriya points out the writing on one side of the coin.

"That's the Shahada around the edge, you see? *La ilaha illallah* – the Arabic for *No god but Allah*."

I know that phrase now. And the stamping of this spiritual

law onto money is fascinating and strange – yet congruent, given that these people seem to embody the spiritual in a way that's not just personal but social. I look at Nuriya with a smile. I can't help but feel excited for her.

"This is a copy of the coins minted by Umar ibn al-Khattab, the second khalif after the death of the Prophet, sallallahu alayhi wa sallam," she says. "It would've bought a chicken in his market, and it would buy one here today. No inflation."

"But this may be worth a thousand pesetas today," I say, "but next week, tomorrow even, it could be worth more, couldn't it?"

"Most likely less," Nuriya replies. "Its value *appears* to fluctuate, but it's the fluctuating purchasing power of paper money that makes it seem so."

A waiter approaches and serves us some drinks. I take a sip, and with the taste of pomegranate in my mouth I glance around at the sea of people. Their presence feels natural and unpretentious. No feigned faces. No masks. Something about the scene strikes me. I think it's to do with honesty: these people do what they say. They don't drink or do drugs – they believe what they profess and act accordingly. There's an integrity about them. Coherence.

Beth passes me the coin and I turn it over in my hand. Its silver has a rich and warming quality, different to the copper-nickel change I'm used to handling.

"But while paper money goes down with inflation," Nuriya goes on, "our coins have intrinsic worth because of the value of their metal."

I understand what she's saying. I *love* what she's saying. But I'm concerned it's too far-fetched. I pass the coin to Chloe.

"I wouldn't mind having one of these," says Chloe

eagerly. "Where can we get one?"

"Maybe ask Aziz?" Nuriya suggests.

Two women come to stand beside us, waiting for Nuriya's attention. We chat with them a while – they're from Denmark – then start making our way out to leave.

Meandering through the groups, we exchange greetings. A group of people standing further off notice us and wave.

As we approach the castle doors I glance back. I can just see Nuriya, now flanked by a group of suited oriental women and a slim, vivacious black lady in Central African dress. Nuriya catches my eye and smiles. I stop a second. Something about her suddenly moves me – how she delights in things. There's not a hint of rebellion about her. No trying to be a certain way. No trying to be different. She's exactly who she is. And she's unlike anyone I've ever met before.

Spinning

It's the morning after and I want to retreat. My mind is overloaded with conversations and opinions: all the things I've heard from the people here. My head feels like it's in a cage.

"I'm going out for some tobacco," I call out, getting my gym shoes on.

"Hey, I've got some you can have," Chloe says, intercepting me in the corridor. Beth appears from the kitchen.

"No, it's okay," I say to them both. "I won't be long. See you in a bit."

The Albaicín beckons. I hurry out into its narrow lanes. Just me and my rubber soles on the cobbles. I try to get a bit lost, roaming alleyways I haven't yet discovered in the hope that their newness will flush my mind of invading thoughts.

Some of the lanes are shaded and damp. Others are bright with the morning sun. I smell sun-warmed stone and hear the clanking of construction work nearby. I glimpse Plaza Nueva far down the end of a thin, high-walled street. I hear children in the playground of a school. I enter a small square and find a few tiny shops, cars parked at one end and washing hanging between some of the houses. A large woman in an apron leans over her balcony, chatting loudly with a group of youths, possibly family, below. A motorbike revs past me and hoots. I go into a shop to buy some tobacco. I come out and keep walking.

I find a small empty terrace – a miniature mirador with grey stone benches around a waterless fountain. Chipped pots are half-filled with dry, hardened soil. I sit down and roll a cigarette, glancing up at a view of the city sprawl and a clipped view of the Alhambra.

I'm at the end of something. The conference has been and gone and it satisfied my desire to return here, but I hadn't given a thought to what might come after. I'm left with a bit of a blank, plus a sinking feeling I can't make sense of.

I take a deep drag of my roll-up. Hold it in. Exhale slowly. Something in me can't relax. I left the flat this morning wanting to get away from it all. But from what exactly? Perhaps it's my growing affinity with the people here. The way they see things. The way they do things. I wonder if part of me is scared of getting drawn in. I've never been one to copy other people and I don't want to start now. I've thrived on individuality. Or at least an attempt at it.

I look down at my shoes and the pretty pebbled patterns underfoot. *I'll be going to Italy soon,* I think to myself. *Perhaps I could stay here a bit longer?* But then what would I be staying for? I've been to the Wird. I've seen the prayer done a few times. I've met lots of the people. I've also walked the whole of this old quarter, learnt some Spanish and seen sights which anyone would delight in, so it can't be about wanting or needing to see or experience anything else.

I notice the band around my wrist. I turn it to read the word I so carefully scraped into its smooth, hard leather. INTENT. Back then, I felt I was etching that word into my very being. I wanted to be awake to the moment. Like a cat at a mouse hole. Whatever it was that was calling me, I was going to find, and when I did, I was going to snatch it right up.

The word is still there. Inside. I feel it. It signposts a slow-burn longing that has been with me far longer than any books, cards or spiritual practice. It has *always* been with me. But this is not the world I thought it would lead me to. When I carved that word, I imagined I was inhabiting a realm of wide open skies, shamans and high priestesses. Meadows, stars and fertile forests. I slept where sunset found me – and shaped my own idea of what it all meant.

Here I've found people whose form is not that of shape-shifters or New Age pagans. They are well dressed, well presented and organised. They appear completely at ease in society – indeed they aspire to a leading role in it – and in many ways they are, for want of a better word, normal. But it's much more than that. Much more than appearances and rhetoric. There's something about them which is profoundly sane. While appearing to be totally in the centre of what I'd call conventional culture, they are profoundly unconventional. And this – *this* is where my intent has led me. This desire for 'knowing' which has propelled me since childhood has brought me here, just as the wave carries the shell to shore.

Yet waves ebb. And when their water washes back, what was lying on the sand is exposed. Is that what I'm running away from – exposure to what I know is true? Am I trying to cover all this over in order to feel safe in my old ways?

I twist the band the other way then back again. My insides are tense and taut. There's a tugging under my rib cage, an energy at work that feels to be pulling the outside in: this place, these people, the things they've told me. I've opened myself up and welcomed it all in. But now I'm resistant.

In trying to make sense of it, I see a part of me trying to split off and escape into my mind – but it can't. I'm present with it. Present with the realisation that the very idea I have of myself is now in question. Churned up. A bit puckered. Skewed.

A dog barks nearby. A little way off I hear more barks in response. I stay with my self-reflection, withdrawing from the sensate world to a deeper place.

I know God here.

I'm familiar with this inner place. Steady and constant. Immutable. From here I can watch all that goes on in myself as though I'm watching actors play out on a stage.

I stretch out my legs in front of me. I can't deny what I've found. It *is* amazing. I agree with practically everything Rafiq and his friends say, unable to find fault. The Muslims I've met – what is it about them? They seem so very much alive. I look up towards the Alhambra, towards the sky. I recall all their faces.

Then I ping back to wondering what's bothering me so tenaciously. My mind starts spinning out all over again. I try looking at my situation from different angles as though I'll find the facet that fits, that feels right, that will make everything once and for all make sense. It eludes me. It's as though I've come to a door that I want to walk through, but all I can do is stare at that door, hearing the words *I don't know* in my head, while at the same time knowing those words are just not true.

I wonder how Matt became Rafiq, what he went through. Was it a process, or something else entirely? Is it happening to me? I try to imagine myself Muslim. I can't quite picture it. Maybe I don't want to. I recall what Zayd said – about discovering Allah. Isn't that what I've always wanted?

I look around at the surrounding houses which form the three walls of this little square. My eyes wander their peeling distemper and rusty burglar bars, but I feel nothing of their charm. I'm penned in. I look out to the view, narrow but spectacular. I see the oldest part of the Alhambra. The mountains. The sky. Birds flying in the valley over the rooftops. But all of it does nothing for me. And nicotine is a useless companion. I stub my cigarette in the pot beside me, covering its crackle with the soil. I pull myself up and, still desperate for distraction, carry on walking.

I pass a carmen on my right. Tall trees rise behind its wall, hinting at grandeur. I wonder if it's like Nuriya's house inside. *Nuriya.*

I try to embody her upbeat energy, try to get in the mood for packing up and catching the train with Beth and Chloe to Florence. That's the plan. But I don't really want to go, and for their sake, I can't change it again.

Italy will be another adventure, I tell myself. There's nothing to lose by going there. Beautiful Italy. Laid back, romantic, dreamy Italy.

The sun grows hotter and I've managed to wander back into familiar territory. Soon I'm walking into Plaza Larga. Casa Pasteles is buzzing. I've developed a soft spot for the place. And the manager is the image of Humphrey Bogart. I glance inside and see him behind the counter, serving customers in full colour while scenes from Casablanca play over in my mind.

I pass the café and walk into the mid-morning market. Its bustle and chatter and its sellers calling out coarsely are a welcome distraction. Locals recognise me and greet me with a nod, a smile. I browse baskets of tomatoes and peppers, aubergines, garlic heads and onions. I decide to look for some pomegranates. Taking my time, enjoying the ambience, I weave amid other customers who are wandering up and down the rows of stalls.

Then, out of the blue, I hear the same recitation our friends do after their prayers. It's as clear as a bell – the prayer on the Prophet. I stop and look around, wondering where it's coming from, expecting to see a group of bearded gentlemen. There are none. A gypsy woman leans over her stall and startles me, asking in a raspy voice if I want to buy some of her prickly pears. I manage a smile and shake my head.

"Freshly picked from Sacromonte!" she barks as I back away. I change my mind about the pomegranates and leave.

I pass through the Arco de las Pesas and make haste up a quiet, dusty lane towards the Mirador. There it is again: the reciting of those familiar phrases. I slow down. No one is around. I stop still, ears pricked. It's still with me. But I can't locate the direction it's coming from. I turn full circle, self-conscious now. Still it is there. A couple of old ladies appear through the archway and start walking in my direction. Puzzled, I turn and set off again.

The lane inclines gently upwards, its cobbles partly broken, its walls crumbling in places revealing a check pattern of fist-sized stones. Ahead it opens up and I can smell lunch at the white parasol restaurant.

Then again I hear the prayer on the Prophet, recited in exactly the same way. Not louder. Not quieter. All around me. I withdraw into myself, scrutinising what I'm hearing. I realise I'm not hearing it with my ears at all. There is simply the awareness of its sound. I steal another glance down the street but somehow I know I won't see any reciters.

In a minute I'm at the Mirador. Only a handful of people are here. I go to sit on its low wall feeling I've got the place to myself. The sky is huge and open, a deep azure with dwindling ruffles of dove-grey cloud above the mountains. My eyes study the Alhambra, taking in every turret, watchtower and crenellations. At the far end of the terrace some gypsies start singing with castanets and a guitar. Their lack of inhibition is relaxing and infectious. Close by, tourists browse local wares laid out on ground cloths: watercolour prints, leather wristbands, painted fans – I watch them choose their mementos. I don't hear the prayer on the Prophet any more. Yet I feel it inside me. I find myself replaying it in my mind, savouring the sense of its sound: layers of reciting voices, in unison, steady, without pausing, overlapping.

I look out to the distant plains and let my gaze relax. I feel more relaxed too. I sit on the wall a long time, enjoying the view and a sense of peace.

A couple of tiny cars rumble past on the lane below. I suddenly realise the sun is burning me. I stretch my limbs and decide to head back to the flat. There's a spring in my step. A gentle breeze has picked up and the air smells fresh and floral. I disappear into the narrow streets, dense and meandering as a labyrinth, their high walls gifting me shade from the sun.

I love it here, I think to myself. And I love what I've found. Surges of delight gush up inside me, and as I stroll downwards towards the square, my heart is pulsing and bursting a little, my mind stilled by a swelling sense of freedom. Tears well up in my eyes which I let wander down my cheeks. As I get closer to Placeta Nevot, they have dried in the midday air.

Pattern

"Where've you been?" asks Beth at the door of the flat.

"Out and about," I reply.

"We were wondering where you were," she says, standing aside to let me in. "You've been gone ages."

"Really?" I say, taking off my shoes. "I just needed some time out."

She smiles a half-smile. "I know, but... hey, you want some coffee? Aziz is here and I've got the pot on."

"Love some."

I put my head around the door of the salon and say hi to Rafiq who's studying at the desk and to Chloe who's drawing the scene from the balcony. I pad into the kitchen after Beth and greet Aziz, who's standing at the stove heating some milk. I pour myself a large glass of water and drink it down with abandon.

Aziz glances at me. "The Prophet would glug milk," he remarks, "but sip water."

"What?" I say.

"How do you *know* that?" asks Beth.

"We know lots of things," Aziz says. "And in detail. That's how we can know the Prophet so well. His companions transmitted everything."

I feel admonished. My cheeks flush. Aziz looks at me but I say nothing. I'm on guard. By the contrite look on his face he must realise he's offended me. I go to rinse the glass and put it on the drying rack, trying to recall what I know of Jesus's behaviour. Nothing so specific comes to mind. It irritates me. Aziz checks the milk. Rafiq comes into the room and sits down at the table.

"There was one time," says Aziz, turning to face me, "when the Prophet, sallallahu alayhi wa sallam, was with his companions, and he was twisting the ring on his finger this way and that. Then he realised that by doing so he was getting distracted from remembering Allah, so he immediately took off the ring and threw it on the ground. One of his companions made to pick up the ring, but another stopped him, saying, 'Would you want something the Prophet disapproved of?' And the man left the ring where it was. You see, that's how the companions were. They followed the Prophet in everything – carefully, meticulously – all because of their love of him and because they recognised who he was."

Beth and I glance at one another.

Rafiq speaks up. "It's a bit like, you know, when you fall in love with someone and you start seeing the things they like and the things they do with different eyes. Like, if their favourite colour's yellow then yellow starts taking on a certain hue, if you get what I mean."

"I *think* so..." Beth says.

"I think you're starting to proselytise," I say, raising my eyebrows.

"Of course you would think that," Aziz continues. "And in a way you're right. But how can you have an opinion about someone when you don't know anything about them? The thing is, when you start knowing the Messenger of Allah – *really* knowing him – sallallahu alayhi wa sallam, you start wanting to be like him."

I wonder what the tipping point for this knowing and this wanting would be.

"He himself said," adds Aziz, "'I was only sent to perfect good character.' That's why we try to emulate his behaviour as best we can."

"Emulate his behaviour?" I say, aware I know so little about this prophet, let alone how he behaved.

Chloe walks in. I tell her what we're talking about and she nods her head and quietly sits down opposite Rafiq. "What kind of behaviour?" she says.

"Well, there are the basic things," Aziz says. "He would trim his beard and nails. He'd wear modest clothes, keep clean, look after his teeth, eat with his right hand..."

"We call that the *fitra*," Rafiq interjects.

"Yes, the fitra is the natural form," Aziz says to Rafiq. "It's the natural humanness taught by all the prophets and messengers. But when it comes from our prophet, sallallahu alayhi wa sallam, together with all the narrations and transmission of how he behaved, then we call it the *sunna*."

"Ah," says Rafiq, nodding.

Aziz continues. "It's the narrations and transmission of life in the great city of Madinah, where Islam was fully revealed and lived out in its luminous entirety. Not as something primative or formative but complete, and the pattern for all Muslim societies ever since."

He goes quiet.

Rafiq smiles at us, seeming almost to apologise for Aziz's forthright words. "Everything that is part of this sunna is noble character," he says.

"You mean, like being polite and generous?" I say.

"Brave and courageous?" adds Beth dramatically.

Aziz blushes. "I mean every noble quality you can think of."

His voice sounds so earnest I feel Beth and I are being impudent.

"How he spoke to people for instance," says Aziz, "that's just one aspect. But we know he always greeted with a smile and that he was the first to shake someone's hand and the last to withdraw it, and when he addressed someone he'd turn to face them completely. He didn't gossip or slander, didn't spread rumours or voice suspicions, didn't tut or huff at people, and he wasn't sarcastic, rude or obscene. He was the slowest person to anger and the easiest to please. He didn't stop a conversation until it petered out and then he'd break it by stopping it or getting up, and when anyone spoke in his ear, he wouldn't move his head away until the person had moved theirs. When anyone came upon him while he was praying he'd shorten his prayer to ask what they needed. He'd come out of his house to welcome his guests and to say goodbye to them. He used to joke with his companions and play with their children, and he was the most smiling and cheerful of people – except when he was giving a speech, when he was admonishing someone or when the Qur'an was being revealed."

Aziz pauses. I'm picturing this man, this prophet whom Aziz speaks of as though he's describing someone he's actually met and spent time with. I look at Chloe and Beth who appear to be waiting for what Aziz will say next. Aziz smiles, his lip quivering slightly. I feel he's trying to stop himself smiling more.

"But he was often silent," Aziz continues. "He didn't speak except when necessary, and he avoided people who didn't speak well. When one of his companions urged him to curse an enemy, he said he wasn't sent to curse but was sent as a summoner and as a mercy. In his gatherings, there was an ambience of forbearance, modesty, good feeling and trust. He mentioned Allah and praised Allah, and he was the most eloquent of people. One woman spoke of his melodious voice and distinct speech and how he didn't speak too much or too little. She said his words were like threaded pearls." Aziz looks at Rafiq. "And his favourite colour was green."

For a moment, we're all silent.

The energy in the kitchen has changed.

Aziz looks at me, eyebrows raised, eyes wide. "We have it *all*, Ally," he says soberly. "How he would give and how he would receive, how he would..."

"So how would he give and receive?" Chloe interjects.

Aziz looks at her, poised to answer. His eyes are alive, and while looking at her, he seems also to look inwardly, as though seeing something in his mind and searching for the best words with which to describe it.

"Well," he says, "he was the most generous of people. He wasn't asked for anything to which he said no."

Then he hesitates, as though calculating whether it's a good idea to say what he's about to say, as though evaluating whether to reveal coordinates to treasure. I could so easily interrupt or try and change the subject but I find myself just wanting to listen.

"For example," he goes on, "a man came to the Prophet,

sallallahu alayhi wa sallam, asking to be given something, and the Prophet gave him a valley full of sheep. Another time, he gave one of his companions so much gold he couldn't carry it."

He clears his throat.

"Yet when it came to receiving, he accepted gifts as meagre as a rabbit's leg, even an invitation to eat barley bread and rancid butter..."

"Yuk!" Beth interrupts. "Why would anyone offer that anyway?"

Aziz beams. "Enormous wealth was offered to him because he and his companions took over the Hijaz, the Yemen, all of the Arabian Peninsula and the areas bordering Syria and Iraq, and he was brought a fifth of the booty from all those areas as well as gifts from foreign kings. But *all* of it passed through his hands to enrich and strengthen others."

Aziz glances at all of us.

"Of course, he kept what he needed for himself and his family, but if he had any unused money in the day-to-day scheme of things he'd give it away before the day ended. Sometimes they had virtually nothing. When he died, his armour was with the pawnbroker to feed his family."

I'm listening carefully. So too are Beth and Chloe. Aziz continues.

"We also know how he was in trade. And in worship. And in marriage, governance, war – it's said that when the enemy drew near, the brave man was the one who stayed near the Prophet since he was always on the frontline."

Aziz removes the milk from the stove, faces me directly and smiles. "And we know how he drank."

The coffee pot splutters.

"And he only used to eat sitting down," Rafiq adds.

"Come, let's go through to the salon," says Aziz, putting

the coffee things on a tray.

We go and sit in the salon, sunlight splaying softly into the room. The conversation has invited a stillness among us such that it doesn't feel right to change the subject. Aziz sits cross-legged, his forearms resting on his thighs, the tips of his fingers pressed together. I wonder if this is how the Prophet sat.

"What the Prophet said and did, sallallahu alayhi wa sallam – his behaviour – was how he taught his family and companions," Aziz says. "His whole life is like a pattern they were imbued with and which they passed on to the next generation, who passed it on to the next generation – and so on – which is how it has come down to us."

We talk a long while, our exchanges more an exploration of Aziz and Rafiq's knowledge than our usual tussle and debate.

"We know a lot about Jesus too," Aziz says, smiling in his particular way.

We finish our coffee and Aziz takes the things away. Rafiq joins him, leaving the three of us alone in the salon. Chloe stretches out her arms.

I'm filled with something I can't place. This prophet – this man of Allah – these people apparently know so much about him. Not just what he said, but what he did. How he behaved. And here they are – endeavouring to copy him.

"Quite intense aren't they," says Beth, going to the balcony and sitting down to roll a cigarette.

"Yep," says Chloe, rubbing her temples with the tips of her fingers. "How do they remember all that stuff when they're going about their day?"

"It's kind of amazing they know so much though," I say. "It's a completely different approach to life."

"Totally," says Beth. "I'm just stuck on how they believe

they actually *know* all these things he did. I mean, how would you *really* know?"

She puffs her cigarette smoke into the square and looks out at the sky. Chloe lies down on one of the divans and starts humming. I run my fingers through my hair, teasing out the knots. For a while we sit in silence.

"I keep going back to thinking how many millions of Muslims there are in the world and that I hadn't heard about any of them," says Chloe.

"Me too," I say. "Weird isn't it. We studied, what, Christianity, Judaism and Sikhism at school but..."

"And how come we hadn't heard about usury before?" says Chloe.

I join Beth on the balcony and roll a cigarette.

"Hey, do you remember in history class, about coins being clipped?" says Chloe, propping herself up on her forearm. "They had that ridged edge so people could tell if their metal had been shaved."

"Vaguely," says Beth. "What made you think of that?"

"I was just thinking about that guy at the conference holding up that gold coin."

"Oh, I remember about clipped coins!" I say, enjoying old school memories. "People would melt down the shavings to sell them on. I drew a sketch of it."

Beth chuckles. "Medieval stealth tax. Aziz would love us talking about that."

"Except shaving coins carried a death sentence, whereas stealth taxes... I don't know." I say.

"I reckon both fall somewhere in that usury category," says Beth.

"Do you think all Muslims know about usury like Rafiq's friends?" says Chloe.

"I guess if Zakat is one of the foundations of Islam and

can't be paid by usurious means then I imagine they would."

"Then what was the conference for?" says Chloe.

"Good point," I say, aiming a thin stream of smoke through the balcony railings.

My eyes rest on the house opposite, the Moroccan-style one with the arched windows. I start thinking about Nuriya and the women.

"I really like Rafiq's friends," I say, thinking aloud.

"Cool, aren't they," says Beth, fiddling with a leaf on one of the geraniums beside us.

Chloe gets up and squeezes in next to Beth and I. "I love this balcony," she says with a contented sigh.

We sit in silence a while longer, puffing on cigarettes and feeling very much a trio.

I think how Rafiq and Aziz talked about emulating the Prophet. Copying his behaviour. But this copying doesn't seem to compromise who they are. They all seem very much themselves, and at the same time part of something much bigger than themselves. Something profound.

"Ally," says Beth, bringing my thoughts back to admiring the Moorish house, and looking at me hesitantly. "Chloe and I have been thinking." I glance at Chloe who smiles. "I know we planned to go to Italy next but, well, we were looking at the map while you were out this morning and Morocco is so close. Wouldn't it be cool if we went there for a couple of nights, touched base back here in Granada, then did Italy afterwards?"

I love the idea. It defers being torn between staying in Granada and leaving for Italy. Plus, Beth's right – it does sound cool.

"But would we have enough time to get back to England?" I ask.

"We'd have a few days less in Italy," says Beth, "but still

three or four days before heading home."

Aziz enters the room. Beth smiles at me, her eyes full of delight.

"Morocco's so different," she says. "It'd be crazy not to go."

"I think it's a brilliant idea," I say.

"Morocco?" says Aziz, unimpressed. "What do you want to go there for? Everything you need is here."

"It's just for a few days," I assure him. "We'll be back before you know it."

"I know backpacking has its allure, but come on – *tourism*?"

"We're travellers!" Beth corrects him.

"I say you're tourists," Aziz counters, "and if you want to visit the sights, then you should visit the people here. Each one is like a city."

"Three days, Aziz," says Beth matter-of-factly, holding up three fingers to him. "Three days."

Tourism

The train journey from Granada to the port city of Algeciras is about five hours long. We arrive in the early afternoon and walk towards the ferry terminal. It's hotter here than in Granada. Drab convenience stores line the streets – a launderette, a hardware shop, greasy-spoon cafés – their flaking frontages painted in gaudy colours. Bangs, clangs and incessant beeping come at us from all sides. A miasma of vehicle fumes and dockyard oil hangs in the air.

We move amid dock workers dressed in overalls, tanned backpackers, suited men and women, and dozens of people clad in jelabas.

At the terminal, we check out the ferry times to Ceuta. With an hour to go, we're at the ticket counter, anticipation mounting.

"Three tickets for Ceuta please... return," says Beth in French, pushing our passports under the glass pane.

"Visa please?" demands the moustached man behind the glass.

Beth leans forward, her face right up to the glass divide. "Please, three tickets for Ceuta," she repeats. Her French is much better than mine.

"This passport is temporary passport," the man replies listlessly, slapping my passport to the glass. "You not allowed in Morocco with this passport." The man leans forward and says authoritatively: "Must have visa."

Beth turns to me, worried. "Ally, he says you can't..."

"I heard," I reply, confused.

Chloe moves up to the counter in a display of solidarity.

"But we don't have visa for that one," Beth says to the man, her face flushing.

"Sorry ladies," he says, shrugging his shoulders. "No visa. No ticket."

He must have seen this scenario a hundred times. His eyes are already looking to the person behind us in the queue. I let my rucksack down with a thud and yank out my inter-rail document listing the countries I should have access to.

"Shit."

"Let's have a look," says Chloe, taking the green, creased paper from my hands and peering at the small print.

"How did I miss that?" I groan.

"Hmm... it's definitely not on here," Chloe says.

I look out towards the dock. "Oh, and there's our ferry!"

Beyond the glass doors of border control is the vessel to North Africa.

"I'm so sorry." I struggle a smile.

Talking my friends out of going to Italy was the first time I've ever felt embarrassed of my actions in the face of friends, and now, in the space of just a couple of days, I'm onto the second. I feel a rug has been pulled out from under me.

"You know what," I say, "considering everything, you should just go ahead. I'll get the next train back to Granada and we can meet up whenever you decide to come back. Don't worry about me."

"You must be joking!" Chloe says.

"No way!" adds Beth, grabbing my arm. "We're not going without you."

"Come on, you've come all this way. I'm not going to hijack your travels again," I say.

"Let's find someone who can help," Chloe suggests.

We look around but see no one official-looking.

"Just go!" I say again, really wanting my friends to have a good time. "I'll see you back in Granada."

Beth and Chloe shoot me a what-are-you-thinking look. I ignore them.

"No, we're heading back together," Beth insists.

"Of course we are," Chloe says, reaching for her rucksack. "Come on, let's go."

I can hardly believe what's happened. It's so odd to have come all this way only to be turned away.

"Well, Aziz'll be pleased," I say wryly.

We pick up our rucksacks and haul them over our shoulders.

"Granada, here we come again."

Checkmate

The journey back to Granada is extraordinarily hot. Every seat in our carriage is taken, forcing passengers to stand in the aisle, lean uncomfortably at doorways and the three of us to sit separately. The air conditioning is off and only two narrow windows will open. It's like a kiln. I concentrate on breathing slowly and try to empty my mind of thoughts.

Eventually I submit. I tell myself the heat will be good for my system. I try to rest, leaning my head against the wooden frame of the window and gazing out through the scuffed glass. The upset of the missed ferry fades into the scenery, and blends into the reality of travelling back to Granada. I find myself thinking how in Valencia I'd chosen to return to Granada, and how this time I'm returning through my own oversight but not my choice. I wonder if there is really any difference.

My dry eyes rest on the blur of wild marigolds and grasses streaking past. Beyond them are fields like leather hides stitched together, tan and tawny, furnished with an occasional olive grove or lush tract of green. Stone villages blend into the parched landscape, and behind them the grainy crags of far-off hills sit along the horizon.

It was on that train, somewhere in the south of Spain, hurtling along in the stifling heat of late summer that something happened. I can't pinpoint the moment exactly.

There was an emerging into my consciousness of a knowing. A knowing that Allah 'is'.

I heard the train wheels clattering on the tracks. I saw the people around me, the outdated seats, the scuffed windows. I felt my sweaty hands, and I was aware of my transient thoughts. Yet it was all *one* experience. Time disappeared. And so, it seemed, did the experience of my self. Nothing was separate and distinct. Everything was sewn together. More than that, all appeared held, suspended in a radiating luminosity that I perceived not with my eyes, but by some inner seeing. All and everything were facets of this: Allah is.

Now I'm noticing my heart in my chest. The name of Allah is in each double beat: Al-lah, Al-lah, Al-lah...

I close my eyes. I sense a realm inside me and it is vast. Formless. Limitless.

Al-lah, Al-lah, Al-lah...

In my mind's vision, I see the letters of the Name of Allah, drawn like the calligraphy in Rafiq's flat, but now almost transparent, colourless. My sense of what it names is washing through me like a dye. I connect to a deep contentment.

I start saying the divine Name to myself.

I know that Allah is Real. Present. Immediate.

I hear Beth's voice and open my eyes. She's sitting two rows in front of me to the left and talking to some man with a ponytail. Chloe is across the aisle reading my travel guide. I look ahead and feel penned in by the high and too-close seat in front. The humidity has risen inescapably. I'm like butter melting on hot sand. I sit up and feel the clothes on my skin, wet, and stuck to my back, stomach and under my arms. I breathe slowly, staying as still as possible, the air in my lungs warm and moist.

I go over what just happened. It wasn't a daydream or fantasy. It was clarity. Deep, piercing clarity.

The door opens and a ticket conductor enters the carriage with a gust of fresh air and the hollow roar of steel on steel. Too soon, the door snaps shut again. I take my ticket from my trouser pocket and wait my turn to hand it over. The conductor works swiftly and quietly through the passengers, sweat glistening beneath his cap. Clunk: my ticket is stamped.

I gather my hair, clammy at the nape of my neck, and twist it to one side. I lean back against the headrest and resume my gaze out of the window. Flocks of sheep season the sloping landscape.

I turn the experience over in my mind. I contemplate the two syllables of the divine Name, silently repeating them: Allah, Allah, Allah. This Name, which had at first sounded so new and strange, now flows through my thoughts with such intimacy, it's as though I've always known it.

Allah, Allah, Allah...

The awareness becomes the backdrop to my thoughts, to my very sense of being, like the pages of a book on which words are printed.

Rafiq, on the first day of our arrival in Granada, had it spot on. He'd likened his whole life up until recently to driving a car with a muddy windscreen, and on entering Islam the windscreen wipers had gone *swish, swish* and he'd seen everything clearly. As for myself, this is true not only of my current state of being but, it seems, my whole life: no matter how colourful my life has been, I can't help but view it now as two-dimensional, cut off from the experience of something far deeper. And without any of my own doing, that deeper reality has inexorably revealed itself to me. Or I have been revealed to it.

Someone behind me coughs, then coughs again. A toddler wakes up crying. Then, as though a balloon has burst, I feel a sudden and terrible physical contraction. I feel jolted, jarred. Alarm bells rattle at my core. Being Muslim? That's *not* how I see myself.

Yet how I see myself has slipped from its moorings, carried away by a tide that is fast going out, leaving on the shore a debris of old beliefs, identities and attachments, dull and somewhat scuffed.

A jagged, unnerving anxiety leeches onto my chest. That earlier illumination seems starkly displaced, lost to an energised internal chattering, a seamless to-and-fro of dialectic: *there's no need to think about being Muslim*, I'm now saying to myself. *I'm fine as I am.*

But I know that's a lie.

If Allah is real, then shouldn't I become Muslim? *But there's no need to 'become' anything*, I tell myself. I begin reasoning that I can surely believe in Allah while not doing the things Muslims do. *Of course I can. Who says I can't?*

I mull this over. It doesn't sit right.

Then more thoughts come, their tone more persuasive: *Being Muslim is interesting and all that, but I'm happy with my life. I can just take what I've experienced here and move on.* The more thoughts that come, the more I try not to think about it, about any of it.

But... I'm flailing. The more I try and convince myself, the more disingenuous I feel I'm becoming. Thoughts eddy back and forth. At the same time, I have a deepening sense of their froth and swirl, their subtly desperate attempts to win me over.

I look out onto the landscape rushing past. I cast my gaze to the horizon and see myself as a churned up flurry of sand that is slowly and ever so gently returning to the depths of the ocean floor.

The game is up.

Fait accompli.

Allah *is*.

And this knowing is undeniable.

Checkmate.

I lose track of time. The light of day is now deepening to bronze. Haloes of sunlight adorn far-off trees. Perhaps hours have passed. I ask the old lady sitting next to me. She looks at her watch fastened too tightly about her chubby wrist.

"Son las tres y quarto," she replies hoarsely, tapping its glass covering with a painted fingernail.

"Gracias," I reply.

Quarter past three. Nearly an hour until Granada. I stand up and look around. A couple behind me are sharing a sandwich. The children next to Chloe across the aisle are leaning in to one another talking quietly. A few are reading. I sit down, the scratchy seat fabric irritating the backs of my legs. Beads of sweat trickle down my breastbone but the air is a little cooler now. I lean back, rocked by the carriage's bumps and shudders as we speed through the sunbaked land.

I start thinking about the Prophet Muhammad. He was the *Messenger* of Allah. So who was he? Who *is* he?

Geography

When we get to Granada, we head out of the station and cross a busy road in the direction of the Albaicín. I'm tired and hungry, my rucksack seems twice as heavy, and there's the embarrassment of our failed excursion.

Nevertheless, the name of Allah is ever-present. Its letters are imprinted on my inner sight. Moreover, my sense of the *reality* of Allah continues to suffuse me. Like light from a lantern. I want to tell my friends about it but the words don't come out of my mouth.

"Hey, I'm really sorry about my passport," I say, genuinely remorseful but also wanting just to say something.

"Don't worry about it," says Beth. "The upside is we'll have more time in Italy."

"I guess so," I say reluctantly.

"It feels like something has pushed us back here, don't you think?" says Chloe.

"*Dragged* us back, more like," says Beth.

I laugh with her but feel false for doing so.

We walk and walk. Past a public garden, a bank and some cafés. Our chit-chat is subdued. Past tall concrete houses and along gum-specked pavements lined with parked cars. All the while, my experience in the train is with me, like a fourth companion.

After a mile or so, we cross a square into an older area. In front are centuries-old terraced buildings painted yellow, their upper storeys adorned with balconies of flowering plants. At the ground floor is a florist with a half-open trellidor, a café and a jeweller. A couple of shops are closed, their rolled-down corrugated shutters covered in graffiti.

Everything feels different. There's an immediacy to my awareness that was not there before. Birds singing close by. Smells of warmed tarmac, stones and fried tortillas. Chloe's sandals looking more scuffed. Everything is amplified.

We bear left and face Puerta Elvira, the original, ancient gateway to the city. It's a huge square block reaching higher than the rooftops, with large crenellations and an archway like a giant keyhole. Its reddish ochre resembles the Alhambra. The plaster has eroded in places, revealing wide, flat bricks, and near to the pavement are cavities where bricks have fallen away.

"Ally?" says Beth. "What are you thinking?"

I stop still. Chloe and Beth stop to look at me.

"Have you thought it might all be true?" I say.

"Being Muslim?" Chloe says straight away.

"Of course I have," says Beth. "Being around Aziz you can't *not* think about it, can you?"

"But what do *you* think?" I ask.

Chloe glances at Beth then readjusts her rucksack. Sparrows sing in a nearby shrub.

"I *have* been wondering why I feel I've met Rafiq's friends before," says Chloe. "Except there hasn't been a before."

"Not unless you count the 'before' that Aziz was on about," Beth grins. "God Chloe, he'd have a field day if he heard you say that!"

Her tone agitates me. I wonder where my friends are actually at with all this.

"I had this thing happen on the train," I say tentatively. "I got a really strong sense that... 'Allah' is real. I can't seem to shake it."

"Why would you want to shake it?" Beth smiles. "You're always having crazy experiences."

"I know, but..." I laugh with her but feel I'm betraying something.

"So, where do you stand with it all?" I ask, still seeking some serious reflection. "Chloe?"

"I don't know enough to say for sure," says Chloe.

"But what would 'enough' be?" I ask.

"Good point," smiles Chloe.

Beth chuckles warmly. "It's pretty wild isn't it."

But Chloe and Beth haven't really answered my question and I get the feeling we're not on the same wavelength. We set off through the gate – keys entering a lock – our footsteps echoing momentarily. Soon we're meandering through smaller streets that more and more resemble those of the Albaicín.

"I wonder if Aziz will be home," says Chloe.

"I'm sure someone will be," says Beth.

I hope they *all* are. I have more I want to ask. I want to know *everything*. "Do you reckon we'll be overstaying our welcome?" I ask.

"Guess we'll soon find out," says Chloe.

We keep walking. My mind wanders.

"You've gone quiet again," says Beth, poking me.

I'm thinking of a gift my father brought back from one of his business trips to the Middle East. It was a black leather diary, heavy for its size with a beautiful smell. The front cover bore two titles embossed in gold leaf, one in English, the other an intriguing set of swirls which, he told me, was Arabic. On the inside cover was a simple map of Arabia depicting its borders and shores, rivers and mountains. Many a time I sat with that book, absorbing the geography of the place and wondering what it was like. It became familiar over time, and one of my childhood treasures. I never used it as a diary – I was too young for that – but it was great for writing stories in.

"Ally?" says Beth.

"Uh-huh?" I say, eyes focussed ahead.

Should I become Muslim? I ask myself.

Something precludes disclosing the thought. It's too big to just chat about while moseying along the street. Nevertheless, the thought keeps coming to me even though my experience on the train suggests that I already am.

Beth prods me again.

I look at her and smile. "Just thinking," I say.

We come to the foot of Calderería Nueva. Now for the uphill slog.

"I swear I see light on their faces sometimes," Chloe says out of the blue.

Soon we're minutes from Hamza's flat and I start wondering about our Italy plans and, more immediately, what our friends will think about us being back yet again.

Rip

Placeta Nevot is quiet. Not a soul in sight. We walk up to the house.

"Hello?" We call up.

The shutters are closed.

"Anybody home?"

Nothing.

"HELLO-OO?!"

My heart is sinking.

Then an upper window door rattles and opens wide. Hamza appears at the balcony.

"Back again?" he calls down, grinning. "Hold on."

He disappears inside. In a moment, the downstairs door opens.

"Hey! Welcome back," Hamza smiles broadly, standing

aside to let us in.

I breathe in the familiar smell of plaster dust and varnish. It feels like home. We explain to him what happened then head up the echoing stairwell to the flat. The Red Hot Chili Peppers can be heard from an upper floor.

"Aziz?" Hamza calls into the flat as we take off our shoes. "We've got guests."

We follow Hamza down the corridor. We enter the salon and Aziz gets to his feet. The look on his face is priceless.

"Well, well, well…" he says, his smile spreading from ear to ear. We greet him, waiting for some form of I-told-you-so.

"My lips are sealed!" he says.

"Is Rafiq around?" Beth enquires.

"He's out, actually," says Hamza, opening the shutters. "Said he'd be back around six. Hey, make yourselves at home."

I go to sit by the back wall and Beth and Chloe join me. On the adjacent wall hangs the picture of the Name of Allah. I see it now with different eyes. It's an indication. A reminder. A portal.

"That's in half an hour," Aziz replies, looking at his watch then squarely focusing his attention on the three of us. "So, tell us about your little jaunt!"

We relate what happened and I get out my interrail pass. "You see?" I say, flashing him the small print relating to temporary passports. Hamza and Aziz listen with amusement.

"So, ladies," Aziz says when we're finished, his tone sober. "Have you realised what you have to do?"

I blush. Beth looks at me sideways. Chloe stays quiet.

"Cat got your tongues?" He smiles warmly.

I feel my heart beating. My secret sense of already being Muslim alarms me.

"Let me just say that whatever you have encountered here is because your heart has drawn you to it."

"Oh, here we go," says Beth.

Hamza smiles sympathetically and excuses himself – he has just started renovation work on another flat. My attention turns back to Aziz, knowing this is a conversation I have to have.

"Your heart has drawn you here," says Aziz again, "because your heart *wants* Allah."

"But..." and I put my hand to my forehead. "I can accept the existence of Allah but... I can't get my head around the whole Islam thing. Being Muslim and all that."

Aziz nods his head. "So you've got half the Shahada."

"What?" I say.

"*La ilaha illallah* – There's no god, but Allah. That's the easy bit," he says, eyes gleaming. "Now for the second half: *Muhammad ar-Rasulullah* – Muhammad is the Messenger of Allah."

"Isn't it enough to know Allah is real?" I say. "Why do I have to give my knowing some kind of practice? Why do I have to become part of some religion?"

Aziz laughs. "That's the most normal thing you've said since you got here."

"What?"

"Well, who wouldn't think that?" he says. "You're facing fundamental change, informed and instructed by divine revelation. It's no small thing. It's perfectly natural for the self, or 'your head' as you say, to doubt and question, to resist and repel – essentially to fight for control over you."

"You make our 'selves' sound terrible," Beth says.

"Oh, well, I apologise," Aziz says genuinely. "I don't mean to." He pauses a moment. "Allah has given us selfhood. Yet it's the very thing that veils us from Allah."

I recall the profound clarity I experienced on that train back to Granada, as well as my fierce reaction to it.

"But where's the heart in all this?" I ask.

"What a wonderful thing to say," says Aziz, pausing again, scrutinising the question. "In one way, the heart is just an organ pumping blood around our body. But for us, it contains something else. Something immense."

He taps his heart with his forefingers.

"Heart in Arabic is *qalb*," he says. "It's from the root qa-la-ba which means 'to turn over', and the heart is just that: it's like the propeller on a ship, a fulcrum that's always turning, and it's only made peaceful by remembering Allah – dhikr of Allah. It'll never be satisfied by this world because that's not what it truly wants. The heart wants Allah."

"But not all the time, surely?" I ask.

Aziz smiles. "And that's what being human's all about. The spirit and the self constantly fight over the heart like suitors."

"The spirit and the self?" says Chloe, leaning forward.

"Two names for the same thing," says Aziz. "When the self is agitated, the name 'self' is true for it, but when that agitation goes away and it becomes pure, the name 'spirit' is true for it."

Rafiq appears at the doorway. "You're back again?" he says.

Chloe explains.

"Well, you can plan," he says cheerfully, "But Allah also has a plan." He then turns and heads down the corridor.

Aziz smiles and rises swiftly to his feet. He excuses himself and goes to join Rafiq.

I take a deep breath and look outside towards the rooftops. I feel the evening air coming in. A bumble bee buzzes through the open doors and bumps into the wall, then it settles, silent, on one of the window panels. Chloe picks up her interrail packet and pores over its contents.

"I think I'm gonna become Muslim," Beth announces, her face full of mischief and delight.

"*Really?*" I say.

"What about you two?" Beth says.

"You decided that just now?" Chloe says.

"It's something different isn't it!" Beth grins. "If I don't like it, I'll just leave it," she says casually.

"But..." I'm cut short as Hamza enters the room with Rafiq and Aziz plus a plate of dates and almonds. I stare at Beth, mouthing a *what?* I'm confused but quietly elated by her declaration, trying to work out if she's serious or not.

Aziz picks up a date, says 'Bismillah' and takes a bite. His eyes then fix on the floor in front of him, concern in his face. I'm about to confront Beth when:

"You have to take a leap," Aziz suddenly says. "You have to *trust.*"

"I do trust!" I counter, wanting to say more.

"Yeah, me too," Beth says quickly, reading the proposition as an oblique insult.

"Then you'd rip up those train tickets right now," says Aziz.

"You don't think we'd actually do that, do you?" I ask.

Beth rolls her eyes and lets out a chuckle. Aziz holds my gaze and I hold his. I want to stare him out but he looks away, and in doing so it occurs to me: this isn't about proving a point over someone else, this is about *me*. I realise that if I leave this place and these people – right now, tomorrow or any day soon – my life will be on hold. I'll be perpetually putting something off, perpetually putting off what I know to be true.

There's nothing else to do: I pick up my blue and white creased interrail ticket and rip it in half.

"There!" I say. "Now what?"

"Allah!" exclaims Aziz, looking at the pieces on the floor then up at me.

Without hesitation, Chloe rips up her ticket too. We look at each other, half delighted, half astonished at what we've just done.

"Well, Beth?" Aziz says. "What about you?"

All eyes are on Beth. The colour has drained from her face and her mouth is open.

"Don't worry," says Aziz. "It's just a piece of paper."

"Oh my God, Ally. Chloe?" says Beth, ignoring Aziz completely. "What've you done? How are we gonna get back to England?"

"We want to become Muslim don't we?" I say. "That means staying here, doesn't it."

"You want to become Muslim?" says Aziz, eyes wide.

"Have I missed something?" Rafiq enquires.

"No," says Beth with a nervous laugh.

"Then we'll be staying!" I say. "What better place to learn?"

"But what about travelling?" she says quickly. "What about Italy?"

I'm confused by her thinking. "Well..."

Beth looks away, leaning back on her outstretched arms and concentrating at some nowhere place on the wall opposite.

"Okay, let's all become Muslim!" she says, as though struck by sudden inspiration.

"Are you sure?" I say, still cautious about her decision but wanting wholeheartedly to embark on this journey together.

"Yeah, I guess," laughs Beth, "Why not?"

"Chloe, what about you?" I say.

"I'm in," she says enigmatically, turning to smile at our two wide-eyed friends.

"Allah!" Aziz gasps again. "Well, we'll have to arrange a big gathering," he says, his face more alive than ever, "for us all to witness your being Muslim."

We look at one another, excited and a little shocked. But for his sense of propriety I think Aziz would jump up and down and ululate. Instead, he remains sitting, emanating joy, his eyes twinkling as brightly as stars.

Muslim

Events have moved swiftly since our return to the flat. Rafiq and his friends are hosting more visitors so they've asked us to find somewhere else to stay until they have more space. I understand the guest arrangements but, having committed to becoming Muslim, the timing feels unfortunate. It's no one's fault. It's just that I've really enjoyed staying with these men, and I've learnt so much simply by being around them, living around them. I'm disappointed to part ways again.

Rafiq and Hamza tell us they have numerous friends who want to meet and invite us for a meal but, for now at least, it feels as though Beth, Chloe and I are on our own.

"I've just met a French girl," says Beth, later the same afternoon. "Her name's Susie and she's doing a Spanish course in the Albaicín and said we could kip at hers while she's up in the Alpujarras. What do you think?"

"It's good timing," says Chloe.

"Exactly," says Beth, excitedly. "We can take our stuff there now if we like. She said she's in until five-ish."

I hesitate.

"Don't worry, Ally," says Beth, prodding me in the arm. "The point is we'll be sorted for a few days."

Susie's apartment is uphill from Plaza Larga on top of a bakery – up an exterior flight of uneven, white-painted steps. It's tiny inside, and although there's no need to show us around, she does so anyway.

"Make yourselves at home," she says, handing over her keys. Then she picks up her travel bag and heads out.

"Well!" says Beth, looking around and shrugging her tanned shoulders. "Here we are!"

The flat feels bereft and there's not much food. I sit down at the little table and roll a cigarette. Beth and Chloe unpack some clothes. An awkwardness settles between the three of us and I wonder if we're all feeling the same way but reluctant to admit it. I pop downstairs and buy a baguette.

After eating we decide on an early night. Susie has locked her bedroom door so we put out our sleeping bags in the living area where there's just enough room to lie sardine-style next to the table and chairs.

"Can you believe we're going to become Muslim?" says Beth. "Wait 'til we tell our friends back home!"

I think about Jake and what he might say. I think of other friends and family and special people who have meant a lot to me over the years.

"We'll be pioneers," Beth continues.

"I like the sound of that," says Chloe.

"Me too," I say. "But... are you feeling a bit odd?"

"What about?" says Beth.

"It's all happened so quickly," I say. "I mean, how long had you been thinking about becoming Muslim?"

"It just came to me," Beth smiles. "Spontaneity!"

And I love her for it. But I still sense an awkwardness, a disharmony I can't place. I can't tell if it's just me or something surfacing between us. I'm reluctant to acknowledge it, let alone mention it. We don't talk much more, and before the light has completely left the sky, we're asleep.

I wake up disoriented with my head beneath something. I rub my eyes, turn onto my front and look out through a copse of table and chair legs to a slurry of clouds. I feel terrible. I'm squashed by furniture, but much more than that, my chest feels pressed in a vice, my mind bound in a straightjacket of anxiety. What happened yesterday? And then it dawns on me: Becoming Muslim.

I look over to Beth and Chloe, asleep, then turn back to the overcast sky. Allah is *real*. I know it. I know it in my heart and my bones – and it frightens me. *How did I allow myself to get into this?* A profound certainty seems to have crept up on me. I know it to be connected to my thought processes, but at the same time it's beyond any thinking in my head.

Allah is real.

Allah is Reality Itself.

Where did this knowing come from? I try to locate where within me it resides. I can't quite tell. It seems indistinct from my very sense of self. The more I try to get a hold of it, the more it feels like it has always been there, like some star gleaming in the depths but which is now light years closer. A sun burning steady. Radiant.

I think how back home I don't know anyone who is Muslim. I have no reference point. It doesn't fit with anything in my life so far. People I know have become Buddhist. That's cool. A couple of friends call themselves pagans.

But *Muslim?*

I extricate myself from my sleeping bag and lumber to the balcony doors, unlocking them with fumbling fingers and pushing them open as though some space might diminish this incoming tide of panic. I step outside and lean on the railing. My body aches. I close my eyes and tilt my head to the sky. The morning air slips across my face, carrying smells of fried food and freshly baked bread. I throw my gaze over the rooftops like a fisherman casting his net, hauling in their rustic beauty in the hope of some relief. A word keeps coming to me and won't go away: *Muslim.*

Muslim.

Muslim.

Muslim.

I miss the view from the other flat. Down below there is a narrow street, tarmacked in places. There are no plants here. Cables hang between the houses. I miss Zayd, Hamza and Rafiq, and although I understand why we can't stay with them, the separation now feels sore.

Thoughts buffet me back to some point before we returned for the conference: *why did I come back? How did I let this all happen?* Then I recall the man in white. Beautiful. True. Beckoning.

I hear myself saying: *You don't need to be Muslim. Leave now! Just forget all this.* But it's a false voice. I think back to how Aziz described the two aspects of self, warring over the heart. I've never experienced that so fundamentally as I do now.

"Allah, help me," I whisper into the air.

Close by, a bird fills the air with its song. With a merry chirp and a *pirrup, pirrup, preeee* it swoops in front of me, darting one way then another like a little jump jet. I watch it career over the rooftops and back before flitting out of sight.

"Morning Ally," yawns Beth, joining me on the balcony, bleary-eyed. "You're up early."

"Yep," I reply, pushing myself off the railing and rubbing my hands over my face. "Sleep well?"

"I did, thanks. You?" She casually stretches her arms above her head.

"Not bad," I reply lightly, reluctant to reveal more. The smell of food wafts up again. "Shall we go out for breakfast?"

"Sure!" She runs her hands through her bed-head hair.

I look back into the room. Chloe's up. "Morning!" I shout inside.

Chloe acknowledges us with a raised hand and heads for the bathroom.

I take a deep breath.

"Sure you're alright, Ally?"

I'm not alright. I'm staying in a stranger's flat, my ticket home is in a rubbish truck and my money is running out. More than that, I'm starting to feel distant from my two closest friends.

Sorority

We find a little café on the lane around the corner and choose a table by the window. The radio is on. A couple of guys in jeans sit at the counter jesting with one another over their breakfast. An old man stirs sachets of sugar into his coffee, his spoon tinkling loudly. I go up to the counter.

"Three toasts with tomato, please," I say in Spanish. I get out my purse and start counting pesetas.

My constricted state isn't loosening. I'm now wedged between it and a paralysing inability to express any of it to Beth and Chloe. I don't think I've ever buried my feelings around friends like this.

"Gracias," I say to the waitress, putting the money into her hand.

I join Beth and Chloe at the table. Beth mentions she

forgot to ask for cheese on top.

"Never mind," she grins. "Next time."

I lean on the formica table and watch the old man sipping his espresso. I smell our bread toasting, cigarette smoke from the guys at the counter, and hear the radio unintelligibly blab and babble.

"Oh, I forgot our coffees," I say, mustering a smile.

"I'll get them," offers Chloe, getting up to order them.

Beth turns to me. Her eyes are full of friendship.

"You're a bit quiet, Ally," she says. "Something wrong?"

I try my best to look her in the eye. "I guess I feel a bit strange we're not staying at Rafiq's."

It's the most I can say. I feel trapped in the resonances of a much younger self. Private. Unarticulated. Not quite in the world. I search for words to bridge it but they seem relegated out of reach.

"Hey, it's no big deal," says Beth. "Why don't we see if they're in after we've eaten?"

I'm about to answer when the waitress claims the moment: "Tostadas!" she calls out, serving our plates on the counter.

Chloe and I fetch our order and we bring the toasts and coffee to our table.

"Here you go," I say to Beth as brightly as possible.

"Ah, thanks. I'm so hungry," she says, eyeing her food.

"Same here," says Chloe. "My mouth is watering."

I sit down and glance out of the window at the people to-ing and fro-ing. If doubts are whisperings, then I have plenty of them. But more and more I'm seeing through them. They really bear no substance. My heart still is pressed by some unseen force, and if I imagine its form I would describe wolves closing in on me. Skulking. Stalking. But it's a well-crafted illusion. Wisps of energy that puff and spume.

If I reach down deeper, I touch bedrock. Luminous bedrock.

'Belief' isn't the right word.

'Faith' falls far short.

Aziz used an Arabic term: *iman*. He said it's to have inner security and confidence in the Truth. Realisation and submission to the will of Allah. He described it as an inner world, a hidden landscape of the Unseen. He said it is certainty in Allah, the Angels, the Messengers, the divinely revealed Books, the Last Day and the Decree. He said that once we accept these realities then the heart begins to move. It made sense to me.

And yet there is still this very physical constriction. This something thrashing around in me like a wild, caged animal. I intuit that like Jason at the mast, I must tolerate it. Bear it.

We sip our coffee, drizzle olive oil over our food and tuck in.

"Hey!" Chloe exclaims, pointing outside. A woman is sauntering past. Nuriya. We jump up and out of the café to catch her.

"I heard you'd gone!" Nuriya says. "Then I heard you're all becoming Muslim. Is that true?"

We fill her in and she exclaims things that have the name of Allah in them and I feel my constriction slacken.

"So, how about you join me?" Nuriya says with a hint of adventure. "I'm on my way to visit a friend."

"Sure!" we say, and discarding the rest of our breakfast, we head off together.

"It feels good to see a Muslim," I say, going to walk beside her.

Cobblestones yield to tarmac, preamble to a clean and modern housing development. Left and right are apartment blocks four storeys high. Shiny, waxed cars are parked outside some of them, and tennis courts are in sight.

"Here we are," announces Nuriya. She steps under a roofed porch and presses the number three on a shiny intercom.

"Si?" comes a voice from the device.

Nuriya leans in: "Soy Nuriya!"

She stands back and we wait a moment. "Allaaah..." she says softly, as though remembering the name of a secret love.

The door clicks open and we enter an air-conditioned lobby. We make our way up a flight of spotless stairs to the third floor. A door opens and Nuriya steps inside exclaiming greetings and embracing her friend. We follow, and Nuriya turns to introduce us: "Girls, this is Hajja Amira."

"Hello," replies the woman, opening her arms to welcome us. "How lovely to meet you."

Her voice is like some great purr. She is dressed in cream, wearing a loose silk blouse tucked into casual, linen trousers which fit her tall and shapely frame perfectly. Jewellery flatters her olive skin: silver earrings and a matching bracelet with dark red stones, ethnic and expensive looking. We kiss on both cheeks then sit down around a large dark table with wrought iron ornaments.

"Hajja Nuriya mentioned you've been staying with our menfolk," she declares. "I bet they have *loved* that!" and throwing a mischievous look to Nuriya she breaks into a rich, throaty laugh. "Oh, but I am sure they have been the perfect gentlemen, no?"

This woman has presence. She has huge, vivid green eyes that seem hardly to blink, and from them charges a powerful gaze that suggests she's lived life on the edge. On the edge of what exactly I'm not sure, but I'll bet she has stories to tell. I feel my mood lifted by her. She leans towards us as though wanting to confide something.

"You are about to set out on the most *incredible* journey," she says, enunciating each syllable and rolling her Rs. "The journey to the King."

Her eyes linger on ours so assuredly that I feel acutely self-conscious. Yet I can't look away. Her eyes are mesmerising. Wide-set and impossibly steady, like those of a large cat. A tigress. This woman is regal, poised, almost predatory.

"To the King," she repeats, those eyes now burning straight into mine.

"I saw you all at the conference," she goes on. "I was concerned for you. What was your impression?"

I tell her a lot of it went over our heads. "But it struck me how politics and economics appear as important in Muslim society as spirituality."

"Politics and economics are not spiritual?" she replies in a demanding tone.

I feel caught off guard and don't know what to say. I try to compute her question but am mostly squirming in my chair. She releases me with a giggle, delight twinkling in her eyes.

"Oh my dear!" she says emphatically. "This way of ours will turn you upside down and inside out."

I laugh nervously. "You mean...?"

"I mean how you understand things. How you understand yourself. How you understand *life*. You think 'spiritual' is sitting on some floor emptying your mind of thoughts and 'political' is taking a stand and exclaiming them?"

I think I do.

"I guess *you* don't see it like that," says Beth, enjoying our host's postulation and turning to Chloe and I with an impish grin.

Seeing Beth so relaxed and accepting of these women is a relief. I just hope this woman won't say anything that will scare her or Chloe off. I imagine she could well do so.

"It's not about how *I* see it," Hajja Amira responds. "Half of Islam is worship, which in the Qur'an is expressed with words like gain, debt, profit, loss – fiduciary metaphors indicating a spiritual transaction. But laws regulating financial transactions are described with spiritual metaphors. It's all opposites."

"*And* complete," adds Nuriya.

"Still," says Hajja Amira, "we have a lot of work to do."

"What kind of work?" Chloe enquires.

"We do not anymore, *anywhere* have Islam," she says matter-of-factly. "In its totality I mean. Due to our political situation, we are being held back from taking on our full responsibilities as Muslims introducing Islam into a world which is at present *deeply* misled about its nature."

"Misled?" I say.

"Islam in many places has been eroded, so that what remains is a cultural muck of post-colonialism and nationalism, paternalism and modernism," her face reddens slightly, "ad nauseam-ism..." She cuts herself short.

"But *this* is our work," she says, wrapping her knuckles on the table for emphasis: "to revive the Deen of Islam and re-establish it."

"And you know what?" she adds, raising her eyebrows. "It will not happen overnight. Allah knows, but we have to see how even in small ways, like taking a homeopathic remedy, we can, by Allah, help make it happen."

"But, *how*?" Beth asks.

"By taking on what we know," she says simply, inclining one shoulder towards us Spanish-body-language style.

"By reminding each other of Allah and His Messenger, sallallahu alayhi wa sallam, which means by extension that we are always striving to refine our behaviour, from the courtesy afforded friends and acquaintances through to international relations."

"And by always learning and always teaching," adds Nuriya. "By making our transactions 'clean' and our environment clean, and by ensuring our youth and our elderly are properly cared for."

"And not for show, I might add," says Hajja Amira, "but because we know that Allah is with us, Allah sees us and Allah is the witness of all we do, and that by acting in a way we know to be right and true and intending it to be *fi sabilillah* – in the way of Allah – we hope for nearness to the Divine in this life and the next."

Nuriya nods and looks at me, affirming our host's words with something unspoken.

"And not least," says Hajja Amira, "by cultivating our homes as places of nourishment and *hospitality*."

She runs her hands through her wavy hair made chestnut-red with henna. If a pin were to drop, we would hear it. This woman fascinates me. Were she to talk about scrambling eggs, I'd be fascinated.

"Society is fast becoming a mess," Hajja Amira continues. "We witness it every day on street corners and every time we turn on the news. But the solution is not in some new law, some new injection of money, some new thing we have to become tolerant of – it is to do with the core of the human being."

"What about women?" Beth says.

"Aaaaah!" Hajja Amira purrs. "How delicious! What *about* women, yes. Because indeed, what I see, and I mean in society at large, are women deprived not of money or position or so-called freedom – although that may be the case – but deprived of womanhood. Woman-ness."

"I wouldn't say I feel deprived," I say.

Concern inhabits her face. "Listen," she says, leaning in and speaking slowly, her hands gesturing with grace. "Woman, like a rose in full bloom, is a powerful thing. It captivates. It elevates. It reflects something of the soul in the beholder. But it is rare, and this creature called Woman is becoming a rare breed. She has been hounded and harassed, plundered and looted, her natural cycles scoffed at and drugged to suit others, and she has been totally covered up or totally laid bare, earmarked for demolition. We are required to spiritually and surgically cut and paste ourselves to fit the tiny mould society nowadays dictates. Woman is being defaced. Literally *de*-faced."

Her eyes hold our gaze, but a quiver in her lip belies strong feeling. Anger perhaps.

"Women have been conditioned to freeze-frame while still tight in the bud," she continues. "They are unable or have been dis-abled to open into their full glory. Like the roses you find in the supermarket they have a certain allure, but no fragrance. All too soon they wither, turning to the latest belief system or self-help book in a quest for meaning. But they will never truly find it in man-made dogmas, because the true meaning of our existence is that we have been created for worship."

She then raises her hand and, graciously cleaving it through the air as if parting an ocean, she pronounces decisively: "L*aaa* ilaha illallah, Muhammad Ras*uuu*lullah. There is *no* god but Allah, and Muhammad is the Messenger of Allah."

I smile sheepishly, embarrassed by the lack of response I feel her words deserve. I'm not sure I agree with or understand everything she says, but I feel no compulsion to argue with her, more a curiosity in what she might say next.

There's also no doubt that, for me, this woman

encapsulates, no, *emanates* Woman. Instinctual. Fertile. Knowing. Her presence reminds me of being back home in rural landscapes, tiptoeing barefoot into the woods, delighting in moist humus underfoot, the moonlit branches overhead and the inky black skies beyond – sometimes overcast, sometimes starry – but always telling something of other worlds, moons and asteroid belts. And beneath them is me; petite atop the undergrowth and full of the wonder of life and death, the cycles of nature, and the sensual, instinctive sense of being a part of it all from beginning to end.

I smile to myself, remembering a time which now seems far away, yet whose meaning feels closer than ever.

I glance around the room. The furniture is solid wood, Indian perhaps. There's a large earthenware bowl on the sideboard, its rim edged in brass. In a large bookcase, ornaments nestle among linen-bound books. A small sculpture of a rearing horse, mane flying. A red porcelain pomegranate, life-size. A framed informal photo of our host and her children laughing altogether.

My eyes return to Hajja Amira. In her I see that naturalness I'd been exploring back home. Yet this woman holds the possibility of more. So much more. Something political. Something relating to society and justice. And something more than any of these things. *She goes beyond herself,* I think to myself.

"So," says Hajja Amira, bringing me back: "with this capitalist society having done away with Woman, the family will be next to go. Just watch."

Her face is animated with concern, and I feel I'm glimpsing in her the great responsibility she feels. It's contagious. I find myself wondering what part I might play in all this.

Beth speaks up. "So you reckon a Muslim woman in this society is better off than a non-Muslim woman? Seems to me we're all kind of subject to the prevailing times."

Hajja Amira listens, eyes wide yet kind. I study her face, anticipating an answer which doesn't come.

"Don't look so concerned!" she laughs, reaching across the table and placing her hand over Beth's.

"Here you all are: young English women in Spain, about to become Muslim. How Allah unfolds the destiny! It's amazing, no?"

She looks at the three of us in turn, holding our gaze, eyes hardly blinking. When she looks at me again, she does so for a prolonged, wordless moment, and it's as though her entire being, majestic and powerful, is imprinting onto mine the profundity of what it is to be Muslim.

Then I feel self-conscious again. I shift in my chair. This woman is like a sun I can't look at directly, the transmission emanating from her like a bright light banishing shadows. I look away but feel her brightness still on me, and I'm thrilled and expectant just to be here.

"We have so many colours, no?" she continues, relinquishing Beth's hand and sitting back in her chair.

"We make such a colourful picture! Of course we are active in the world. We work. We speak out. But we are not afraid to put our attention to our home. Our nest. Our warren!"

She looks to Nuriya and laughs heartily, shaking out her hair. "We are not afraid to make it beautiful and welcoming and fragrant and joyful and to dance barefoot in the kitchen to the sounds of salsa and bubbling pots on the stove!"

She inclines her shoulders as though dancing flamenco and clicks her fingers so loudly I jump in my skin. Beth blushes.

Hajja Amira sits back a little. We go on talking. At some point, Nuriya looks at her watch and says she needs to get going. Hajja Amira smiles serenely at Beth, Chloe and I.

"Well!" she says, breathing through the word with a note of finality then looking to Nuriya who's now on the far side of the room in front of a mirror putting on her scarf. "I think it's time these girls stay with our women, don't you think? Instead of the men?"

"I was thinking the same," says Nuriya, tying the ends of her scarf into a neat bow at the nape of her neck.

Hajja Amira looks back at us with authoritative concern. I feel uneasy, wanting to tell her we've already moved out of the guys' flat and are staying somewhere else, but she intercepts me.

"You get a different transmission from women," she says.

Do you? I think to myself. Part of me doesn't want to agree, but I can't deny how she is stoking my interest. I've never encountered women like the ones I've met here, and I have never moved among a group of people who at times separate off into male and female groupings. But what at first felt odd and a bit worrying, now intrigues me. With Nuriya and her friends I feel a sorority I've not tasted before, and a world of wisdom particular to my own sex. Still, I do wonder what implication this will have.

Hajja Amira reads our quizzical looks and her countenance softens. "I know, it's the thing to view man and woman as the same these days. But we're *not*, hey Nuriya?"

And they look at each other and burst into laughter.

Goodbye Beth

Plaza Larga, post-siesta. There are more tourists here these last days. Chloe and I have been waiting for Beth for ages. She has gone to the phone box near the Mirador to tell her parents about becoming Muslim. I'm not sure it's the best thing, given how little they must know about Islam. I've decided I'm not going to tell my mother yet. She'll just worry. I'll wait until I'm home and can tell her in person. It seems more fitting.

"Maybe I *should* tell my mum now," says Chloe, watching another group of tourists entering the square.

"It'll just stress her out," I say. "Besides, we don't know when we'll be going home. It might be a few weeks, months even."

"You're probably right," she says. "I just don't like the

feeling I'm hiding it from her."

"But how could we possibly *show* our parents what we've experienced here, over the phone? Remember how we felt about Rafiq when we first arrived?" I look out on the square. "If anything, I think we're being considerate."

The tourists, a crowd of about twenty Japanese, are taking photos and turning this way and that, smiling and commenting to one another. I enjoy watching their admiring expressions, remembering my own delight when we first arrived here. Chloe goes quiet. Her large grey-blue eyes roam the square and she's frowning slightly.

"You are sure about it, aren't you?" I say. "Being Muslim?"

"Yes," she says. But the way she says it has me expecting a 'but'. I wait, but she says nothing. Then she sighs and gets to her feet, stretching her legs.

My turmoil from the morning has left me, but a residue of disquiet remains. I still haven't voiced it. Something keeps stopping me. I look at Chloe and wonder how come she doesn't talk about all this with me either. I wish she would tell me how she feels, what she thinks, the way she understands this whole experience. But she's not forthcoming. She sighs again and I suppose she's preoccupied with thoughts of her mother. They have a close, almost sisterly relationship, and what we're embarking on is no small matter. I hope she doesn't bail out.

I look around the square with my mother on my mind. Then I think of Nuriya, mother of four, standing in front of Hajja Amira's mirror tying her scarf. It stirs an old memory of a white woollen shawl my mother had when I was a child. It was a big triangle, it's shorter sides edged with tassels. I loved using it for dressing up. I'd put it around my head like a mediaeval lady. I remember my reflection in the mirror.

"I'm actually quite worried what my mum will think,"

Chloe says eventually, nudging me from my daydream, sitting down again and watching the tour guide herd his flock downhill. "Then there's my dad too..." Her voice trails off.

There's something in the way she says this that tells me our worries have a different nature. I'm worried for my mother's sake, whereas I think Chloe is worried for her own. For me, no matter what anyone thinks of my decision and no matter what conflicted thoughts I may have, no one could possibly change it. I don't think I myself could change it.

Two old local women walk in our direction, greeting us as they pass. Decades ago they were probably sashaying through these streets all long-haired, leggy and lithe, Mediterranean charm from top to toe, but they have grown stout and tense-shouldered, their legs bowed so that they rock from side to side as they walk, like little boats caught in ripples. We return their greeting.

"Where *is* Beth?" I say, glancing around the square and it's four approaches.

"Maybe we should go and find her?" says Chloe.

Flamenco music starts up from the bar and more people are coming through the square. Behind us, through the windows of Casa Pasteles, Humphrey Bogart is starting to serve coffee again. I think he's noticed I look at him a certain way.

"At last!" Chloe says.

I turn to see Beth walking briskly from Arco de las Pesas. Her long hair is flapping behind her, the sun shining through the wisps escaping her messy beehive.

"Sorry!" Beth calls out as she approaches, raising her hands, face flushed. "I had to wait for someone to finish their call."

She sinks down on our bench with a loud sigh. She runs her fingers through her hair and rubs her face.

"Everything alright?" I ask.

"Well, it was a long conversation," she replies flatly.

"Did you tell them about becoming Muslim?" Chloe asks.

Beth avoids eye contact. "Can we not talk about that right now?" she says, puffing out her cheeks and looking irritated. She reaches into her trouser pocket for some tobacco.

"Yeah, sure," we reply, stealing each other a glance.

Beth fumbles for some rizlas then lowers her head, her hair falling over her face.

"Something wrong?" I ask.

She covers her eyes with her hand and shakes her head. Chloe sits down and puts her arm around her.

"Beth?" I say gently.

Then she tosses down her bag of tobacco and begins to cry.

"What's going on?" I say.

"You've used me," she mumbles, burying her face in her hands.

I look over at Chloe. "What?" I say. "What do you mean?"

Beth gasps then holds her breath. "You don't really care about me," she says, crumpling into stifled sobs.

"What on earth do you mean?" I say, sifting through recent events at high speed in search of something I might have said or done. "Of course I care about you! How could you think otherwise?"

I sit down beside her and throw my arms around her in a hug, but she feels rigid and I let go.

"It's just... it's how you became with Jake. And how you made us come back here for that conference." She lets out a gasp, her face contorted. "Your messed-up passport... and now there's hardly any time left for Italy." She gasps again. "Then this whole thing about becoming Muslim..."

"You said you wanted to be Muslim!" I interject. "And

you said it first!"

Beth shakes her head, grasps the tobacco and papers and starts vigorously rolling a cigarette, her hurt giving way to anger, tears rolling down her face.

"And what do you mean about Jake?" I say. "You were working, Beth. You weren't around. I'd moved out of your house."

"You just don't get it, do you!" she blurts out, shooting me a look from reddened eyes. "You always have to have everything your own way."

Her words cut. I don't know what to say. Defending myself seems off point.

"I'm really sorry," I say tentatively. "But... I've never meant to hurt you, or *use* you." I wait a moment then go on: "How could you possibly think that?"

She shakes her head again and clenches her teeth. "My mum sees how you use me."

Her mum?

"And what do *you* see?" I ask, my body starting to shake.

Chloe and I look at one another again. Beth cries more and my attempts to talk the matter through are rebuffed. I suggest we head over to Nuriya's to talk it over, but Beth's not having it. It all seems so ridiculous and twisted that I'm sure she'll see sense soon enough. Chloe seems as surprised as I am, which is a relief of sorts. I wonder why Beth's mother said those things about me. I thought we got on well.

Beth clears her throat, sits up and composes herself: "I'm gonna go," she announces, looking straight ahead and taking a deep drag of her roll-up.

"Go where?" says Chloe.

Beth looks up at Chloe. "To Italy, of course. Or as near as I can get. I worked my butt off for this trip. If I leave now, at least I can get *some* travelling in."

The colour drains from Chloe's face.

"Hang on, we need to talk about this," I protest.

"Talk about it? We haven't been *talking* about anything lately."

I feel a huge hole opening up between us. "But you can't leave *now*," I say. "Not after everything we've experienced."

"You're at it again!" Beth interrupts. "Wanting everything *your* way." She taps her cigarette and the ash blows away on the breeze. "I'm gonna get the night train and leave tonight."

"Wait, all this from a phone call?" I say incredulously.

"What did your mum *say*?" says Chloe, visibly shocked.

"And what about becoming Muslim?" I say, tasting defeat, the dread of her leaving turning my blood cold.

"I don't want to talk about it!" she cries, raising her voice. "I don't know what I was thinking!"

She gets to her feet looking this way and that, flustered. "University starts in less than two months," she says, "and I need to get back to sort things out."

"Sort things out?" I say. "Think of what's happened here! Aziz was right when he said we didn't arrive here by accident."

Beth stares at the middle distance, seeming to think about something else.

"Look, I'm really, really sorry," I say, desperate to salvage something.

Beth doesn't respond.

"Anyway, how could you think..." My reasoning trails off.

Beth shakes her head and brusquely wipes her face. Her sobs are gone.

"It's no big deal," she says eventually. "We'll see each other back home."

"No!" I say, feeling the nervous urge to laugh. "Stay here! Please... sleep on it or something."

"Exactly," says Chloe. "I'm sure you'll feel different in a bit."

"I don't think I will," Beth says, determined. Then she looks at me and says gently: "Ally, I'm going to leave."

That evening we all meet up with the guys in Casa Pasteles for a little farewell. The place is buzzing and everyone seems in good spirits. For Beth's sake I try to be upbeat, but the whole thing is gouging my insides. I can't believe what has happened. I'm gutted. My own sense of hurt is only beginning to sink in. Smiling feels false.

Beth doesn't mention any more of what happened in the phone call, and that has me feeling all the more awkward – we always share everything. To my bewilderment, she seems genuinely excited at the prospect of leaving. She's her happy old self, eyes sparkling with unconscionable mischief. I'm glad she's not feeling so upset – the thought of having hurt her is still mortifying. I wonder if she knows how I feel? She hasn't asked.

I watch, a shade removed, as she chats and laughs with our friends. Rafiq is in good spirits. Aziz exhorts Beth to stay, then reluctantly accepts her decision. He manages the best of parting words: "May you find what you're looking for." Ever the gentleman.

"Take some photos," I say, my heart caving in.

After hugs and farewells, Hamza drives her to the train station. I feel I've lost an arm.

River

It's nighttime now. Dark. Quiet. Emptiness cramps the tiny flat that only yesterday Beth was so excited to have organised. Lying in my sleeping bag, I go over in my mind what Beth said in Plaza Larga. I'm still mortified. But now I'm angry too. I turn to face Chloe.

"Do *you* think I always want things my own way?"

"Well," she says, seeming to give my question some thought, which troubles me. "I guess you just know what you want."

"But it was Beth's idea to go travelling," I say quickly, my eyes roaming the ceiling then fixing on the whirring fan. "And she was the one with Rafiq's number."

"Yeah," says Chloe. "I guess she was referring to other things."

"Like what?" I say, suddenly worried that Chloe may feel the same way.

She lets out a little chuckle. "Well, you can be quite forceful."

"Yes, but... so can she, don't you think?"

"Of course," Chloe grins sleepily. "And I kind of love it."

"You do? So... you mean..."

Chloe yawns. I'm hoping she'll say more because I don't want to ask – I'd be fishing for compliments.

"I'm really tired Ally," she says, her voice almost a whisper. "I'm falling asleep."

"But you'd tell me if you had some problem with me, wouldn't you?"

"I'm here, aren't I?" says Chloe warmly. "Don't worry about Beth. She just had to do something on her own terms. It'll sort itself out."

"But she's not becoming Muslim," I say, feeling the enormity of it more and more.

Chloe doesn't reply immediately. "Yeah," she says eventually with a sigh.

I lie on my back. Chloe's breathing deepens and soon she's asleep. I narrow my eyes, watching the rhythmic shadows the fan casts on the ceiling, replaying Beth's words in the square. She's gone. Just like that. It feels like a death. I imagine her mum saying I use people. I recall Beth's smiling, happy face at the café and I want to cry. But nothing comes. I count the days remaining on Beth's interrail ticket – maybe four – then wonder how many days Chloe and I will stay here in Granada. Many more than that, I imagine.

I feel I'm standing at the edge of a giant crevasse. All that is known is on the far side of it moving further and further away. I have no idea what lies ahead.

I start thinking about the Muslims I've met, then about our

time earlier with Hajja Amira. I remember almost everything she said, word for word. I replay bits of our conversation, feeling the buzz of her wild energy.

My imagination takes over and projects me into nature. My love of the forest. The hidden creatures and their sounds and song. Unknown, uninhabited places. I see myself standing at the cusp of a north Norfolk marsh, looking out over wet sands stretching out to the sea and a pale and pure horizon. Then in my mind's eye I go back to breakfast in the café this morning. It feels an age away.

I look at Chloe, asleep, and wonder if she experiences any of this inner turmoil. I wonder if the Muslims I've met have also felt and faced similar things.

I recall my encounters with them all. How our conversations have opened doors onto worlds I didn't know existed. Their hospitality and ready welcome, their sociopolitical knowledges, and what I've glimpsed of their spiritual practices and aspirations are, I'm sure, just tips of icebergs. But there is something else. Something existing alongside those things which bears a catalytic element of truth. What *is* that?

I think of Hajja Amira again, then Nuriya, and more generally of all the women. I think of Rafiq and his friends, particularly Aziz and his unrelenting drive to inform – I might say *convince* – us of the reality of Allah, and how he described the teachings of the Messenger of Allah as being 'like the banks of a river.'

I imagine myself beside that river. I'm watching its clear waters moving past. Then something in that image gives me a sense of that element I'm trying to pinpoint. It's what flows alongside these people's words and gestures; what resides, gently humming, in their presence: an energy, warm and golden, which I perceive in and around my heart and solar plexus. An invisible, luminous transmission awakening me to something I've always known yet at the same time have forgotten.

My mind goes back to Beth. I feel the pang of her absence, the fear that our friendship will be forever changed. Plus, I feel she's missing out. I'm sad about that. I lie awake, turning over events and encounters, far from sleep.

Sometime later, I hear the solitary song of a bird outside. Then a duet.

Dawn.

I'm about to enter Islam. This is *real*. I feel the magnitude of this threshold and it makes my body tremble. My journey is no longer a gap-year escapade, an adventure between one backpackers' den and the next. It's an arrival. Right now it's the only thing I'm sure of.

I remember what Beth said the other day at the guys' flat: "If I don't like it, I'll just leave it." Those words made me uneasy at the time. Now they make me recoil. I can't think like that at all and I don't want to. Then I remember her words in the square: "...this whole thing about becoming Muslim."

But it's not about 'becoming' anything. I'm not taking something on as though I'm putting on a new suit of clothes. If anything, they've been taken off. Something in me has been uncovered. Freed.

For me, this is not about deciding whether or not to become Muslim.

I *am* Muslim.

PART IV

Albaicín

It's the following afternoon and Chloe and I are out and about in the Albaicín. Beth's departure weighs heavily on us. We're hoping that walking will do us some good. Maybe it will help me get out of my head, overthinking things.

"I still can't believe she left," says Chloe, bringing the matter up again as we start striding downhill towards town.

"Me neither," I say. "I keep thinking what I could've said to persuade her to stay."

"We did try," says Chloe.

And deep down, I know I couldn't have persuaded her. Being Muslim isn't a matter of persuasion.

We come to Placeta Nevot and pause in the middle of the square, drawn to the familiar sight of the guys' flat.

"It's been only ten days since we arrived there," says

Chloe, shaking her head. "Weird how time does that."

I picture us arriving fresh off the train from Madrid and meeting Rafiq, Hamza and Aziz. Compared to the person I was, insisting I'd met Rafiq's friends before, I realise how different I am now. It's as though I've shed a dozen skins, and with each peeling off I've seen things with new eyes.

A couple of backpackers enter the square behind us. I think they're chatting in Dutch. They're in bright T-shirts and dark cargo shorts, their hair mousey blond. One of them has dreadlocks just past his shoulders with small silver bands clamped around some of them. Passing us they say hi, and we say hi back. I smell patchouli oil and sweat. I watch them leave the square, a familiar feeling of tribal identity coming over me. But it no longer has any traction. I really notice that. There's something old about it now, like clothes I've loved but have worn out.

"Beth's probably in Barcelona by now," I say. "I wonder if she's enjoying travelling by herself."

"She's pretty independent," says Chloe. "I think she'll be okay."

"But I wonder if she misses us, if she regrets leaving."

I look around the square, feeling the warmth of the sun on my face.

"I guess we'll find out back home," Chloe says. "Hey, do you reckon the guys are in?"

"Could be," I say, looking back at the house and observing the half-closed shutters on their floor. "But let's catch up with them later."

We turn away. I glimpse a view of the Alhambra. A sleeping cat twitches its ears.

We continue downhill, still raking over what happened with Beth. Before long we're at the area of Moroccan tea shops where the smells of cinnamon and cardamom hang in the air. Minutes later we're walking into Plaza Nueva and squinting in the bright, white sunlight.

"So," says Chloe, "I wonder when we'll be saying the Shahada? Aziz did say he'd talk to some people about it."

Time has taken on such a different quality. I feel we were talking about being Muslim last week, but it was only the day before yesterday. I smile on recalling Aziz's awestruck face.

"I hope he has," I say. "I'm ready."

We cross the big square towards the tall, Renaissance buildings painted two-tone ochres and earthy pinks. We pass an old Catholic church, its stone saints standing rigid above the doorway, its bell tower dark and distinct against a deepening blue sky.

"Have you thought about what we'll do next?" says Chloe. "I mean, after our Shahada."

"Not really," I say. "I imagine we'll be learning and absorbing for a while. How about you?"

Chloe pauses a moment. "Do you think we'll meet the shaykh?"

Her question brings something I've been vaguely thinking about into focus.

"The guys haven't mentioned anything, have they," I say.

"Maybe it's not for them to say," Chloe says.

I picture the two photographs in Hajj Abdullah's place. I remember how Hajj Abdullah spoke of the shaykh and how Aziz distinguished him from a guru. I remember Hamza reticent to describe him, as though his humility prevented him from doing so.

"I wonder what he's really like," I say.

"I know," says Chloe. "It's a bit daunting, isn't it."

The possibility of meeting the shaykh is suddenly an exciting one. I realise I really do want to meet this man.

Daunted or not, I want to meet this man of Allah the people here so often refer to.

"Let's ask Nuriya about it," I say, quickening our pace.

We leave the square along an old, uneven street which narrows to barely two armspans wide. On our left is a terrace of archaic houses adorned with mounted coats of arms, dark wood balconies hanging over the street and cornerstone quoins so pitted and pocked they resemble rocks eroded by a tide.

To our right, below a low and similarly weathered wall, is the river. The heat has reduced it to a trickle along rocks and pebbles and the roots of tall grasses, scrub and fig trees growing thirstily at its edge. The giant, solid square towers of the Alhambra loom high, high above it, casting much of it, and us, into shade. A little further and the street opens up to a broad and sunny esplanade.

We stop a moment and take in the view. A sign says this was a place of bullfights and jousting, even public executions. Now there are family restaurants and cafés with red parasols.

"You realise we'll have to call our parents soon," says Chloe, shielding her eyes from the sun.

"You think so?" I say, still reluctant. "We could just tell them we love it here and we're extending our stay, can't we?"

"That's not gonna work, Ally. Think about it – Beth will be home in a few days and she'll be telling her mum what happened, and our parents are all in touch with one another."

I think back to standing in the kitchen with my mother, drinking tea, her asking me to keep in touch. News about me being Muslim will surely confuse and worry her.

"Let's say the Shahada first," I say. "We can call them after."

We continue along the river as far as we can, then bear left up the steep Cuesta del Chapiz. On either side are traditional limewashed houses. Birdsong trills from tall cypress and firs. At the church near the top, the road levels out and we pass some artisan shops and a cheap snack kiosk, then a little plaza with a water fountain, some chained-up bikes and a bus stop. Far off to our right, just visible above the rooftops, I make out the cave dwellings of the Sacromonte.

We turn off into backstreets and weave our way along familiar lanes towards Plaza Larga. A woman on a balcony swishes a mop, dripping water to the ground. Someone strums a guitar. Then I'm aware of something else.

"Can you hear that?" I ask Chloe, putting my hand on her arm, stopping still.

"Hear what?" she replies, turning to face me.

I stare into her eyes.

"The prayer on the Prophet," I say. "Don't you hear it?"

Chloe looks around then scrutinises my face.

"Er, no. I don't," she replies. "I think you're hearing things."

But I'm not hearing things. I perceive it clearly. Instinctively I know not to look up and down the street in search of its source. The reciting voices are not physically here. Neither are they voices in my head. It's like a window is open onto another realm – and I hear them. They're for me alone.

"Hola!" calls a man from a tiny tobacconist next to us. I wave to the man and we turn to face the street again. I no longer hear the recitation. But it's presence stays with me. I decide not to mention it again.

At Plaza Larga, we come across a lively group of women.

"More Muslims," I say, stirred by their presence.

"Shall we go and talk to them?" says Chloe.

We approach, and one of the women notices us. "You

were at the conference!" she says, turning to her friends who welcome us. "I see we haven't scared you off?"

I tell them how Chloe and I are soon saying the Shahada.

Responses with the name of Allah ripple through the group. Chloe and I find ourselves a focal point of attention. I ask what they're doing here, given that the conference ended days ago.

"I stay on after all our events," says a forthright Malaysian-looking lady with large pearl earrings edged with tiny diamonds.

"It's so nice to just spend more time with people, you know?" adds the woman standing next to her, holding a little boy on her hip.

Then an ancient desert-looking woman, Moroccan perhaps, starts speaking in a language I don't recognise. Her voice is slow and shaky, her expression triumphant. She stands a little bent, one hand leaning on a wooden cane, the other held by a much younger woman at her side who translates her words:

"My grandmother is very happy to meet you."

I start to reply but the old lady speaks over me, her phrases propelled by sudden bursts of energy.

"My grandmother says to look around you."

The old lady extends her cane towards the women around us, continuing to speak while her granddaughter translates:

"She says that these people are lovers of Allah and His Messenger, sallallahu alayhi wa sallam. When you come across such people you must hold to them. *Cleave* to them. Even if it's by one hair's breadth."

I look around at the people, then glance at Chloe. The old woman bangs her cane on the ground, nodding her head, not smiling, but looking at Chloe and I, eyes lit and searching, demanding something.

"Inklisiyya?" she says.

"You're English aren't you?" says the granddaughter.

We nod and describe where in England we're from.

"Hmmmmm," says the old woman, light pouring from her milky eyes.

She seems moved. She then hobbles towards me – though I feel something about her is gliding – her gaze directly on mine while speaking more words in her native tongue, slowly, surely.

"My grandmother says she could travel the earth and not find a more blessed people. Wherever they sit, those places remain fragrant from their traces."

I take her words in. I feel I'm taking *her* in.

"Always seek out good company," she continues, her voice becoming a hoarse whisper. "This is our strength. And it will be *your* strength. And also your safety."

The granddaughter starts excusing her grandmother's forwardness but the old woman talks over her.

"Keeping company is like the coals of a fire. When one is removed and put on the hearth, it goes cold."

The old woman steps back, saying the name of Allah under her breath. Something in me feels connected to another plane. I sense this woman tasting something of the beyond, something of the next life. Maybe all of these people are. *She'll get her reward in heaven,* I think to myself.

Chloe and I watch as she turns to the little boy in the arms of the woman standing next to her, and tenderly passes the palm of her wrinkled hand over his face. She then runs her hand over her heart and lowers her eyes.

"Allaaah," she says again quietly. For a moment no one speaks.

"So... tell us what happened to you both here," says another of the women, and we start chatting.

The clatter of a shop-front shutter rattles across the square. Siesta is coming to an end. I turn to Chloe and stretch my arms.

"I don't know about you," I say, "but I still feel like walking."

"Yeah?" says Chloe. "I think I'll stay here a bit longer. We could meet at the Mirador in an hour?"

"Sure, let's do that," I say. "See you later."

I head off along one of the square's side streets, intending to take the longest route up to the Mirador and looking forward to a bit of time to myself to reflect.

"Alison?" says a voice behind me.

I turn around.

A woman dressed smartly in white with navy trims and delicate gold accessories is hurrying up to me.

"I was hoping I'd see you," she says breathlessly, coming right up to me and putting both hands on my arms. "I'm Jamila."

Before I can reply she's taken my hand firmly in hers.

"I hear you're about to say the Shahada? Is there anything I can do?"

"I... don't know," I reply, taken aback.

Small hazel eyes search mine.

"Well, has anyone taught you the prayer on the Prophet – what we recite after the Prayer?"

"No, actually," I reply, a bit thrown.

"Well look, I'm on my way somewhere," she says, still short of breath, "but let me write it down for you."

She opens her bag and scrabbles for a pen and paper.

"It's best to sit and learn it face to face. But in the meantime..."

I glance at Chloe on the far side of the square. She's still talking with the other women. Jamila sits down at the nearest table and beckons me to join her. Mouthing words under her breath, eyes focussed, she starts writing. For a moment she looks up briefly, as though double-checking her words, then she continues in haste.

"There!" She clicks the top of her biro and slips it back into her bag.

Standing up with a big smile, eyes fixed directly on mine, she hands over the piece of paper in the deliberate way you might hand over the deeds to a house.

"Bis-mil-lah!" she says, her eyes still holding my gaze.

I take it.

"Oh, but wait," she adds quickly. "Let's read it through together."

She moves to my side. I hold the paper in front of us, feeling I'm being entrusted with more than a house. She glances at me and pronounces the sounds. I start repeating them with her, their familiarity inspiring me.

"We recite this three times after each of the five daily Prayers," she explains. "But there's benefit in reciting it whenever you can: walking in the street, driving, alone in the night – it has a lot of light."

"What does it mean?"

"It means *Oh Allah, bless our master Muhammad, Your slave and Messenger, the unlettered Prophet,*" she shuts her eyes, concentrating, "*and his family and companions, and grant them peace.*"

Of course. Hamza told me that up on the mountainside. But, "unlettered?" I say.

"He didn't read or write," says Jamila.

She then slings her bag on her shoulder, her bracelet tinkling, and reties the bow of her scarf at the nape of her neck. I thank her.

"It's a pleasure. Thank *you!*" she smiles.

I want to ask Jamila more but we part ways. I glance at the paper again and feel excited. In my mind I recite the words, my own voice blending with the reciting I've been hearing in the streets.

"Oh, wait!" Jamila exclaims, walking back to me. She reaches into her bag, draws out a book and thrusts it into my hands.

"You *must* read this," she says emphatically.

Then, poised to head off, she puts her hand on my arm and says calmly and quite precisely: "As-*Salaaamu* 'alaykum."

Barely have I returned her greeting when she's gone. I open the book at the beginning. It appears to be transcripts of some of the shaykh's talks. What I read starts drawing me in. But standing here doesn't feel the right time or place for it. For the moment I'm wanting to stay with the prayer on the Prophet.

I close the book and look down the street to the square. Chloe and the women are gone. I clasp the book to my chest and continue on my way.

Blossoms

I decide not to visit the Mirador. I head straight for Nuriya's house and on the way I hold the piece of paper from Jamila in front of me, saying its phrases over and over. By the time I pass the huskies dozing on the steps, I'm familiar with the pronunciation and so engrossed that reaching the door to Nuriya's house comes almost as a surprise.

On entering, some women relaxing around the pool greet me with Spanish hellos. "Join us!" calls one of them. At first I don't recognise any of them in their swimsuits.

"¿Dónde está Hajja Nuriya?" I call back.

"She's inside."

I make a beeline down the steps, through the lemon trees and to the house.

Just before I reach the front door I hear water hissing

in the walled garden. Curious to see an unexplored nook of the property, I follow the sound and put my head around the trellised wall. In the middle of a courtyard, wearing a pale orange, floral dress, is a young woman standing with her back to me. She has an even tan and long, thick, burgundy-brown hair that curls in ringlets at her waist. Humming to herself with hand on hip, she holds the end of a hosepipe, capping it with her thumb and wiggling the spray over the blossoms and climbing foliage that surround her.

"Hello?" I call out.

The woman spins around in surprise.

"Nuriya?" I say.

"Ally! What a lovely surprise. I was about to go and try find you."

"You look so different without your scarf," I say, staring at her.

Nuriya laughs, closes the tap and coils the hosepipe over a hook.

"Do you want to swim?" she says.

"No, I've come to ask you about something."

"Aha?" she says. "Then let's go inside."

The entrance room is cool and smells of roast chicken and rosemary. Nuriya leaves the door wide open and I hear a splash from the pool.

"So!" she says, facing me directly. "We have to arrange your Shahada."

"Well, mine and Chloe's," I say. "Beth left last night."

"She left?" she says, her face full of concern. "What happened?"

"Well, I guess... I don't know... she..."

"You don't have to explain," Nuriya interrupts. "We can't choose who becomes Muslim."

"Well, I'm pretty gutted about it."

"I'm sure," she says. "Gosh, I'm sorry too."

We talk more about it, then she gets up and goes to the kitchen. "I was just making tea. Let me fix one for you too?"

Copper pots hang from an iron rail and above the oven are dark blue and white tiles.

We sit at the head of the dining table. Rosehips and hibiscus scent the air.

"So this is why I'm here," I say, producing the piece of paper Jamila gave me.

Nuriya takes it and glances at the writing, curling a lock of her hair this way and that around her finger. *"Alhamdulillah,"* she says, putting it down in front of her.

I repeat her expression inside me, savouring its meaning I now know: *All Praise is to Allah.*

"So why do we recite this?" I ask, tapping the paper.

Nuriya puts her mug aside and leans forward. "Because the Prophet Muhammad, sallallahu alayhi wa sallam, is our doorway to knowledge of Allah."

She smiles with deep warmth, her gaze sealing her words. "He is the best of all Allah's creation."

Swifts hurtle this way and that outside the window.

"We recite this because it increases us in our love for him. Being Muslim is *based* on loving him."

She sits back, her eyes becoming moist.

Then she continues: "The Prophet told how people would come to him on the Day of Rising that he would recognise just by the prayers they did for him."

She gestures to the paper. "And he said: *'Whoever blesses me in a book or a letter, the angels will continue to ask forgiveness for that person as long as my name is on it.'*"

I examine the writing on the paper. I think of Jamila.

Nuriya watches me. "So look after what you've got there."

There's a knock at the door and we turn around.

"Hello-oo!" calls Chloe from the open doorway.

"Oh, Chloe!" I exclaim apologetically.

"I thought I might find you here," Chloe grins.

Nuriya invites her in. She slips off her shoes.

"How are you doing?" Nuriya asks her.

"Fantastic!" she says. "I've just been at the Mirador."

"I'm so sorry I wasn't there," I say. "I got distracted."

"It's fine," she says breezily. "I would've left earlier but there were some guys playing some great guitar."

"We should tape the music that goes on up there," I say.

"Listen," says Nuriya. "It's good you're both here. I want to talk to you about something."

Chloe comes to sit beside me. Nuriya clears her throat.

"You know how we were talking about you girls spending time with women? Well, a lady I know wants to invite you to stay with her."

"Oh, but we're fine where we are," I say quickly.

"I'm sure you are. But this is a special time for you both, and you'll benefit from staying with Muslims. It's like when a baby is born – you want the best possible environment for it because those early days are so precious and formative."

"Rafiq did say we could go back to their flat in a day or two," I say.

Nuriya smiles sympathetically. "And I'd also love you to stay with me," she says, "but I've still got a full house of conference guests." She puts her hand on my arm. "Look, there's a difference, staying with men and staying with women."

I feel how I did when we went to the Wird and Aziz told us the men and women sit separately: off kilter, apprehensive. Nuriya tilts her head affectionately.

"It's better this way," she adds, straightness in her eyes. "Come on, keep spending time with the men and other energies start creeping in. You know what I'm saying, no?" She laughs. "It's just – you're women. It's best to get this thing from other women."

I feel thrown.

"Well, it's really kind of you to help us," says Chloe. Then she turns to me. "We just have to remember to give Susie's keys back."

"Sure," I say, still uncomfortable, but encouraged that Chloe seems okay with it.

I finish my tea and look at Nuriya. She smiles reassuringly.

"I just feel a bit awkward at the thought of staying with strangers," I say, "that's all."

Nuriya chuckles. "Don't worry, this woman won't bite."

"Yes, but..."

"And in another way, we're all strangers," she interjects. "'*Islam began as something strange,*' said the Prophet, '*and will return to being strange. So blessed are the strangers.*'"

"Can you say that again?" I say.

Nuriya repeats what she said, blessing the Prophet after. I turn the words over in my mind.

"So what's happening about our Shahada?" Chloe asks. "Do we need to do something about it?"

"Good point," says Nuriya. "There's a wedding tomorrow night, so we're thinking of holding your Shahadas at the zawiya the following morning – if that's alright with you both?"

"An extra day to wait?!" I say.

Nuriya smiles. "Saying the Shahada is just a formality."

"It feels important though," I say.

"Yes," says Nuriya in earnest. "But it's best not to mix the wedding with your Shahadas, you know? Being publicly witnessed as a Muslim is a significant step. And there's wisdom in giving each event its due."

Mizan

At the Wird that evening we meet our new host. She's a tall, Italian business woman in a camel tailored suit and matching heels. She wears an elegant beret rather than a headscarf, which adds to her height and compliments her high forehead and large round eyes. We walk with her to her house, close to the zawiya.

"My home is your home," she tells us as we step through her front door.

She takes off her beret and slings it on a stand alongside a trench coat and denim jacket.

"Kinza!" she calls out, going to the foot of the stairs and looking up. "We're all here!" she says in Spanish.

Then she turns to us, running her hands briefly through her dark, shoulder-length hair.

"I hope you'll feel comfortable here. I'm at work most of the day but my daughter will look out for you." Then, "Excuse me," she says, going into the next room to switch off a television.

At a glance the house has a modern feel: monochrome colours, angular furniture, sleek silver fittings.

She joins us again. "Ah, your rucksacks," she says, eyeing our luggage. "I remember those days. Let's share travel stories over supper."

She goes to stand in the doorway by the stairs. "Kinza!" she calls up again.

"Si, si!" exclaims an exuberant young teenager, bursting into the hallway with a toddler on her hip and shimmying up to Chloe and I.

"Ohhh, I'm so happy you're here, this is so cool!" she exclaims, her husky voice booming melodiously.

"Look, mi amor," she says to the little girl, "these are the English girls!" Then to us, "Meet my niece."

Then taking my hand and grinning at Chloe, she pulls us away as though we're to be coveted, and sets about showing us around.

After supper, Kinza teaches us the movements of the prayer. Chloe and I have seen it done several times but doing it ourselves is another matter. Kinza stands and bows, stands and prostrates, and we copy her, her niece at her feet, pulling at her dress. Kinza picks her up and continues with the prayer, setting her down beside her when she prostrates, then putting her back on her hip when she stands up. Kinza's mother pops into the salon several times to see how we're getting on, and seeing that we are, she nods, smiles and bids us goodnight.

"Enough for now," says Kinza at last. "I'm going to put this little one to sleep."

She gets up, and holding the little girl's hand she gently shakes it to wave at us.

"Buenas noches," she whispers into her little ear.

"Kinza," I say, hesitating. "Does it matter if you're carrying her in the prayer?"

Kinza laughs. "Of course not!" she says, her face lighting up. "That's what the Prophet did with his granddaughter."

She laughs, rubs noses with her little niece, then goes upstairs.

Later, I hang out with Chloe in her room. We write down the movements of the prayer, acknowledging with a quiet sense of awe how we'll be learning passages of the Qur'an to accompany them.

Sometime after midnight I withdraw to my room. I light the candle on my bedside table and turn off the light. It feels strange to be apart from Chloe. I'm not lonely. But I feel my aloneness. For the first time since staying with Beth and working at the chocolate factory, I'm not sharing a room with anyone. The candle flame stills. I wonder about Beth and where she is right now. I wonder if she's feeling her aloneness too.

I become acutely aware of my unfamiliar surroundings: a futon mattress with Egyptian cottons. Large, goose-down pillows. A steel chair by the door stacked with neatly folded blankets.

I go to the window. On the windowsill are delicate, exotic-looking perfume bottles. I carefully open one and smell something woody. I open another and it's floral, sensual. I open the window and breathe in the warm night air. I look up at the night and let my eyes roam the stars. I play at making my own constellations. But the ancient ones say more.

Then I remember the book of the shaykh's talks which

Jamila gave me. I get it out from my rucksack and go to sit on the floor by my bed. The page before me is thick, crisp and white, the text generously spaced and with large margins. I hold the book up to the candle flame and start reading.

Islam, by definition, is not and can never be in crisis or need of revisionist change.

I read the sentence again, making sure I understand each word. Then I go on.

Islam is immutable in all places until the end of time. The mizan of Islam adheres in every age, personal and social. It is itself a critique and balance principle against which all human ventures must be measured and themselves revised and changed.

I think back to the conference and picture the shaykh sitting at the speakers' table, eyes wide and surveying the auditorium with concern, his voice rich and stately, his bearing formidable.

At no time and in no place do the moral and political limits become altered to suit the latest fantasies and ambitions of men.

I'm struck by his boldness of expression. He doesn't mitigate any of his statements with explanation, defence or political correctness. I recall the two photographs in Hajj Abdullah's house and how, although one appeared 'spiritual'-looking, the other more contemporary and intellectual, Hajj Abdullah did not see them like that. He mentioned how a true shaykh has both inner and outer knowledge. That he has reached direct knowledge of Allah. That his profound insight into current times enables him to read clearly what is happening and so to forewarn.

Limits of human behaviour remain decreed by the Revelation until the end of the human situation.

There's a glossary at the back. I read it in almost equal measure to the text. *Mizan* means balance. I read on until my eyes grow heavy. Then I get into bed. A small jug of water and a glass have been left for me on the bedside table. I pour myself some and take a sip, mostly to savour my host's thoughtfulness. I lie down. I hear the bathroom door open and shut along the landing. I hear water running gently. I turn onto my right side, the way the Prophet did when he went to sleep. My mind turns over phrases I just read.

But I don't sleep. I realise a crack of light shining through my door is keeping me awake. I get up and go to the door. From the room opposite I catch a whisper of Kinza's voice: *Allahu akbar.* She must be praying. I close the door as quietly as I can and get back into bed.

Kinza's words stay with me. Allah is greater. Lying on my back, looking at the ceiling, my thoughts roam.

Allah is not a concept. Allah is not an idea. Allah isn't about finding a new god that suits. There are no gods. There is only Allah, only Reality. And Muslims submit to the Real. But they don't own this reality. What I now know about Allah doesn't change Allah in any way. But it changes me.

My thoughts go again to the Prophet, the Messenger of Allah, Muhammad, sallallahu alayhi wa sallam. He was sent by Allah to exemplify how to submit to what is truly Real, how to live harmoniously with oneself and with others and with the whole of creation – the seen of it, and the unseen of it. What I know of him so far isn't from any book, but simply from keeping company with the people here. I close my eyes and see their faces. All of them, in their own way, have something of the flavour of him, the scent of him, that ineffable luminosity which seems to me to be his very proof.

My mind goes to my conversation with Bilqis and the women at Nuriya's house – about the angelic realm, about the Unseen. It seemed theoretical then. Biblical. Now it's different. I sense those worlds present, close. I blow out the candle. Soon I'm drifting along the edge of sleep.

When I was a child, my mother took my brother and I for a trip in a glass-bottomed boat off the Balearic coast. It was a hot, sunny day, with a clear view to the horizon. We motored out to the coral reefs, not far from land. Our guide then switched off the engine and gathered us around a glass pane in the boat's hull. We peered through that window, and suddenly, beyond it, I saw a whole world of life that though ever-present, is normally entirely hidden from view.

That is what this is like now.

"Bismillah," I whisper, and fall straight to sleep.

Meat

The next day, Chloe and I meet up with Rafiq in Plaza Larga. He has something to give us.

"The title is dreadful," he says, "but I found it useful at the beginning."

He hands us an A5 booklet.

"Spot on about the title," Chloe gasps. "Islam Starter Kit?"

"Yep," Rafiq frowns. "But there it is: how to do wudu and the prayer – the women will teach you that – and there's a transliteration of the Fatiha, which is the opening verse of the Qur'an, then the last three surahs of the Qur'an, also called the surahs of protection."

He pauses, watching me. "It's good to have as stand-by if no one's at hand to ask," he adds.

Chloe flicks through its pages. "Thanks," she says. "But I think Kinza's going to teach us."

"I hope so," says Rafiq. "Can't beat face to face."

I ask how he's been and how the guys are. We chat a while.

"So I hear your Shahada is happening tomorrow?" Rafiq says. "We'll all be there you know."

"Will the shaykh be there?" I ask.

"I'm not sure," he says. "But it's not about the shaykh," he adds. "It's about you."

"I know but... we'd really like to meet him," I say.

"And I'm sure you will at some point," he says.

Night has fallen by the time Chloe and I arrive at the wedding celebration. It's being held on an open tract of level land in an upper part of the Albaicín. There must be several hundred people present. An enormous barbecue is underway, with spreads of hot coals and wood-burning fires roasting lamb on spits and grilling sausages, kebabs and vegetables. We spot the newlyweds. They have so many people around them that we have to wait our turn to congratulate them.

Sounds of merriment and flamenco guitar spill through the warm night air. The atmosphere is relaxed. We stroll among the guests, chatting to those we know and acquainting ourselves with some we don't. Their easy presence feels so good-natured, so normal – like a temperature I can barely feel because it's the same as my own.

It comes to me how when we first arrived in Granada, especially when we began meeting lots of people, everyone seemed similar in a way. Perhaps it was just my unfamiliarity with trimmed beards and headscarves. Then as I got to know them and discovered who they are as individuals, I began to recognise another sort of similarity, not of outer appearance but of an inner kind. I feel it now.

Rich. Warm. Luminous.

We stay near to the barbecue, its lambent light and warmth drawing us close, the steady amber flames like a lighthouse in the darkness. I think back to the beach in France, hanging out with the hostellers around their campfire, a silhouette of dancers by the flames. There, we were all revelling in the freedom of that wild and foreign place, strangers together for a moment in time. Here, everyone is perfectly contained, but I feel that openness inside. Instead of fleeting encounters, ships passing in the night, this companionship feels more like coming in to harbour.

I listen to the sounds of their voices – the animated conversations, laughter and discussion. Everyone dresses so well without seeming to try. And there's no awkwardness. There's no affectation, triviality or attention seeking. I feel close to them in some innate and timeless way, recognising who they are in the same way I recognise my own reflection in the mirror.

The evening grows late and the food is ready. Four very long rows of tablecloths are laid down on the ground and groups of servers place huge, oval platters of food along them: salads, pasta dishes, meats and sauces. Older children put down forks and glasses. Everyone sits down. The groom calls out "Bismillah!" from the far end of one of the tables, and we eat.

Appreciative comments about the food mingle with a melodic hum of conversation. Chloe and I sit with some of the young women and a particularly courteous and refined lady I've not met before. We talk about Spanish history. She tells me her family fought against Franco, the Spanish dictator.

When our platters are nearly empty, servers begin walking up and down the rows, filling them up for those who want more.

"Good evening," says a man's voice, deep and resonant.

I turn and look up to see Nuriya's husband silhouetted by the wood fires. We greet him.

"I see you are not eating the best part?" he says to me. Then he calls over a boy walking up the row towards us with a platter of carved lamb.

"Bismillah. Give this young lady some of that please," he says, gesturing towards me.

"No, I'm fine thanks," I reply, touched by his care but a little embarrassed. "I'm vegetarian."

"Not anymore," he declares.

I'm taken aback, wondering if he's joking. "I'm really okay, thank you."

He pauses a moment, looking at me. "You're about to become Muslim, are you not?" He says it rhetorically, his tone imposing. "Well, you don't want to be *munafiq*, do you?"

"Hajj Abdulmalik!" I hear Nuriya exclaim admonishingly from somewhere up our row. "Hajj Abdulmalik!" and she's up and quickly making her way over to us.

Her husband smiles amiably, waiting as she joins us. I get to my feet and Nuriya is standing at her husband's side. I greet her, and he looks at her with admiration.

"I was about to tell our friend here," he says to Nuriya, his Spanish accent thick, almost poetic, "that a munafiq is someone who says they believe in Allah's law then contradicts themselves with their actions."

"Come on Hajj, she's new!" she says. "Leave her alone."

"I believe the English word is *hypocrite*," he continues, without a trace of self-consciousness.

Nuriya looks at me, shaking her head apologetically but smiling too. I'm wanting to defend myself but I don't want to offend my hosts. I certainly don't want to be a hypocrite.

"I think there's been a misunderstanding," I venture, not sure how to continue.

Hajj Abdulmalik clears his throat. I've got that squirming feeling of being put on the spot that I got with Hajja Amira. Except this is much worse.

"Islam," he begins, "is nothing other than the crystallisation and clarification of a teaching that has been perceived in all religions and by all great cultures."

He talks clearly, deliberately, his demeanour devoid of any flurry of expression. I'm wondering what this has got to do with my food.

"It has been described in very clear language in all the great texts of the human situation. Yet there are rules. And those rules form a template which is not for a particular climate or race, but for any human situation in any social nexus in any place in the world, and part of that template is that Allah has made animals permissible for you to eat."

He speaks carefully. I sense his words are prelude to something I'm going to find difficult. Accordingly, I feel as though I'm in the presence of a large hammer slowly and precisely tapping in a nail.

"So do not make them forbidden," he says.

Then he smiles and gestures towards our tablecloth spread with food. "Bismillah!"

I laugh nervously, uncomfortable in my own skin.

"It's just I hate what happens in abattoirs," I start, "and that profit-making greed that goes into animal production," I add, now feeling the indignance-fuelled thrust of a familiar rant coming on. "And then there's the..."

Hajj Abdulmalik listens, his eyes fastened on me.

"Hm-mm," he says, smiling warmly, listening politely, his eyes widening.

I keep talking but realise my heart's not really in it. And the man in front of me isn't interested in arguing.

I've been vegetarian for six years. I know Muslims don't eat pork, or scavengers, carnivores or carrion. But what Hajj Abdulmalik says shocks me. I glance down at Chloe who's watching the exchange. She looks a little startled, but smiles in sympathy.

I look back at Hajj Abdulmalik and see clearly a man endeavouring to transmit what has been divinely revealed to the Messenger of Allah, sallallahu alayhi wa sallam. I trust him mainly because he's married to Nuriya. And I feel a respect for him which goes some way towards assuaging my theoretical outrage. But there's something in his direct and unwavering presence which fast-forwards me to a clarity: I can do what I want, but in truth there is only one choice: the revealed knowledge of which he speaks will have to supplant my own high-minded opinions.

"Okay," I say simply, nodding my head and thanking the boy who has given us more meat.

"Good," says Hajj Abdulmalik, and with a courteous nod: "Enjoy the evening."

He turns to Nuriya, inviting her to something with his expression. Arm in arm they stroll off together, the light from the fires illuminating the outlines of their forms.

I sit down.

"Wow, are you okay?" says Chloe, seeing I've gone quiet.

"I'm not sure," I say with a little laugh.

I feel in shock, like I've survived some disaster and am about to start picking over the wreckage.

"That was a bit heavy," she grins, concern in her eyes.

But there is no wreckage. The old me would be ranting about that encounter. But I don't feel angry. A bit bruised maybe. More than that, I feel something new in myself.

Something new in me is emerging and it has sparked a tingle of excitement that I can literally feel coursing around my body.

"Ally?"

"Oh, sorry," I say, discombobulated. "A bit heavy, yes."

Then I do something which for many is entirely normal and inconsequential, but for me is not: I pick up a small piece of lamb.

"Bismillah," I say, taking a bite and slowly chewing it, then slowly, slowly allowing myself to savour its hearty flavours.

"Wow, Ally. Do you realise how many people have become vegetarian because of you?" Chloe chuckles. "They'll be horrified."

"Noooo!" I laugh and start blushing. "Well, bismillah. So be it," I say, still incredulous at what has just taken place, and pushing a bit of lamb Chloe's way. "It's actually really good," I say wryly, making her laugh.

"I mentioned you could be a bit forceful," Chloe says, "but I think Nuriya's husband might have outdone you."

"He's quite something," I say, nodding.

The more I think about it, the more I see his words coming from a place quite detached from any channel of argument or debate. It's as though his words flow from another source, unadulterated.

"How're you doing with that new food in your tummy?" Chloe asks.

"I'm okay... I think."

I'm concerned how my body might react. I wait for something dramatic to happen. Minutes pass. But nothing happens at all.

Later, I leave Chloe with the young women we met the other day. I wander around, enjoying the night air and atmosphere.

"Hello?" says a woman softly, appearing at my side. "Are you one of the girls who're friends with Rafiq?"

"How did you know?" I reply.

She smiles, curiosity flashing in her deep-set eyes. "I'm so pleased to meet you."

She leans in to kiss me on both cheeks. I smell lavender. The woman is English, slim, her demeanour intelligent and composed.

"Welcome," she enthuses. "I heard you and your friends were travelling and, well, it's wonderful you're here."

"It certainly is," I say. "I've never met people like all of you."

"I'm sure," she says warmly, surveying the gathering.

Lines in her countenance hint at past struggles, yet her eyes are like portals to meadows. There's a luminosity about her. And it's interesting to meet an English person again. I'd almost forgotten what we're like. The Spanish are more sensual and expressive than us, but this woman has a sobriety and depth I find comforting.

She turns back to me and smiles. "I'd never met people like this either. And here I am decades later, and I'm still moved at the sight of our gatherings."

Midnight comes and goes. The air is still warm but there's a gentle breeze. The bride and groom are long gone but many people remain, chatting in the mellow ambience. Children chase one another and shriek with glee. Some of the young men have gathered to sing and play guitar. They do it so well.

A group of servers start tidying up. Chloe and I offer to help but they decline and gesture for us to just sit with the other guests. We go to sit with the girls we met in the square, talking a bit, but mostly just listening to the music.

"So, all set for your Shahada tomorrow morning?" says

one of them.

"All set, yes," Chloe says. "Right, Ally?"

She turns to me and smiles. I see a mix of quiet excitement and trepidation mirroring my own. I nod, and we relax back into the ambience, talking every now and then, the young men continuing to play and sing, although more softly now.

Cinders from the barbecue float upwards into the night. They disappear into the blackness, leading my eyes to the stars. For a while I roam their constellations. Then I start thinking about the Prophet's Companions, those people who kept company with him and loved him. Who were they? How were they with one another? I reflect back on the evening. They must have gathered like this. I begin to imagine it. Gazing into the starlit depths, I feel curiosity. Awe. Wonder. My sense is that they will be limitless.

Soon, a yearning to know the Prophet and his Companions and all of how they lived and breathed is rising within me. It courses through my veins. Tingling and sparkling, it feels as though something in my very cells is coming alive. In a moment my heart is swelling. Becoming as big as an ocean. Filled and flooding with love.

Aisha

I open my eyes. Soft sunshine is at my open window. All is quiet. The house. The street outside.

Blinking, I turn my head on my pillow. I follow the stream of sunlight to the floor where it gathers in a pool of gold. I stare at it a moment. It's so intense I almost hear it. I put my hand behind my head, absorbed. Then I smell in my hair the bonfires from last night. I see in my mind's eye the dancing flames and white hot coals. I smile to myself, recalling the sense of togetherness. The laughter and the music. The children playing. And some subtle, transcendent energy woven through it all.

I sit up and run my hands through my hair. I look to the window and see above the ridge of roofs a pale cerulean sky. In the distance, circling high, high up, is a flock of birds.

Silent silhouettes, I watch them a while until they gradually disappear from view. I hug my knees to my chest and notice my leather wristband pressing into my skin. I turn it so I can see its engraving.

INTENT.

For a while I stare at the letters, contemplating the meaning of the word. The Prophet, may Allah bless him and grant him peace, said that each of us gets what we intend.

I look at the wristband some more. I see it as a signpost for the journey. A pointer on the map. I realise I no longer need to wear it. Its meaning has internalised. I turn the wristband around and undo its small buckle.

"Bismillah," I say to myself, and put it down on the bedside table next to me.

The bedroom door opens a little. "Ally?" says Chloe, coming into the room.

"Hi," I say, moving to put my feet on the floor. "What time is it?"

"Getting on for eight." She smiles. "You slept well."

She comes to sit next to me, sunlight illuminating the side of her face and highlighting the copper shades in her hair.

"How are you doing?" I say.

"Fine, thanks," she says.

"Sure?" I say.

"I'm worried about my parents. I woke up wondering what they'll think about all this, you know?"

"They love you, Chloe," I say.

"But that's exactly why they'll probably freak out." She sighs deeply.

"We can cross that bridge when we come to it," I say. "I'm sure they'll come to understand."

Chloe looks down at the floor in thought. I start feeling

anxious and wonder if the anxiety is mine or hers.

"Are you sure you're okay with all this?" I say. "Being Muslim, I mean."

"Of course," she says simply, taking a deep breath.

Then she exhales slowly, her large blue-grey eyes resting on a landscape painting on the wall in front of us.

"I feel like... I'm kind of deep sea diving."

"You mean, you need to come up for air or something?"

"No, not that," she smiles, pausing in thought. "I keep getting this image that I've swum almost to the bottom of the ocean, as though my realisation of what it means to be Muslim is being somehow arrived at, but when I get there I find the ocean floor isn't solid. It's just a threshold. And there are further fathoms of water – or knowledges, realisations, whatever – beyond it."

She shrugs her shoulders.

"But that's... kind of wonderful isn't it?" I say, relieved by what she's saying, her experience reflecting much of my own. "It's a good thing, right?" I add.

Chloe hesitates. "It seems to ask something of me," she says slowly. "I don't know what."

She glances at me, and I sense a cautiousness.

"Like at the conference," she continues. "I'd had quite a nice, romantic idea about Rafiq's newfound spirituality up until then, when suddenly these people are talking about politics and economics, about usury and how it's forbidden in all revealed religions and how it's the task of our time to reestablish financial justice, and I felt so energised but... so completely at sea. I suddenly saw Islam less as an ideology but as something real and tangible – and so where did that leave me?"

"Why didn't you say anything?" I say. "I was so worried about you."

"You were?" says Chloe, turning to face me, her eyes full of relief.

"Of course I was! I didn't press you about it because I felt you didn't want to talk about it. Actually, I was ready for you to turn around and say, 'Okay, we're leaving for Italy right now!'"

"Really?" Chloe says, still surprised. "Oh, I'm sorry, Ally. I just... got overwhelmed I guess. Everything I'd planned suddenly seemed meaningless. I was seeing my whole future unravelling. I mean, what about going to university?"

"Tell me about it!" I say. "I'm down for studying English and Philosophy but now I'm asking myself how I could possibly spend three years hypothesising on the meaning of existence after all this."

Chloe and I hold each other's gaze, acknowledging our shared experiences, our shared concerns. At the same time, I feel our journeys becoming more separate.

"You okay?" she says.

"Yes," I say. "And no," I add, her question eliciting a pulse of nervous excitement. I run my hands through my hair again. "I feel... Well, I feel I should get dressed."

An hour later, just before nine o'clock on this Tuesday morning, Chloe and I close the door of the house behind us and walk with Kinza down to Qudra's house to get ready.

"You've met Hajja Qudra, hmm?" says Kinza, her espadrilles slapping the cobbles as she walks, her voice even huskier in the morning.

"I think so," I say. "When we first went to the Wird."

"Ha, well she was one of the first people to become Muslim in our whole community," says Nuriya, flicking her hand in a Spanish 'wow' gesture.

Chloe speaks up: "Do you think we'll see the shaykh at

the zawiya?"

"No idea," laughs Kinza. "If you do, you do."

I want to ask more, but we arrive at the house and Kinza knocks on the door. She turns to us with a chuckle. Chloe and I look at one another saying nothing. I enjoy the look of anticipation in her face. I imagine she sees the same in mine.

The door opens and Hajja Qudra appears before us. I feel something whoosh up in front of me and it takes me aback – not an external sensation, but some unseen energy jolting me inside.

"Come in," she says.

I glance up at her as we step through the doorway. In the half-light her eyes are luminous, like a torch shone through water.

Inside, a group of women are sitting on cushions underneath a window which looks out onto the street. Nuriya is here. Firdaws and Hafsa too. They stand up and come to greet us, expressing their pleasure at what we're about to do. Perfumes mingle with the smell of fresh coffee.

"So you both know what you're doing with your *ghusl*?" asks Hajja Qudra, wasting no time with pleasantries. "It's like wudu but for the whole body."

"Yes," we reply, having been briefed by Kinza.

"I think so," I add.

"Good," says Hajja Qudra, her demeanour almost stern. But then she smiles, a playful look coming to her eyes. "So you first, Chloe?"

They go through the order of the full, ritual wash: washing the private parts, passing water over the head – forehead to the nape of the neck then back again – the wudu wash which the old woman showed us when we first went to the Wird, then, before finishing with the feet, rubbing water over the whole of the right then left sides of the body, concluding by saying the Shahada phrases.

I watch Hajja Qudra with interest. She's tall and has a swan neck. I find myself mapping the details of her face: long but not horse-ish, her high cheekbones and angular jaw lending her a regal, authoritative appearance. Her eyes are large and outlined with navy kohl, their generous lids darkened with brown eyeshadow so that the whites appear whiter, and the irises all the more translucent. Arched eyebrows frame her eyes' changeable nature. In one moment I see vulnerability. In another that is gone, and something strong and resilient is in its place.

There's something else about her. I'm not sure what. She goes to get us towels. The women glance at us, not quite watching, mostly talking among themselves.

The salon has a simple feel. Whitewashed. Wooden beams overhead. Not one item seems superfluous: the dark leather furniture, dark-wood lampstands, a full bookcase and the calligraphy – one piece inscribed on animal hide.

Chloe takes it all in. The women go quiet, taking books out of their bags and opening them, then flicking backwards and forwards through the pages as though deciding on something. I saw the same book at the flat. *The Diwan*. It's a collection of divine praise and sufic instruction – the shaykh's inheritance from his two shaykhs before him. Hajja Qudra appears and hands us our towels.

"So, once you've finished your wash," she says to us, "you say *'Ash-hadu an la ilaha illallah, wa ash-hadu anna Muhammad ar-Rasulullah'*. Alright? Say it in English if you can't remember: 'I bear witness that there is no god but Allah, and I bear witness that Muhammad is the Messenger of Allah.' If you forget what to do, just give me a shout. Once you're done, we'll leave for the zawiya."

She speaks with a let's-get-on-with-it attitude and

seems accustomed to this situation. She shows Chloe to the bathroom along the corridor then comes back to me.

"Ally, you can sit there while you're waiting."

She gestures to the women. Nuriya looks up and beckons me over. I hear Chloe's shower water running and go to sit down. Hafsa begins to sing and the women join her, all except Hajja Qudra – she stands close to the bathroom, hands on hips, listening out for Chloe.

The women glance at their books and close their eyes, some swaying gently, their song sounding tribal, maybe mediaeval, sometimes futuristic – I can't quite pin it down. I wonder what the words mean. Although I don't understand them on a cognitive level, on another I feel some pure, uplifting element moving my heart. After each couplet there is a chorus of the divine Name, and I join in singing it.

Chloe reappears with a smile and a look of accomplishment. Hajj Qudra stays with her. Now it's my turn. I go into the bathroom and close the door. I take off my clothes and hang them on the hook. The floor is almost warm. I step into the shower, close the curtain and turn on the water. *This is it*, I think to myself. I make the intention to do the ritual act of washing then begin rubbing water over all my body, making sure to cover every inch.

Soon I'm finished.

I turn off the tap and say the words of the Shahada.

I step out of the shower. Fresh. New.

I dry myself off and put on my clothes. I go to the basin and pause to look at myself in the mirror. I search for outward signs of my changing inner world. I lean in. My face is lightly tanned, my freckles pronounced. Gone are the sunken eyes – they're larger and brighter now. My expression is calm, belying a tremendous sense of anticipation.

"All done?" says Hajja Qudra as I close the bathroom

door behind me.

"Done!"

Hajja Qudra looks amused, and I see the humour of our circumstances.

"Do you often get people turning up at your house for a shower?" I say, rubbing my damp hair with the towel.

Hajja Qudra laughs, and as though a floodgate has opened, an unexpected warmth gushes from her being and I laugh with her.

Greatness. I think that's what I was wondering about. And now I sense it. Something of her spirit. Powerful. Like magma beneath tectonic plates.

"Come," says Hafsa appearing at my side and looping her arm in mine. "I help you get ready."

She takes Chloe and I to the back of the salon and puts us in front of a long mirror. The women continue singing.

"Bismillah," says Hafsa, handing me a cotton scarf with a flower pattern. "For you."

I'd brought my minidress, but her gift feels so apt. Then she turns to Chloe, giving her a dark blue scarf with a white batik design. We thank her and she kisses us on both cheeks.

I hold my scarf between my thighs as I run my hands through my hair, teasing out knots. Gone is the salty residue from the French Atlantic and the curls it kindled. It feels silky now, returned to its familiar and distinct waves, except more golden and sun-bleached.

Looking at myself in the mirror, I gather my hair briskly into a high pony tail and tie a hairband over it, looping it around twice. I look different without a mane framing my face and neck and falling over my shoulders. My cheekbones are more prominent, the shape of my forehead more visible. I coil the length of my hair into a bun and tuck in the end.

Hafsa watches my reflection in the mirror as I fold the

scarf in half to make a triangle, lift it above my head then set about placing its long edge at my hairline. She looks on patiently, as though watching a young child tying their shoelaces. Chloe attempts to put hers on too. She tuts and starts again. Hafsa chuckles and says something in Spanish that sounds reassuring. Hajja Qudra comes to join us. She stands arms folded, amused.

I take the ends of the scarf and tie them at the nape of my neck. It crosses my mind how from now onwards I'll be clothing myself like this every time I leave my house. Men will not see my hair. Only women and children and close male relatives like my brother, uncle and eventually my husband – if and when I get married. The thought is rather prosaic. I find myself wanting to explore the notion further, probing for some sense of shock or trepidation I might be feeling. But there is none.

For a moment I take in my reflection. I see little trace of personas I might previously have inhabited. I see little trace of those parts of me which dressed a certain way, which identified with certain kinds of people. I will my reflection to yield more of what this means. Then I'm content simply to see me as I am.

I adjust the scarf around my face so it looks symmetrical, then take its lengths and wrap them around my head. I'm a bit fingers and thumbs, but less so than last time. I tuck the ends into the wrapped material.

"That's it," I say, looking at Chloe who's already got hers on and is waiting for me.

"Looking good," says Chloe with a broad smile.

Hafsa turns away from the mirror and looks at us directly. "Si, si," she says warmly.

Nuriya comes up to us. "It's time to go," she says.

The women finish singing, raise supplicating hands and

say something in unison. I watch as they put their books away and gather their things. A wave of gratitude comes over me – gratitude to have arrived here, to have met these people, to have discovered what they have.

Soon we're at the door, slipping on our sandals.

Outside, the air is fresh and warm. I smell jasmine and sun-warmed stone. We all set off uphill along the street we've now walked so many times. I start feeling nervous: not really knowing what to expect, imagining people will be there to watch us, and knowing that what I'm taking on is so big I can't truly comprehend it.

Chloe and I hardly talk. The women do, but not too much. I feel supported by them, as though we're migrating birds flying in a V, moving together with purpose. None of the women say anything about Islam. They don't have to. They exude it. They *are* it. My excited apprehensions ripple and swell. But they do so on the surface of a deep, inner security.

The zawiya is flooded with light from the mid-morning sun. Thirty or so women are sitting in groups in the middle of the floor and along the back wall. On the other side of the curtain are a similar number of men. Some are talking quietly. Others sit in silence. I spot Zayd and Hamza.

We walk with Hajja Qudra and Nuriya to the far side of the room and sit down by the window. We wait as more people enter. Then Hajja Qudra motions for the women to gather about us and everyone goes silent. The whole zawiya goes silent. The atmosphere is hushed. Expectant. Sunshine falls on my shoulder, my lap. Birds sing outside the window. From a few streets away comes the revving sound of a passing scooter.

Then Hajja Qudra speaks. Everyone is listening. She tells me I'm to say the Shahada first. She gestures for me to come closer. We sit cross-legged, our knees almost touching. I sense everyone looking at us.

"Are you ready?" Hajja Qudra asks me.

"Yes," I say clearly.

"First of all, I'll go through the five pillars of Islam which you must agree to. Then I'll ask you to say the Shahada three times after me. Do you accept this?"

"Yes."

My heart beats stronger.

Hajja Qudra takes my right hand in hers and closes her eyes for a moment. Then she looks at me directly: "Do you testify that there is no god, only Allah, and that Muhammad is the Messenger of Allah?"

"Yes."

"And do you accept to do the five daily prayers?"

"Yes."

"And do you undertake to fast the month of Ramadan?"

"Yes."

"And to pay the Zakat tax if and when it applies to you?"

"Yes."

"And do you undertake to do the Hajj at least once in your lifetime, if you are able to do so?"

"Yes."

"Good."

She smiles briefly.

Her eyes look carefully at mine. "We're going to bear witness that there is no god, only Allah, and that Muhammad is the Messenger of Allah – and you're going to say it after me."

"Alright," I say.

Hajja Qudra pronounces the first phrase.

I repeat after her: *"Ash-hadu..."* I bear witness...

Then she says the next phrase.

I repeat after her: *"...an la ilaha..."* that there is no god...
Then she says the next.

Again I repeat after her: *"...illallah..."* but Allah...

She nods and continues with the rest of the Shahada.

And I repeat that as well: *"Wa ash-hadu anna Muhammad ar-Rasulullah."* And I bear witness that Muhammad is the Messenger of Allah.

We say it three times. As soon as I say *'Muhammad ar-Rasulullah'* for the third time, Hajja Qudra's face softens. With a bright smile she announces: "Your name is Aisha."

The women start ululating. One of the men behind the curtain exclaims something and the men respond jubilantly with a chorus of "Allahu akbar!" Allah is greater. I look around and see a sea of smiling, radiant, welcoming faces.

Now it's Chloe's turn. I move aside.

Once more the room falls silent. Serene. Hajja Qudra goes through each of the five pillars. Chloe then says her Shahada three times and Hajja Qudra names her: Safiya.

I glance at Chloe and repeat her new name to myself. More shouts and ululating fill the room and soon we're surrounded by a throng of women helping us to our feet and taking it in turns to embrace us. One is a short, stout lady with large kohl-lined eyes. She hugs me tightly saying, "Marhaban: welcome!" Another is Malaysian, with hooded eyes and cheekbones the size of apple halves. She gives me a peach scarf with pearls hanging at each corner: "Bismillah." Another woman kisses me on both cheeks then steps back and puts her hands on my shoulders, looking at me directly. "What a gift," she says with an expression of wonder, her face streaked with tears. She slips a tasbih into my hand then disappears into the crowd.

Several women give us jewellery. Others give us perfume bottles and scarves. A slim, dark-skinned lady with a proud nose and gleaming teeth says "As-Salamu alaykum" three times, addressing us but also seeming to say it to herself.

There are women I've met and women I've never seen before. Their outpouring is overwhelming. Then Nuriya steps forward and hugs me.

"Allah," she whispers in my ear. "Allah, Allah, Allah." She stands back to look at me, her face full of joy, her eyes brimming with tears.

Hajja Qudra and Nuriya lead us out of the zawiya. We put on our sandals and head towards the entrance of the building, followed by a crowd. The smell of perfume mingles with that of the wooden panelling in the anteroom. Rays of sunlight from some unseen window reach down upon the throng. I see Rafiq. He nods his head in acknowledgement. So many people are here and all of them looking at us, but I'm not uncomfortable or embarrassed. The attention seems part of a more general sense of celebration.

Before we reach the atrium, the older gentleman who spoke at the conference appears in front of me. There is an urgency in his voice.

"There... there was a lot of light at your Shahada," he stammers.

He intones the end of his words with a certain finality and looks at me earnestly. I don't know how to respond.

"Thank you," I say, then I am carried away by the tide of women.

Chloe and I – *Safiya* and I – are accompanied out of the building by a small group and together we start walking downhill towards Casa Pasteles. I don't feel particularly different. In fact, there is a surprising normality to this moment. But at the back of my mind are that man's words, about there being a lot of light. They linger, carving out some deeper part of me and entrusting to that place something weighty: responsibility.

Peace

I love my new name. Aisha means *life*. It is the name of the Prophet's wife, and half of Islam came to us through her. She was highly knowledgeable in medicine and poetry too. Chloe's name – Safiya – means *clear*, and carries also the sense of *serene, pure*. It suits her.

"It feels strange but I like the sound of it," she says in the café.

Back at the house there's a knock at the door. I go to open it.

"Hamza!" I say.

"I didn't get a chance to speak with you at the zawiya," he says, "so I thought I'd come by and, well, *congratulate* isn't really the right word but..."

"Oh, it is," I interrupt.

Safiya appears at my side.

"So, are you both getting on alright here?" he asks.

I think he feels bad we didn't come back to stay at the flat. I reassure him we're fine.

"But we miss all of you," says Chloe.

"Well, maybe we'll see you tonight?" he says. "Are you both coming to the Wird?"

"We intend to," I reply.

Hamza inhales deeply and pulls his shoulders back.

"Well, I'm on my way to catch up with Aziz," he says. "Just wanted to wish you both well and hope everything ahead is easy for you. If you need anything..."

He pauses and a smile spreads on his kind face. "Wow, who would've thought it?"

"I know," I say, with a laugh.

For a moment none of us speaks.

"Thank you Hamza," I say soberly. "Thanks for everything."

"Thank you to both of *you*," he says. "It's a great reminder for us all." He jingles his keys in his pocket. "Well," he says, "As-Salamu alaykum."

We return the greeting. He lingers for a moment, looking at both of us and smiling, then he heads off uphill. Chloe goes inside. I stand and watch Hamza a moment. Leaning slightly forward he hastens close to the wall. Someone told me that the Prophet walked like that when he was in town. I wonder whether he emulates him on purpose, or whether it just rubs off on people. I close the door and go to get a drink of water. Standing in the kitchen, I feel I should be doing something.

I look at the clock. It dawns on me.

"Chloe!" I exclaim. "I mean *Safiya!*"

"I'm in the lounge," she calls out.

"Hey," I say, poking my head around the door. "It's time for the midday prayer."

We go into the bathroom to do wudu. Together we revise the order of washing and I look on as Chloe goes first. Then it's my turn.

I turn on the tap so that just a trickle comes out – the Prophet wouldn't use a lot of water. "Bismillah," I say under my breath and start washing my right hand then my left. Then I lean down, scooping shallow handfuls of water into my mouth, three times.

For the briefest moment, the sparse, cold water takes me to wet and rainy woodlands back home, tilting my head under half-unfurled ferns to catch raindrops on my tongue, feeling so much a part of my surroundings – natural, and deeply alive.

I continue with the washing, and alongside the invigoration of cold water and the brisk rubbing of my skin, I sense an inner cleansing too. A clearing. I tie my hair in a loose bun then catch up with Safiya in the salon. Kinza and her mother are working, but we'll see them tonight. For now, Safiya and I are alone.

"I'm sure its fine to use these," she says, kneeling at a wooden box in the corner of the room and taking out two prayer mats; one of them undyed wool, loosely woven, the other made of straw. We know the direction of the prayer – the Ka'ba in Makkah lies roughly east-south-east from here – but it comes to me to check with my compass. I go and fetch it from my rucksack. Holding it in my hand I remember the morning I bought it, striding through town in my cowboy hat and blue sunglasses, the pale morning sun on my face.

"Check this out," I say to Safiya.

I turn the compass and align its 'N' for north with the red arrow. We look for east-south-east.

"It's there," says Safiya, gesturing towards the corner of the room and the direction of the prayer.

I take a length of soft, salmon-pink cotton and wrap it over my head and around my chin, the ends draping down over my chest. Safiya does something similar. We lay out the prayer mats then look at each other a moment, sharing something unsaid. Back home, we used to get ready together for nights out. Now we're preparing to put our heads on the ground.

We place the booklets Rafiq gave us as reminders a little way in front of us, then stand in the direction of Makkah.

"Allahu akbar," we whisper, bringing our hands down to our sides and entering the state of prayer.

I look at a point on the mat in front of me, an indentation formed by the prostrations of others. My feet are shoulder width apart, relaxed. The upper part of my palms rest lightly against my thighs. I'm conscious of the material swathed loosely about my face. It's as though I'm looking out from the mouth of a secret mountain cave.

I silently recite from the Qur'an: first the Fatiha, its opening part. My face is still moist from doing wudu, and as the water dries, my skin tickles. I want to rub my face but resist the urge. The sensation recedes. Then I recite more, pausing halfway, trying to recall what comes next. It comes to me. And I go on. I'm aware of my chest moving with my breathing, my heartbeat rhythmically quivering my top. I hear teenagers passing by on the street outside.

Safiya bows. But we're not praying together. That happens when there is a man leading the prayer. Soon I bow too, whispering, "Allahu akbar," as I move, pausing a moment with my back horizontal, legs straight, eyes ahead, my hands gripping my knees. I say some Arabic phrases, glorifying Allah.

"Allahu akbar," and I stand up.

I pause here. Upright. My eyes again on the mark in the straw.

"Allahu akbar," and I go down and put my forehead and the tip of my nose on the ground, palms flat on the floor near my face. More phrases of glorification.

"Allahu akbar," and I move to the sitting position, my lower left leg tucked beneath me, my right foot resting vertically on my toes behind me. It feels odd at first, my left side stretched up and leaning a little to the right.

"Allahu akbar," and I'm prostrating again with my forehead on the floor. Then I'm pushing myself up to my feet to do it all a second time. When I come to prostrating again, I wonder if my eyes should be open or shut. I keep them open.

At the second sitting, I recite some words from the booklet Rafiq gave me: a transliteration of a blessing on the Prophet Muhammad and his family, and a blessing on the Prophet Abraham and his family. Then I stand up and repeat everything another time.

All the while there are the sounds of our moving clothing. Voiceless recitation. Moments of silence. Our first morning at Nuriya's house comes to mind, when we came upon the women praying downstairs in the salon. There is now what I sensed with them then: a lustre in the air, a rich quiet. I perceive those qualities all around me, and now also within me.

I hear more youngsters walking past outside, their voices raised and cheerful. Soon they are gone, their voices and footsteps fading to quiet.

"Allahu akbar," and I bow.

My sense of body shape recedes under my extra garments and I feel free of it. Anonymous. Standing again, my breathing is slowed. I'm motionless but for my reciting and my body's subtle muscle movements keeping me upright and balanced.

"Allahu akbar," and I go on.

Later, we take a walk to the Mirador. We have lunch with one of Nuriya's friends on the outskirts of the Albaicín. I notice how I'm watching for the end of the day. I'm feeling for where the sun is in the sky, noticing how I'm aware not only of what my eyes can see, but how something inside myself is also seeing. I sense something new about external north, south, east and west – an internal geography consisting not of imaginary forest, hill and skyscapes, but a deep and universal sense of place.

Setting Out

In the very late afternoon we return to the zawiya for the sunset prayer and the recitation of the Wird. Safiya and I have prayed twice now. We're about to pray for the third time. But instead of standing alone, we're standing shoulder to shoulder with upwards of eighty people. A man at the front of the zawiya says, "Allahu akbar," and we all raise our hands near to our ears and, saying the same, bring our hands to our sides. The man starts reciting Qur'an. I recognise it and bring to mind its meanings. He has a steady voice, rich, and doesn't rush the silences between phrases.

As I listen, I'm feeling the rough sisal carpet under my feet. I'm smelling a musky fragrance. From an open window to my right comes the sound of birds singing sunset songs. I'm distinctly aware of everything around me. At the same time, I feel I've stepped away from it all.

Again I hear 'Allahu akbar', and we all say the same, the sounds of moving clothing and tinkling jewellery as we bow. This is different from praying alone. I don't have to try and remember what comes next. I don't have to reach for a booklet to remind me. I'm part of one entity. Moving as one body. I let go to it, to this sense of expansion, and the thought comes to me how there must be countless other bodies of people like this one, all facing the same point and oscillating like a wave that is sweeping around the planet with every rising and setting of the sun.

We rest a while, bowed, my eyes fixed on the sand-coloured fibres on the floor a little in front of me – I don't let my gaze move at all – and in my peripheral vision there are rows of feet. We stand up straight, pause, then bend and go down to the floor with the sounds again of moving materials and the just perceptible draught of air displacing, seeming also to push some other energy through me.

Then our palms come to the floor and shush slightly forward against the carpet as our knees go to the ground. I place my forehead on the ground too, my eyes open and looking somewhere beyond, my nose pressed against the carpet and smelling dry summers. Then there is stillness. Whisperings of glorification. A residual sense of kinetic energy.

It comes to me how Muslims have been praying like this for over fourteen hundred years. I then wonder how many times the old woman next to me has prayed in her lifetime. *Hundreds of times*, I think to myself. Then I realise it's more likely to be thousands. A tingle glistens and surges up my spine and up the back of my neck, and my hair, though covered, feels like it's standing on end.

I'm with these people, I think to myself. These fascinating, extraordinary, wonderful people. My whole body relaxes. The air leaves my lungs. My tear ducts sting as water fills my eyes. Then I realise that the tears are distracting me, and I turn away from them too.

"Allahu akbar," and we're pushing ourselves off the ground to return to standing.

During the Wird, Safiya and I join in by reading a transliteration of the Arabic text. It uses Spanish phonetics, but we manage.

Afterwards, some of the younger women gather around us. Mishka is here, sitting closer to me than the others. Her yellowy green eyes are inquisitive, deer-like, striking next to her clear, suntanned skin. She sits cross-legged, hands curled in her lap. Something in the way she looks at us tells me she's wondering what to say, or how to say it.

"Shall we go then?" Safiya says to me.

But before I reply, Mishka interjects.

"I can't imagine what it must be like."

"What do you mean?"

"To discover Islam by yourself."

She looks at us, the searching look still in her eyes.

"Well... yes," I say, unsure how to respond.

Mishka smiles, not saying anything, her eyes studying us.

"We were just saying the other day," says Safiya, hesitating like me, "that we could never have imagined this is where our travels would be taking us."

But neither of us really know what more to say. She's looking for an answer and I want to give it, but I don't know how.

"It's just that all of us were brought up with it," Mishka says. "It was all there for us, laid out."

I look at her, trying to imagine.

We chat a little longer until most of the women have

got up and left. I find myself wondering what it must be like to have been surrounded by this for as long as one can remember. Would one's familiarity with it mean missing out on the wonder of discovery? I look at our new friend. She doesn't seem jealous. But perhaps there is a rueful look in her eyes, as though she recognises our delight and wants to taste it for herself. But then I imagine it to be the same for all Muslims, whether born into it or not – at some point there has to be that confrontation with Reality, whereby one decides to take it on or reject it. I look deeper into Mishka's eyes and I see inquiry and hope. Perhaps her encounter is yet to come.

Outside the zawiya I hear lowered voices speaking quickly. There is a sense of excitement. The next thing I know, Nuriya is at our side telling us that the shaykh is coming down from his apartment to greet us. My heart is suddenly thumping in my chest. I really wasn't expecting to see him. Nuriya ushers us to the atrium at the entrance of the house and invites us to sit at the small wicker table and chairs.

"Okay, just stay there," she says.

She positions one chair on the other side of the table in front of us, arranges its two linen cushions so that one lies flat on the seat, the other against the back, then leaves us to the tinkling water fountain, the pebble-patterned floor and tall potted plants, some tree-like, standing to our right in the corner. The ambience is similar to a conservatory, and a little humid.

In front of us is the large doorway to the street. The door is open, its pewter studs and hinges in full view, the viewing grille protruding several inches from the dark wood. A group of men are leaving. Others stop, sensing something about to happen. They stand where they are, talking quietly among themselves. Some women come through the doorway next to us, saying very little to one another and going to stand by the wall next to the plants. I think they're hoping to see the shaykh too.

Safiya and I watch people fill the atrium. They are not exactly looking at us, but they are waiting here because of us.

My heart is pounding. My best friend is gone. My money has run out. My ticket home is in a bin somewhere in the city. And because I've abandoned going home for now, I'm also foregoing my place at university, and with it, all ideas I had of my future.

But I feel totally at peace.

All is well.

There is no loss.

There can only be gain.

We wait. Sensing the anticipation of others increases my own. There is no jostling among the gathering crowd, just a courteous making of space for as many as possible. Hushed voices. A sparkle of laughter. Whispering. My heart continues to beat hard, its pulse now in my throat.

Nuriya appears again, crossing the gathering to the door to the street and unfastening its large hook from the eye on the wall. She closes it slowly and secures the latch on the door frame. A sparrow swoops from one corner to another, tweeting and perching on a wooden beam which juts out of the wall opposite. It turns its head this way and that – all escape routes closed off – then flits from view.

Nuriya finds a place among the people. I notice Aziz is here now. I catch his eye and I see recognition in his face. He then lowers his eyes, and I feel something of his inner being: humble, courageous, acting not from a place of what people might think of him but by his awe of Allah. I see him as wholly part of this gathering yet, for a fleeting moment, entirely alone. Then I see more: a man standing in solitude and company before his Lord.

I look back at Nuriya. She looks between Safiya and I and the doorway which leads through to the hall and zawiya. When she looks at me I see love for me in her eyes, pride too, and perhaps concern. She looks expectantly towards the doorway.

Then there is the sound of hastening footsteps and everything goes very still and quiet. I already know it's him. The shaykh comes through the doorway at our side and appears in front of us, his tall form outlined by the backdrop of onlookers behind him. Everyone is motionless. Silent.

He sits straight down in the chair in front of us, nimbly, without ceremony, his gaze settling on us. I can't take my eyes off him. His face is long and noble. He has high cheekbones with no puffiness or fat, his skin taut to his cheek and his beard neatly trimmed, tapering beneath his chin and reminding me of knights of old. Large eyebrows protrude over his eyes as if guarding them, his look still and penetrating, disarmingly intelligent. As I meet his gaze, I feel I'm witnessing eyes that have seen rare things. More than that, I sense in him an inner vision that informs all his sight falls upon.

"Well," he says, smiling broadly, delight enlivening his whole face. "Your becoming Muslim is a *wonderful* event."

His eyes sparkle as he smiles, and he looks steadily at me then at Safiya, then at me again. His diction is precise, his voice a little gravelly. Straight away I feel myself wanting to sit well and speak well.

He looks straight at me, pinning me to the moment.

"Welcome," he says. "I'm very glad to meet you both." His voice seems propelled by something from within.

He crosses one leg over the other and clasps his forearms

in either hand. There is excitement coming from him, like the prelude to something. I recall the colour photograph in Hajj Abdullah's house, the one of him resting on the edge of a boat, looking straight into the camera. And the black and white one of him, so different, so hidden, enwrapped in a cloak, eyes down, sitting cross-legged on a floor, disappeared in a world of contemplation. This man in front of me appears most like the former. But my memory of the latter is foremost in my mind, like knowing a secret about him.

"Thank you. Thank you so much," we say.

He leans towards us. I notice on his tie a small coat of arms, its outline silver grey. His face turns serious.

"You must know what an important thing it is you have taken on," he states gravely. "But you must also know that it is Allah Who has taken *you* on."

He raises large eyebrows, revealing all the more his twinkling eyes, and I feel I have stepped onto a boat and he is the boatman, and we are sailing down a river.

He says no more, so I begin to talk. I say how happy I am to have become Muslim, how I always knew I'd find the Truth and how at last I've found it and how amazing it all is. I go on enthusiastically. He listens carefully, the skin beneath his eyes drawn up in concentration, his eyebrows in one moment knitted together, musing; in the next, raised in a startling expression of surprise at something I say. As I gush on, he nods in acknowledgement, giving me fuel to continue. Several times he looks at Safiya. She hardly says a word.

Then he interjects: "Well!" and looks at Safiya and I with a studious look. I stop talking and smile back.

The shaykh uncrosses his legs and places his hands purposefully on the arms of his chair, poised to push himself up to leave.

But before he does, he looks straight at me and says:

"You will have success."

Then he rises to his feet, smiling broadly at Safiya and I. "I won't take up more of your time," he says. "I shall leave you in the good care of our excellent ladies." Then he acknowledges the people standing around us by looking at them warmly and addressing them with "As-Salamu alaykum."

"Wa alaykum salam," we all reply.

He leaves.

Everyone watches him go.

The energy around us relaxes as though the wash of the sea is receding down the sand. People turn to one another and begin to talk quietly. Some smile at Safiya and I. Someone coughs. There's some quiet conversation. Then people start talking freely and moving to and fro. Someone opens the door to the street and a cool breeze comes in.

I look at Safiya, lost for words. Then some women are surrounding us, welcoming us, filling the atrium with warm, feminine voices. One of them invites us to her house for supper.

It's late. In my room, I unfurl a prayer mat for the last prayer of the day. I bow, stand, put my head on the ground, sit. I concentrate on the meaning of the words silently leaving my mouth. That is the first cycle: one, I count. I continue the movements, soon completing two. I linger while I prostrate, looking into the prayer mat, focussing somewhere beyond it. Three. It's as though I'm pressed against a window, looking into the universe. Four. And I'm merely a dot. An intrepid, fleeting little speck of a dot in a vast experience.

After, I don't get up straight away. All is quiet. It's dark outside but I'm not tired. I go over the evening and find myself dwelling on the encounter with the shaykh. Perhaps my excitement veiled me from him, because now, with stillness, I seem to see more of him. I see him before me, his presence commanding. I see his face, full of interest and attention. Even when he's listening to me going on, his eyes are full of expression and seem to respond to my every word. The more I think of him, the greater my sense of his presence, his force. It's as though he is imprinted on me. I think of the Prophet, sallallahu alayhi wa sallam, and wonder what it would be like to meet him.

My thoughts wander. I find myself looking ahead, wondering what the future will bring. I wonder what fasting will be like, when we don't eat or drink between first light and sunset. Ramadan will be in early spring next year. Then there is the Hajj, the pilgrimage to Makkah, and inshallah I will see with my own eyes that curious, square, black building I saw in the photo in the flat, and join the millions of people going around it.

I feel I've come to the top of a huge hill. But now I'm starting to see another perspective: a vast and magnificent mountain range before me.

My thoughts return again to the shaykh. I recall his words: "You will have success." I wonder what exactly he meant. It would be easy to take it as an affirmation of sorts. But I don't feel it was meant that way – and it certainly wasn't flattery. No, it feels more like an instruction. Perhaps an invitation. The words take root in my mind.

A gentle breeze blows in through the window and I savour its coolness on my face, tilting my head up and breathing in the night smell.

I think of home. Norfolk.

At some point, I know I'll return. I need to speak with my mother in person. That feels the most courteous approach – towards her and towards what I have done. Maybe she already knows I'm Muslim? If so, I know she'll be concerned, maybe frantic. I imagine meeting up with Beth again and hearing about her travels after she left us. I hope I can make up with her.

Then there is Jake. I'm nervous and excited to meet him. Where will I start when I tell him all that has happened? Will he understand?

I think back over these last months and try to pinpoint when the seed of all this was planted. Was it in those conversations with Jake? Was it in those mind-altered states? What about those chance encounters – like with the man on the bench and the woman in the doorway? Did my years of church-going create fertile soil? Perhaps when I was out under the stars, alone, my heart searching the skies, the wildness of nature whispered the Truth.

I go back further and think of my mother's love – selfless and unconditional. I reflect on what my father taught me, and what his death and all that came after taught me too. And I remember how, as a small child, the sunlight would sparkle and dance through summer trees and I would lie on the grass gazing up at it, feeling its quiet, golden, rippling stillness inside me. Then I think of my ancestors, of what prayers they may have done for their descendants. I carry all this in the marrow of my bones.

Looking back, events in my life seem to have been perfectly shaped to prepare me for this – being Muslim – and yet in another way, they don't seem to have anything to do with it at all.

There's something else about my meeting with the shaykh. I can't place it. It plays on my mind, agitating me. There was nothing in what he said or did that offended or disappointed, but there was something in the meeting that did.

I decide to revise some of the Qur'an I've learnt, thinking of my lesson tomorrow with Mishka. I recite the Arabic, bringing the English rendering to mind:

Say: 'He is Allah. One.
Allah, the Everlasting Sustainer of all.
He has not given birth, and was not born.
And no one is comparable to Him.'

I savour these meanings. Then I think to read a bit. I reach for the book of the shaykh's discourses. But there is still that something else, something unsettling coming to the fore. I feel I'm waiting for it to emerge. I put the book back. I look down at my prayer mat and move my hand over it, feeling the natural fibres under my palm and recalling again the shaykh getting up to leave.

Then it comes to me.

The shaykh had ended our conversation so abruptly: after I'd been talking, he just got up, said goodbye and left. *Why did he do that?* I ask myself. I get the lurking feeling I did something wrong.

Some young men pass by on the street outside. One of them laughs. The others hush him and soon I'm smelling cigarette smoke. I look up at the window to the outside. Above a silhouette of rooftops I see the moon. Solitary, it shines radiantly in an empty sky, a bright pearl in a sea of black. My eyes map its contours, then its rim, sharply defined but for one small edge – one more day and it will be full.

The voices on the street recede, then my room falls silent. I close my eyes, aware that the silence has a richer quality than before.

And then I realise.

When I was talking to the shaykh, I became so full of my own journey. I became so full of my own discovery – basically so full of myself – that I made the meeting all about me.

A wave of mortification breaks.

The shaykh must have seen all this and, in his courtesy, allowed it. And that meant I missed out on *him*.

The realisation sinks in – excruciating, inevitable, unstoppable – and as it does I feel a huge part of myself crumbling, collapsing, then falling away, crashing like a chunk of land into the ocean.

My heart beats stronger, unmoored, then is flooded with yearning to see the shaykh again. I sense he knows something I want. Something I have yet to understand. And something I have yet to taste.